Happily Married
with Kids

Collection Management

Happily Married

with

Kids

It's NOT Just a Fairy Tale

Carol Ummel Lindquist, Ph.D.

BERKLEY BOOKS, NEW YORK

B

A Berkley Book
Published by The Berkley Publishing Group
A division of Penguin Group (USA) Inc.
375 Hudson Street
New York, New York 10014

This book is an original publication of The Berkley Publishing Group.

First Edition: January 2004

Library of Congress Cataloging-in-Publication Data

Lindquist, Carol Ummel.
Happily married with kids : it's not just a fairy tale / by Carol Ummel Lindquist.—
Berkley trade pbk. ed.
p. cm.
Includes bibliographical references.
ISBN 0-425-19395-0
1. Parenthood. 2. Parenting. 3. Marriage. 4. Interpersonal relations. I. Title.

HQ755.8.L543 2004
649'.1—dc22
2003057845

649.1

PRINTED IN THE UNITED STATES OF AMERICA

10 9 8 7 6 5 4 3 2 1

Acknowledgments

This book is a love note to my husband, Neil, who never read a whole self-help book in his life, until this one. He skillfully guards the happiness of our marriage, puts up with my experiments, and helps me laugh at myself.

Ira Poll, the best and most fun therapist I know, believed in this project when it was only an idea. A warm friend, she made me read the first pages out loud and provided encouragement, endless inspiration, great stories, gentle critiques, and laughter.

Marni Jameson, a real writer and mother of two brought both her professional touch and her mothering experiences to the whole manuscript. I loved that she has girls and so a different experience from me. She reread the manuscript endlessly. She and Dan helped me carry it over the deadline to the finish line and encouraged me when I needed it most. She coaches, teaches, and empowers. She suggested the Tips, so I have nicknamed her Mother of the Tips.

Deborah Allen, another fabulous therapist, read every word of the book and contributed many perfect phrases and experiences. She is a wise and funny lady and should write her own book.

Two terrific dads and very fine husbands, Doug Anderson and Neil Poll, read chapter after chapter on the computer and gave me detailed feedback, catching me when I didn't speak to the male ear.

My sisters, Allyn Kahle, Gay Ummel, and Larke Recchie, are wonderful moms and a genuine inspiration. Each had the wisdom and good fortune to marry excellent husbands and dedicated fathers. Jim Kahle and Ron Mieloch read early drafts and provided encouragement. Our parents, Clark and Carolyn Ummel, gave us everything we needed. We feel so lucky.

My New York partner, Ellen McGrath, a great coach, author, and therapist continues to make important contributions to the field. Her experience as an author gave me the courage to start my own book. Both she and my writing and coaching buddy, Ginger Sherman Silverman, read early drafts and encouraged me with media and marketing ideas.

Besides Ira, my other sisters of choice, the Bad Girls, Judy Anderson, Linda Bennett, and Lucyann Carlton, great moms and therapists all, read early drafts and provided warm encouragement. Suzy Willhoit, queen of "fight like the windows are open" and very happily married, marched up and down hills listening to all my writer's quandaries. Two other good therapists, Geoffrey White and Michelle Massey, gave me positive feedback and supported my writing. Jeanne Reiss, Sari Poll, and Ruth Rich kept my days on track so that I could write. Giselle Russ read the manuscript from the client perspective more than once. I would like to thank all my clients who shared their stories and eagerly read early chapters.

My agents, Jean V. Naggar and Jennifer Weltz, who loved the book, guided me with enthusiasm, gentle realism and professionalism. My editor, Christine Zika, has such a light and positive professional touch and knows best how to put a book on a diet and keep the flow amazingly smooth. My copyeditor, Bert Yaeger, after all the previous help and edits, could still find wonderful improvements of word and phrase. I appreciate everyone's gentleness with my neophyte status.

I feel that by writing this book I stand on the shoulders of many giants in the field of psychology and self-help. I have tried to make their work simple and accessible and to credit their wonderful ideas each place I have mentioned them. The really special ideas become so familiar that they seem like part of my own practice and coaching. So if I have inadvertently omitted credit to anyone, I apologize. The responsibility is completely my own.

Contents

Author's Note

I still remember the mysterious way people said, 'Boy, is your life going to change!" when we said we had a new baby. Some said it with awe, some with dread, some with a laugh. That's when I first became interested in writing this book. I wanted to delve into that mystery, magic, and laughter.

As my own motherhood adventure evolved, my work as a clinical psychologist compelled me to take an almost voyeuristic interest in other parent's lives. I began to notice that what other couples fought about were exactly the same things that triggered fights with my husband, Neil. What's more, the particular fights couples seemed to have when their kids were two, three, or five were the same fights Neil and I had had when our kids were those same ages. For example, as each of our kids reached two and my husband and I would go out with them socially, there was the "who doesn't pay enough attention to the children and whose turn is it to talk to the other adults" fight. At three, it is the "you are too lenient and no I am not" fight. Then, when our youngest was four or five, another couple visited with their two-year-old and had the same "whose turn is it" argument. And so it was with the couples I counseled.

For some couples these normal stresses in new parenting seem like just a little rough asphalt. For others it seems like a big pothole or even a dead end. For still others it seems like they would go suddenly off the road and over a cliff into the fiery crash of a hotly contested divorce.

I also began to notice common threads among my happily married friends who seemed to roll right through the universal problems. They resolved issues in similar ways. I also noticed people began to resolve their fights and crises when their kids hit certain ages. For example, parents aren't arguing about who is watching four-year-old Johnny when they are out as a family anymore, though they may be arguing about who picks him up from preschool and who arranges for the baby-sitter when they both have a breakfast meeting.

By their child's fifth birthday, mothers began to feel their children's independence. When the youngest child reached five and a half or six, moms often reported that this was the best year of their marriage since kids. I also found similarities in couples who didn't seem to make it or who drifted apart—some just seemed to blow apart.

When I shared early drafts of this book with friends and family, even though they were right on schedule with their discomforts and disagreements, they frequently said, "Our problems are a lot bigger than these you write about." I noticed that conflicts that they had successfully handled before the stress of the new baby now seemed to loom too large to manage. Stress also made them treat each other differently when they disagreed. Their conflicts rolled around on schedule too. If the examples here seem too mild, I would encourage you to try a few of the tips and see if things get better for you and your spouse. Or take

**At last, gift balloons that reflect
the reality of parenting.**

heart that your marriage just might get better anyway by the time your youngest is six.

I was most curious, though, about those couples who rarely fought, or fought a lot but made up so fast between the sheets it hardly seemed to matter. I decided to write this book to try to describe what I have discovered about how to be "Happily Married with Kids." I hope you will laugh a bit, nod a lot in recognition, and benefit from the helpful bits of wisdom I have gleaned as a mother and a psychologist. I learned a lot along the way that I wished I had known when we started our journey. Here is what I have discovered.

Introduction

Kid Crisis—What Is Happening to Us?

Not long after our first child arrived I began to wonder what had happened to our marriage. Although I was totally absorbed in and happy with our son, for whom we had waited ten years, I found myself reading those magazine articles at the check-out stand with titles like "*How to Put Romance Back in Your Marriage,*" or "*Is Sex Less Fun?*" Just less, I thought, a whole lot less.

A very famous (and over-fifty-year-old) sex therapist was quoted in a women's magazine saying, "Just set aside time for sex and make it a priority . . . If you are tired, you are ambivalent about sex." When I first read this, I was standing in a check-out line, by now with *two* sons, each wrapped around one of my thighs. I thought, "Boy, has it been a while since *this* woman had small children! I am *always* tired." I felt guilty, frustrated, and sad. Sex wasn't the only joy missing. I missed long talks with my husband over dinner and movie marathons. We had so looked forward to and rejoiced in our kids. The kids weren't the problem. We were crazy about our kids. So what *was* the problem?

Looking back, I can see that we were so wrapped up in the kids, we had no relationship. We lived in the same house but we rarely spent any time alone with each other. We had high standards for what it meant to be good parents. Our kids had no problem letting us know when they needed parental attention. We just weren't giving or getting attention from each other. Our marriage wasn't even on the to-do list. Like most dedicated parents, we couldn't see the problem. We thought we were good parents and that should be enough.

Sometimes I enjoyed our kids more when I was in charge alone or with my girlfriends and their kids than when I took the kids out for the day with my husband, Neil. I knew Neil was great with kids. He was a former kindergarten teacher. So what was my problem? Gradually I started talking honestly to my friends. Sometimes I even asked their husbands questions: "Are you having fun?" "Why aren't we having fun?" "Do you have a life as a couple anymore?" "Do you ever get to spend time just talking?" "What do you argue about?" One perceptive guy said there were times he felt like he and his wife, both with demanding careers, had become just two laborers in the baby business. He no longer felt a connection as a couple, no longer felt like best friends, or like lovers. No kidding.

Other husbands often said it seemed their kids were more important to their wives than they were. These were solid marriages. My clients with young kids felt the same disconnection, although by the time they came to therapy they were often in serious trouble and ready to divorce. Couples in my practice who sought help with their marriages said their problems started when their children were under five. The most together, apparently stress-free couples confided that they, too, had struggled and then had counseling after the children were born.

I began to read about marriages and children in the psychology literature. My reading confirmed what I had been hearing from my clients and friends. I even found a book about "Supermom" and "Stuporman" by columnist Susan Maushart that made me feel that there were soul mate couples out there who felt like we did. Although many couples have a brief and blissful honeymoon period after the birth of a child, research studies show that the time married couples are most likely to experience problems is when they have children under age five. People are more likely to seek counseling when their children are young. If their children are stepkids or special needs, the odds of marital discord and divorce climbed even higher.

In my own work with clients, I noticed that people who had strong marriages or even just adequate marriages usually ran into trouble shortly after the birth of their first child. Their second child typically intensified the problem or triggered the final meltdown. Some flared with anger; others drifted into divorce. Couples often linked the beginning of their emotional separation to the time their kids were small. Like us, they didn't see that the children had anything to do with the problem. Many times they didn't seek counseling until the kids were older. Then it was often too late. They chose divorce when the kids were small. They only acted on it later.

My experience convinced me Nora Ephron was right when she said that having an infant is like tossing a hand grenade into a marriage.

So Kids Kill Marriages?

Children themselves are not the problem. The parents' reaction to the children creates the problem. Adding one or two new little people to a relationship creates a normal crisis, but a crisis nonetheless. The Chinese symbol for crisis combines the symbols for danger and opportunity. This normal, albeit often unrecognizable, couple crisis of having children provides both danger and opportunity for the marriage. The danger is that the demand of raising children will lead to conflict and emotional distance in the marriage. The golden opportunity is that confronting the normal stress of raising children will create a happier, stronger, and more intimate marriage for the long term. Psychologist David Schnarch describes the conflict and demands of normal couples as a crucible that either melts down a marriage or forges a steel bond.

Absorbed in their children, partners miss the clues to this crisis. They may sense a problem but can't pin it down. Many a new father has said, "You pay more attention to the kids than me!" His wife may respond with a gentle version of, "So what is your point? Kids need more attention." He might be thinking, "Boy is she *overinvolved*." She's likely to be thinking: "Maybe if you'd help more, I would have more time for you." If he doesn't start helping more, she begins to have thoughts like, "Oh great, now I have *two* children instead of one, and the big one *whines*."

What they each missed was the red flag, the opportunity to notice and address the anger that signals a problem. The husband's statement about attention to the kids could be a signal to look at the marriage together. But it is a disguised signal. Though he meant no harm, his first comment, which felt like an admission of vulnerability to him, probably sounded to her like he was criticizing or blaming her. Now the signal might have been easier to read if he had said, "I miss my time with you." Similarly, her responding to his need for attention with "You're right! I miss you, too. What can we do about it?" would have started the process of working on the real problem together. These niceties of communication tend to evaporate with sleep disruption and the new workload. Either partner can refocus the couple to "What are we going to do about our marriage?" Rather than opponents, they are allies, cooperating and struggling with the same issues. Both may be tired, cranky, overloaded, and with little left to share. However now they are on the same team, struggling against the same problem rather than against each other. This understanding can bring them closer even if they just flop on the bed for ten minutes of cuddling and talking about how overwhelming it is. But stress tends to make people irritable rather than reasonable. That irritability is like a small flame that can be fanned into a huge fire.

Instead, the normal parental stress and lack of time causes a mom to wonder privately, "Who *is* this person who thinks he isn't getting enough attention?" He thinks, "She loves the kids more than me," or worse, "She doesn't love me like she used to." And the flame grows. Both begin to think, "Who is this person I married?" Many people decide somewhat grimly that they will focus on the marriage again "after I get this kid thing going smoothly." Unfortunately, it may be another three to five (or eighteen!) years before things start to feel a little bit smoother, enough to think clearly and discuss calmly. And that may be too late.

The Good News

The good news, for me at least, was that the research showed that my marital discomfort after having kids was typical. I told myself a lot of marriages made it through many years and mine would too if I just figured out how to cope with the dual demands of marriage and parenting. I also learned that because Neil and I were older when we became parents (we were forty and thirty-nine), we were at risk for a more intense crisis. I had assumed being older would make us calmer and wiser. Studies indicated just the reverse. The older you are when you start having kids, or the longer you have been married, the worse the discomfort. Apparently having a long time to settle comfortably into a marriage makes it harder to adjust to children.

At the other end of the continuum of years married, those with almost no time to become a couple before babies arrive and very young, teen couples also have a very hard time. Couples in the middle who have plenty of good times together to remember BK (before kids) but are not yet settled into a rigid, yet comfortable, pattern have a little easier time.

Another point discussed in the research was that women tend to feel upset first. Men feel it later. When I tried talking to Neil, my husband, about our marriage and these facts, he didn't get it. From his point of view, if I would just be nicer everything would be fine. He wasn't that unhappy, he said. Neil was right on schedule. The timing of post-child malaise is different for women and men. Women become unhappy first and men follow. It is as though a man's unhappiness mirrors his wife's discomfort.

Studies of depression over a woman's lifetime show that women experience the most depression when their children are under age five. (See Baby Blues box, Chapter 5.) Menopause and the empty nest are nothing compared to what a woman experiences when her children are little. It appears to be a case of "If Mama ain't happy, ain't nobody happy." If she doesn't share her concerns and he doesn't notice, both of them are often quite surprised when she either blows up or becomes depressed and critical. If they don't attend to her unhappiness and both of them don't deal with it together, he becomes unhappy living with someone who is so unhappy and/or grouchy. The questions still nagged at me: Why does marital satisfaction go down when you have a baby? Why doesn't it bring you closer? Why isn't it one more wonderful thing to share? Like our friends, we were thrilled with our children. So why weren't we happier as couples? I was further intrigued to discover that while parenthood led some couples to divorce or put them on the rocks, 33 percent of couples experience intense happiness in their marriages after having a baby and were headed for a lifetime of greater closeness. So why weren't we one of the couples "chosen" for greater closeness? How do you get to be like them?

Happily Married
with Kids

Part One

Baby on Board: Using Chaos to
Create Couple Closeness

1

Baby Bliss vs. Baby Blues

What was I thinking? Before our first child, I had visions of candlelit dinners with a little angel dozing peacefully nearby. When reality hit, we were lucky to get dinner made. Real life included drippy noses and stain-encrusted clothes. I wanted to fall asleep before the kids did, and snarled if my husband suggested I stay up with him. Like most couples, rosy daydreams arrived with the news we were pregnant. But like most new parents, we became dazed and disillusioned because our dreams and fantasies of parenting and partnering didn't match reality. New parents expect cozy and blissful and get disruption and exhaustion.

On top of that, each partner changes in unexpected ways. Having a child tends to clarify, crystallize, or capsize a person's ideas about what is important in life. Sudden changes in values and habits sometimes occur. Nonreligious people get religion. Formerly flexible people become rigid about eating schedules. Reasonable people disagree about medical treatment and what is healthy to eat. Fearless people develop fears. Travelers refuse to travel. Dedicated career women sometimes decide to stop working. Sexually enthusiastic couples lose their sex drive.

Worse, partners sometimes assume that certain "natural" changes will occur in their spouses that just don't happen. I assumed that after we had kids, Neil would *naturally* want to stay home more. But he still wanted to work ten- and twelve-hour days and have us run around on the weekends. I was perplexed and exhausted. A friend's husband told me, "Even though we always ate in restaurants a lot, I just naturally thought Susan would like to cook for the kids." But the reality is workaholics rarely stop working and fast-food fanatics rarely become cooks. Conflict follows when one spouse feels tricked or confused by the changes or lack of expected changes in their partner.

However, if the disappointment can be expressed, the conflict can be addressed directly and resolution will be more likely to happen. If I could have said to Neil, "I'm really disappointed that you are still spending so much time at work. The vision I had of our family life was spending more time as a family. I am curious, though, what you want our family life to be?" I would have started a discussion that might have led to a clarification of our shared hopes for our family. But fatigue and stress led to irritability so my first attempts to resolve this sounded much more like, "Where the heck have *you* been?" Not a good conversation starter.

Neil tended to view these attempts as a rhetorical question and thought it safest not to answer. So we had no discussion and I felt more frustrated. Other couples start small wars over this issue.

If these assumptions and expectations are not addressed tactfully, the changes and conflicts accumulate over the first two to five years, as the child becomes more mobile and demanding. As the emerging little person requires more attention, parents feel more justified and comfortable expecting change in each other "for the sake of the child." Often the person requesting change has little awareness that they want the change as much for themselves as for the child. For example, one parent might say to the other:

- "You know kids need time with their family at dinner, so I think *you* need to get home sooner."

- "I want our kids to remember their Christmases at home, so let's not go to *your* parents' this year."

- "Kids need a neat house and an orderly schedule, so *you* need to keep *your* stuff picked up."

All these points may be legitimate concerns, but sometimes the needs of the child get tangled up with the wishes of the parent requesting a change. Requests for change sound more like demands. If the wishes of the parent are disguised and expressed as if they are needs of the child, the partner is likely to feel manipulated and resentful. When a request is presented as a demand or a rule rather than a consultation or suggestion, it is also more likely to create resistance or explode into a battle. Listen to how different these issues sound rephrased:

"I think it is hard on all of us to travel at Christmas. I want the kids to have memories of Christmas in our house with us. Do you have any ideas about how we could do Christmas differently to accomplish that?"

Conflict in the first years of parenthood is expected and natural. According to one of my favorite authors, Harriet Lerner, in *The Motherhood Dance,* unless both parents make a deliberate effort to defy traditional gender arrangements, they are likely to fight about six things:

1. *Money* (Mom has lost earning power; Dad has gained earning power.)

2. *Childcare and housework* (Mom notices and does more; she feels more responsible.)

3. *Work outside the home* (Dad's job comes first; he feels more responsible.)

4. *Extended family issues* (Mom overdeals with his family and Dad underdeals with his family.)

5. *Sex* (Mom becomes uninterested as the unequal distribution of domestic tasks takes its toll.)

6. *Deciding how to spend what little free time the couple has together* (Dad and Mom go out for the evening and argue about the previously mentioned items.)

"Oh, *yes*," I thought as I read that. Fights explode about trivial issues like the soda can someone left in the wrong place, but these six core issues underlie most conflicts.

Unlike previous generations, when parents expected child-rearing to involve hard work and sleepless nights, current generations don't necessarily expect this. We like to believe we have evolved to a new social order, or at least can buy greater comforts. While our mothers say that parenting is hard work, we think it will be easier for us.

Today, people are having children a bit later in life. Women spend more time in the workforce childless and are therefore somewhat removed from the reality of parenting. We may spend the first years of marriage without children nurturing our partners. We love both the spoiling and being spoiled. When children arrive, such cherished time together often takes a multiyear vacation. This loving attention is instead lavished on the child.

Most men and women remember their own childhood from the time they were nine to twelve, when children are the easiest. Parents do not remember their own infancy and toddlerhood, so they are blissfully unaware that chaos theory may have been invented while watching a two-year-old. Unless they have spent time with young children recently, they often have hilariously unrealistic visions of parenthood. I have had childless twenty-somethings announce to me that, unlike their niece, *their* children will have perfect table manners at the age of three. I smile politely and think, "Just you wait, honey."

I remember thinking: I would have it made with childcare a few doors down the hall at work. Despite my training with children, I failed to fully realize until I had my children what "difficulty separating from Mom" meant. Having Mom so close could just as easily mean they will lie outside the door and sob to get your attention. Nor could I imagine the glorious relief of a few hours of uninterrupted adult time. In fact, I was surprised that work often felt much less stressful than being home with the kids.

New parents imagine that their children will happily go out to restaurants. Instead, the dining experience degenerates until they find themselves diving desperately into the balls at a McDonald's playpen to retrieve a lost treasure they have allowed their daughter to wear. They imagine hours spent cuddling and reading. In reality, reading is usually less than half an hour of a parent's day with a toddler.

As nine-to-twelve-year-old children, many of us watched our mothers do most all of the housework, while Dad did very little. New parents tend to expect more equality between partners. Before kids, working partners experienced more equality. Children disrupt this. Instead of experiencing how similar we are to our partner and growing closer, we begin to discover fundamental personal and gender differences. What's more, the busyness and stress of caring for children doesn't bring out the best in our coping and communication skills, which are sometimes too short and abrupt. For example, "I am getting something from the garage, you've got Zoe." Such terse and practical communications don't create intimacy.

Deeper intimacy comes not from what we share by having children, but from how we resolve the many new conflicts and changes that children bring to our relationship. How parents deal with the mixed blessings of children determines who will survive as a couple. The violated expectations, the conflict, the frustration, and the anger all become the workshop for developing the relationship, bringing new opportunities for laughter, insight, and intimacy. Yet most couples don't see the opportunity for growing closer. Instead, partners see the conflict and think that they are somehow failing. They do not see that intimacy is an accomplishment couples literally fight for (and pray for) by resolving the inevitable disappointments and savoring the moments of happiness that come with their children. Thus I learned that couples aren't *chosen* for greater intimacy, as I had erroneously assumed, they must create it themselves.

A mother, now a grandmother with two grown and successful sons, told me about the day she brought those twin sons home from the hospital. She and her husband were lying on the bed together with the twins between them. She felt panicked and said, "How am I going to do this?" He replied, "I don't know but there are two of them and two of us and we are going to do it together." That wasn't a big plan, but it laid the groundwork for intimacy and a feeling of support that she still treasures. It was hard work, but what she remembers is that they were in it together. Kindness, and recognizing that we are both at our limits, strengthens the relationship and helps weather the inevitable disruptions.

The Core Fantasies

After working with hundreds of couples, I've found that the disappointments from a few core fantasies are the seeds of the disagreements most couples have in those early parenting years. Finding ways to laugh together about your unrealistic fantasies may be the best way to grow closer. When couples understand and come to terms with these core fantasies and the unrealistic expectations they bring, the six common fights (about money, sex, extended family life, childcare and housework, career and time alone) are more easily resolved. When they don't understand them, couples can become caught in a cycle of disappointment and blame that makes problem-solving impossible.

Sometimes before we can grow closer we need to reflect on what seems wrong or out of kilter. Reflecting on which expectations aren't being fulfilled, either with or without a professional's help, may give you helpful insight. (Neil says just don't tempt fate by doing it too often!)

Whether or not you solve them, looking at the issues as a couple and learning to laugh at your differences creates closeness. After you identify the ways your days fall short of reality, you can begin to create the life you can really enjoy with your partner and your kids. Facing the fact that kids don't magically appear in clean pajamas, sweet-smelling, and ready for you to tuck into bed allows you to decide how much you will share in getting them clean and developing the routine to get them to sleep.

Some people just give up their expectations and enjoy life as it is. To them a messy house means love and kids. Others change their life dramatically by revising their careers and broadening family life to give it more meaning. I remember a young man who looked at his wife with a twinkle in his eye when she was grinding away about their dire financial straits, and said, "I get your point. You have the crazy idea we should spend less than we make!" She started to laugh. Once they began to laugh together, he explained that he had always figured that if they wanted something, then his job was to make more money. This cut into their time together as a couple and a family. It doesn't

EXPECTATIONS VERSUS REALITIES

Here are the five core fantasies along with a dose of reality, as I have come to appreciate it over time. They don't always fall neatly into these categories. Some couples manage to feel all five disappointments acutely, while others may focus on only one or two. I am always curious how people react to these issues.

WE EXPECT:

Tender family time: We'll have many tender moments together at home with a cooing baby.

Closer soul mates: We will share all the fun we had before but have even more in common after the baby.

Continued equality: Our relationship will be more equal than our parents' marriages were.

Support: We will be each other's main emotional and practical support.

Our family/new start: We'll do things better than our parents and make up for things we missed.

WE GET:

The red-eye special: Sleep deprivation, crankiness, irritability; less—not more—quality time and falling asleep during tender moments.

Unexpected differences: Children change us in unexpected ways. We each experience parenthood differently than our partner.

Tag team parenting: A new workload and a new definition of fairness.

Community: We learn "It takes a village to raise a parent."

Ghosts from the past: Finding out our past car powerfully disrupt the present.

---

matter how they resolved the issue, spending less and/or working less. Once they began to take both expectations into account, they could work out the problem together.

One valuable set of expectations from before kids (BK) does not change for happily married couples with kids.

- Happy couples maintain a certain standard of civility or caring, a set of unwritten rules about not hurting too deeply or irreparably, or allowing themselves to be hurt too deeply during their conflict. After a fight or discussion they can reconnect and respect each other again.

- Happy couples disagree and set limits with each other in ways that leave each person's self-respect intact. In fact, research suggests that couples don't last when the husband can't indicate disgust or displeasure. Happy couples know that it is not whether you disagree that matters—because you will—but how you work things out.

- Happy couples resolve the demands of parenting in many fascinating ways. The following chapters are filled with normal conflicts and the ways that couples resolve them to create happiness in their marriage.

2

The Real Parent Trap

Fantasy 1: New parents expect to have cozy time and grow closer because of the baby. Reality: Disruption and exhaustion arrive with baby.

Dreamy visions fill parents' heads, visions of playing together with a cooing baby or out strolling blissfully as a couple with a new baby. While these things do happen occasionally, a lot of things that don't fit with this picture occur as well. Sleep deprivation, the crunch of endless toys underfoot, and chronically disrupted conversations have led more than one young parent to feel that watching the baby sleep is the best parenting time, if you can stay awake to enjoy it. The word *cocooning* conjures up a picture of warm family time at home with "just our family." But, finding "just our family time" isn't that easy. Some parents have a hard time enjoying extended time knee-deep in clutter, interacting with a two-year-old. Others love that time but feel they lose touch with each other. It is normal to want to flee occasionally to moments of drool-free, uninterrupted adult conversation. Cocooning as a couple and as a family is possible, but it requires careful attention to the need for parents to spend time alone together as well as time with the family.

There may be a few walks together in the beginning while the baby is in the backpack or stroller. Unfortunately these times fuel expectations that soon won't be met. Most young couples, even those with hideously stressful schedules, have far more uninterrupted talk time and fun time together before kids than they will for many years after the baby. When the baby begins to toddle and talk, new parents find themselves walking alone while their partner stays with a (finally!) sleeping baby. Instead of growing closer, many couples become a sophisticated tag team, competing for personal time: "I'll cover ten until noon while you go to the gym, and then you take them to the park while I go shopping." Each partner vies for the hour or two of "free" time that is rarely enough to get the necessities of family life handled, much less their personal time, time with friends, or the extra hour needed at work. Going to the grocery *by yourself* may be as good as it gets some weeks.

But, one partner's free time may become the other partner's burden. Sometimes it feels like "Oh you need a haircut? Well I need to go to the hardware store to get parts for the toilet!" Sometimes the bottom line is there isn't enough time to go around even when both partners believe they are doing more than 50 percent. It is not surprising that many couples become adversaries who blame each other for shirking their share of the new burdens. Paradoxically, while all this pulling apart and competition for time is happening, the world still treats them as a couple, they see each other as a couple, and they have these wonderful kids they share.

Each parent's dream may be a little different. Now that she is home more, Mom may fantasize that she will work on all

FOR BETTER OR FOR WORSE By Lynn Johnston

those creative projects she put aside during her busy "work" life. Dad may fantasize that now that she is home more, she will take his stuff to the dry cleaners, take over bill paying, and be home when he gets there. Instead, both feel frustrated as less gets done, not more. Bottles and toys encroach on personal space and routines are disrupted. Mom may feel she doesn't deserve to go shopping or hire help because she is making less money. She may feel frustrated and isolated because no one is listening to her or asking her opinion as they used to at work. Because she is staying home, she may not ask for or expect her husband's help, and thus she grows more exhausted. Dad may be frustrated because they have less money and aren't filling the retirement account and college fund or even meeting the bills.

They may not have the money for a getaway dinner or weekend away. Mom may not be ready to leave the baby for fear of interrupting the bonding or because she likes to be available to the baby.

Whether working outside the home or inside the home, exhaustion and illness are common complaints of new parents. Parents often aren't prepared for the new germs kids bring home from daycare or the playgroup. Parents snuggling their child typically catch the bug, too. Three to four colds a year is considered normal for kids but is quite a disruption for working or formerly working adults who were used to averaging one sick day off a year. Exhaustion and flu *don't* make for greater closeness, exciting sex, or better relationships. Nor do they leave much time for leisurely reflection about how your life is changing.

Baffled, parents sense their reality falls far short of their dreams. They love their kids more than they could have imagined and focus their attention there. Compromise and expediency become the order of the day. Everyone compromises and all feel resentful.

Babies' Golden Slumbers

Experts hold very divergent views of how to get children to sleep well. Dr. Richard Ferber, director of the Boston Center for Pediatric Sleep Disorders, recommends a number of strategies that involve putting children down for naps and bedtime and letting them cry it out. His recommendations are more sophisticated than I describe here and vary with the age of the child. Many loving, tender parents haven't got the heart for this approach, however.

Conversely, the family bed approach, also known as attachment parenting, suggests that children sleep in the same bed with parents until they spontaneously give it up sometime before puberty (or college?!). Then there are parents who fall asleep

THE RED-EYE SPECIAL: SLEEP DISRUPTION

Our friend Bill described his lovely and cheerful wife, Maria, as a "pit viper" without adequate sleep. In other couples we knew, although more rarely, the dad could not function without regular sleep. I noticed, as my girlfriends' kids arrived, their idea of a dream vacation shifted from Tahiti with their man to sleeping in any clean, quiet hotel room, *alone*.

This is a critical issue for some couples. Sleep deprivation causes moderate to severe problems for 30 to 50 percent of new parents. Mothers often report never sleeping as soundly after the arrival of their first child. This lack of sound sleep may not feel like a problem at first, but it often becomes more severe and chronic as the child grows. In addition, sleep deprivation, whether caused by not enough sleep or by constant sleep interruption, often causes inhibited sexual desire, frequent headaches, irritability, depression and poor judgment.

Sometimes couples argue about the "right" amount of sleep a person should require rather than accepting they have different sleep needs. Other couples argue about who needs it most or that it is an absolute necessity for work. Successful couples make a plan that realistically accommodates both parents' sleep needs and accept that kids will disrupt both the sleep and the plan frequently.

SLEEP SOLUTIONS:

- If partners don't share a similar vulnerability to sleep deprivation, the two can use their natural inclinations to become a good tag team. The person with more tolerance for sleep disruption handles night duty and naps during the day. The sleep-requiring partner can do the early morning or weekend duty.

- Some couples alternate nights they get up with the baby or one partner takes night duty on weekends while the other partner takes weekdays.

- Dad can bring crying baby to bed so Mom can breast-feed without fully awakening, and Dad can then comfort Junior and put him back to bed.

- If both partners have a problem with sleep deprivation, they may need extra help. One exhausted mother of twins hired a baby-sitter every day for two hours, hoping to get some housework done. She slept instead, felt guilty but was less grouchy. This was an adaptive, healthy solution.

- Natural sleep remedies, like Valerian Root or Melatonin work for some people, although others experience significant side effects. *Be especially cautious of these solutions if you are breast-feeding!*

- Prescription antidepressants like Zoloft or Prozac can help insulate against the irritability and depression of the sleep disruption for some people. Ironically, these both may cause weight gain and further inhibit your already diminished sex drive.

- Antianxiety drugs like Valium and Xanax will give a good night's sleep in the short term, but most are addicting and create insomnia if used repeatedly. They also may dramatically *increase* depression.

If you choose to live better chemically, some careful reading and a good health care professional to help you evaluate the remedies you choose are essential. I cannot list all the side effects here. *Again be especially cautious if you are breast-feeding.*

Work together making this decision. Often a spouse de-
tects changes in a sleep-deprived or depressed partner's
mood more accurately than the affected person does. If you
plan to sleep through the night soundly with medication, be
sure your spouse or someone can and will wake up when necessary and that you do not sleep with the baby in your bed.

---

every night on their kids' beds. These choices have a significant
impact on your marriage.

Research in the personality development of children reared
under either extreme method is nonexistent, though both approaches appear to have adherents with happily married couples
and reasonably well-functioning children. The reality is your
kids will learn to sleep through the night *and* occasionally your
kids will be waking you up at night right through college.

How the two of you deal with this will affect your relationship. Clearly, if you insist your child be allowed to scream and
your partner feels that letting the child scream is child abuse, you
won't be getting much sex anyway! Likewise, if your partner requires eight to nine hours of uninterrupted sleep to be a civil human being, the family bed will probably cause family discord and/
or distance. Indeed, early proponents of the family bed approach
report their kids loved it, but it led to the end of their marriage.

Since the time my children and I struggled with this, there is a
wonderful book that addresses several simple solutions tailored for
the ages and stages of your child: *The No-Cry Sleep Solution: Gentle Ways to Help Your Baby Sleep Through the Night* by Elizabeth
Pantley. She places great emphasis on safety and gently teaching
your infant to fall asleep alone sometimes. I recommend it.

I advocate, as does Pantley, helping the baby become familiar with different ways of falling asleep. You can both comfort
your children and get them sleeping well in their own beds. Start
early and vary your routine. Have more than one person put

them to bed. Make sure each parent participates at least some of the time. Occasionally let Granny or a beloved caregiver put them down for a nap or the evening. Letting young children fall asleep on your bed or their bed while you rub their back is okay as long as they can fall asleep in their own beds alone sometimes, too, so that when they are too big to carry they still have a comforting sleep ritual. Be forewarned that this process is imperfect and will fall apart when kids are sick.

I know many parents who have fabulous sleep routines with their children: special songs, foot rubs, reading and "cozy time" for reviewing the day. I noticed though that happily married couples tended to include both parents in the evening ritual, even to the point of having Daddy sing or read from a story over the telephone if he is on a business trip. Such a routine needs to take into account the natural talents and inclinations of the family. My son, by age one and a half, clearly announced to me more than once, "Don't sing, just rock!"

Unhappily married parents had elaborate routines that did not include both parents or any routine to touch base with each other. Moms who were scrupulously regular about rubbing their children's feet or giving massages never did that with Dad. One couple, now separated, slept with their five kids in the bed with them. Another woman, now separated from her husband, woke with her child each night and got up and sang to him when she changed the diaper. By the time the second son arrived, there was a child party every night in the middle of the night.

Happily married couples have their own good night connection routines and unhappily married couples don't touch base before bedtime. I was curious why women usually would be so careful about their children's routines and not recognize their own or their spouses' needs for connection in the marriage.

When you choose sleep solutions for your child, be sensitive to the impact on your relationship. As mundane as it may seem, I have known several lovely couples to break up over this issue.

They didn't always disagree about the children's routines. They simply didn't create times for marital contact or think about the marriage when solving the sleep problems.

If your child has special needs, night terrors, or you can't get them sleeping alone in their own bed, talk to other mothers or professionals. Be sure, in any case, to work out a plan with your partner that allows you each to take good care of your kids and also have tender times for just the two of you.

> Planning ahead together to have warm couple and family time, however you manage it, prevents the need for crisis time and pays big dividends in family closeness and fun.

BABY BLUES By Rick Kirkman and Jerry Scott

Fostering Tender Time

For Couples: Time alone as a couple is the link that makes a marriage strong.

- Carve out two kinds of time together: time to just "date," for fun and romance with little serious talk, and time I call "staff time" to organize for the family needs. Make this staff time independent of your date time so you don't spend date time battling about parenting. Daily, weekly, and quarterly times are important. Successful couples often have some combination of all three.

Daily: Happy couples make regular time for each other in different ways. There is no one right way to make time.

- Some couples have telephone-free time each day together.

- Some have twenty minutes together in bed either early in the morning or late in the evening while kids are sleeping.

- Some take walks before breakfast or after dinner. These walks are wonderful, but as you start including kids in the walks and kids become more verbal you will need to find a new time that is just yours.

- Some people romance each other via e-mail during the day.

- Rare couples commute together or have lunch together regularly.

Whatever your style, you need this time to stay connected. It was interesting to me that 20 minutes seemed to be a time most often mentioned by satisfied couples.

Weekly: Many people think of childcare as something t   need so they can go to work but they don't see it as something they need for their marriage.

- Successful couples often have a standing date with a baby-sitter one night a week. Couples see this as especially necessary before kids are four.

- Some couples go out right after work on a weeknight so they don't have to say good-bye to the kids twice.

Having regular family time the day or the afternoon before date time alleviates parenting guilt and makes the date flow more smoothly.

- **M. A. D.** This tip to *Make a Date* is so important that I will repeat it frequently throughout the book. When you see M.A.D., know that it stands for *Make A Date or you and your partner will end up mad at each other much too frequently.*

- **Quarterly and Yearly:** Some couples wait for a marital crisis to schedule their first overnight or long day or evening away from the kids. A healthier approach is to schedule trips to prevent crises. When kids are older, some happy couples balance couple and family time with a three-day or weeklong parent vacation once a year while the kids visit grandparents, stay with friends, or go to camp. These first trips are often a source of conflict and must be scheduled carefully taking into consideration the age of the child and the issues of the parents. I know several happy couples that didn't schedule a trip alone until the kids were ten but had such great daily and weekly habits for connecting that they felt very close.

For Family: Good family time makes the time you spend away as a couple better because you feel connected and happy in your relationship with your kids.

- Create "just our family" time. Families need both fun time and "teamwork time," when the family pulls together and works. Make sure you have both. Though kids can't help much at first, the time you take with them to do small tasks together pays big benefits later. Kids also need one-to-one times with a parent each day. Time with each parent is better.

Daily: Many studies show that families that have a meal together each day have healthier and better performing kids in school and life.

- Some heroic parents get up for work at 4 or 5 A.M. to be home for dinner.

- Others change their jobs to eliminate a commute.

- Breakfast works as well as dinner for some people as family connection time.

- Consider not answering the phone during meals and/or for an hour at bedtime. Kids and partners are frustrated by interruptions. Imagine how you feel when a movie is interrupted. When you don't answer the phone, they feel very important to you. Friends and family get used to it quickly, especially if you tell them why you are doing it.

Weekly: Designate a family day or a family evening. For one night a week, let the machine get the phone and don't answer the door.

- When kids are older, don't let them have friends over during this special time because it's "just our family time." Couples say this tradition or habit works at all ages of children's lives. Family activities will change when kids are five versus ten but the togetherness is what's important. I have known both an insurance executive and a real-estate broker who took every Wednesday off because they had been gone on weekends so much when the kids were young. Both have great relationships, and are in the top 1 percent in their field in earnings. That Wednesday became a symbol to all of them that family was a priority. They only wished they had done it sooner.

Quarterly and yearly: Weekends and family vacations create memories that hold the family together. Some vacation time needs to be "just our family" if you want to foster a feeling of family closeness. However, vacations and weekends with family friends are great fun for kids and parents. They teach kids (and parents) a lot.

3

Can We Stay Best Friends?

Fantasy 2: Couples believe a baby will be a new, common interest that will bring them closer as soul mates. Reality: Men and women change and grow in different directions and in ways they never expect.

New parents expect to continue as friends who share the same interests and the same experiences. They used to share their workdays, work problems, and marathon movie weekends. They expect to continue to have fun in the same ways. Now the deck is stacked against this easy sharing. Whether she works full-time outside the home, part-time, or not at all, a mom's experience is just not the same as a dad's. What a new mom and dad in fact share is a greatly increased and dramatically changing workload.

Differences in experience begin in pregnancy. For many women, pregnancy brings nausea, napping, swollen ankles, and other discomforts not usually mentioned in mixed company. Even if Mom loves pregnancy and is perfectly healthy, the sheer weight gain and the rioting hormones cause a woman to slow down and turn her thoughts inward. For some women, each task she performs while moving around like a hippo raises questions about how this baby will change her life. People begin to respond to a pregnant woman differently. Still, it is impossible to imagine how your life will change.

Men, on the other hand, often begin to focus on making money or career advancement. If a man doesn't focus on this spontaneously, he often feels a not-so-subtle social pressure to do so. "Have you started that college fund, yet?" people joke. But the point is not lost. He may panic about money. He may think about what kind of model of career success and status he will be for his child. Even when the man has a well-established career, he may decide that the birth of his child signals a time to expand or change directions. "Even though I own a restaurant, I had better start another for my son." Psychoanalysts speculate that this is because the father is competitive and wants to be as creative as the mother who is creating a child. Whether or not competition is the root of the change, after seeing hundreds of couples, I am certain change begins to happen.

Dependency Issues

Often pregnancy is a period of incredible dependency among even the most independent women. The mom may crave reassurance that she is attractive, feel very physically and emotionally vulnerable and want extra help with decisions and duties. For most couples, the fact that the wife can burst into tears over a funny look upsets both the woman's sense of herself and the man's sense of her independence. Several women reported to me that they never regained their early sense of self-assertion after their first child and this lead to great unhappiness in the marriage. How the couple handles this period of emotional dependency can set the tone for the rest of the relationship.

These dependency issues can be a special strain on a relationship if, for example, the wife experienced an early trauma involving dependency. Being punished for normal needs as a child or, more commonly, having a parent abandon the family often create significant difficulties depending on a partner. In either of these cases, the new mom might be unable to talk about, or accept, that she feels very dependent. If she is uncomfortable about feeling dependent, she can become quite critical of her partner's efforts to be supportive or she might withdraw completely in anticipation of being abandoned.

Likewise, if the husband was required to be an emotional caretaker for his mother, he can be quite upset by his wife's new needs. He can feel like, "I married her because she was independent and now it turns out she is not!" Clear communication of respect and an understanding that the dependency is temporary leads to closeness and a positive outcome.

If either Dad or Mom had difficulty with the dependency, the change in their relationship may make them too uncomfortable to resume sex. I have heard of a woman deciding that she couldn't ever count on her spouse, because of the way her husband reacted at the hospital or on the way home.

However, when the mother is encouraged to talk about her sensitivity and feeling of dependency, and the father enjoys being attentive and nurturing, she experiences her partner as responsive and supportive. He experiences her as appreciative. The couple can emerge from this period stronger than ever. Together they can both feel more secure in the knowledge that when things change, they can both adapt and be there for each other.

As one woman described it, "It felt like a huge leap of faith. For the first time I really needed my husband. I think I liked knowing that, and I got better about trusting since he came through so well. Very scary though."

After the first child arrives, these differences between men and women intensify. Breast-feeding sends a clear biological message that Mom has a different role from Dad. Even in adoption or with bottle-feeding, Mom, not Dad, more often takes several months or more from work to bond with the new baby. Mom is likely to weigh more than she ever has in her life and this can become a source of conflict or an unspoken fear: "Will I (she) ever be thin again?" (See Chapter 14 for the answer.)

Because couples may spend more time home together than they had previously, they also sometimes become locked in struggles over small issues that hadn't bothered them before. One of these issues often is snoring.

Typically, dads are treated in ways that tend to drive them out of their marriage and into their cave. Whether his cave is golf, a garage workshop or the TV, it is his emotional safety zone away from talk and intimacy. As one comedian quipped the night after the arrival of his baby: "Ever notice how when a baby arrives, men suddenly become useless around the house."

In fact, a new dad is often treated like an idiot. Frequently the arrival of the child means that his mother and mother-in-law are around more. Men tell me that having their wife, mother, and mother-in-law all giving sometimes wildly contradictory advice and detailed "suggestions" is intimidating and humiliating. Most wives and mothers are eager to share knowledge and don't see themselves as humiliating anyone. The new mom is often in an experimental mode and excited to share what seems to be working for her baby—not the one right way or only way to do things. She may sound more certain than she is. Grandma may be excited about sharing what worked for her. While this enthusiasm is wonderful, their numerous suggestions often cause men to retreat. This creates more distance between the new mom and dad. Because of her initial enthusiasm, New Mom may encourage or allow Dad to be unskilled so that when he actually tries to help he has a bad experience.

SNORING

After the birth of the first child, snoring is a remarkably common issue for already sleep-deprived couples. Mom sleeps more lightly now, listening for the baby. The dad's snoring, or her own, may awaken her, disrupting sleep even more. Of course, in some couples, Dad gets up with the baby and experiences this problem. In either case, the discovery of what sounds like a dying seal in your bed is disconcerting. There are many solutions:

- **Separate bedrooms:** Mom may move out of the bedroom occasionally. This is a practical move with obvious potential negative consequences for the relationship. Dad thinks they will never have sex again. Paradoxically, if Mom requests Dad to sleep elsewhere and he agrees, she may then feel both relieved and then abandoned. Talking about this and having tender time before you sleep elsewhere helps.

- **Earplugs:** When the baby grows enough to get out of the crib safely and come tugging on your sleeve when he or she is ill or needs you, or if your husband will wake when the child calls for help, the newer soft gel earplugs work very well. I trained myself to sleep with a pillow over my head and face to muffle sound but it isn't a solution I recommend.

- **Snoring Cures:** With a vested interest in this problem, I discovered many purported cures. Breathing strips that attach to your nose, eliminating alcohol prior to bedtime, nutritional supplements available at health food stores called SNORE, even a mist you can spray in your husband's face that promises not to wake him up, den-

tal plates that position the jaw, losing weight, evalua-
tion for sleep apnea, and surgery are all solutions that
work for some people some of the time.

A snorer often has trouble accepting any of these solutions (except earplugs) since he or she may have been cheerfully snoring for many years without complaint. The snorer
usually views the complaints with mild bemusement or disbe-
lief. The snoring cures are seen as personally intrusive, critical,
belittling, and unnecessarily extreme. The snorer is also not desperate from sleep deprivation and therefore lacks empathy.
The light sleeper can grow quite resentful and enraged if the
snorer ignores the complaints or treats them lightly. Mock suf-
focation by pillow may result. If your wife moves out of the
bedroom the problem is serious for her. Try to keep some perspective as a couple. This is only one of many mundane problems you get to share after kids. Work on a solution together,
and be very grateful if you don't have this problem.

If Mom has excluded Dad and then Mom suddenly does decide to let Dad step in and take care of the kids, it is a setup for
disaster. No way can Dad step into the parenting and housekeeping job suddenly and do it as well as more experienced
Mom. He is even less likely to do it the way she wants. She is
likely to compare his attempts unfavorably to other mothers or
childcare workers. If she suddenly steps aside after she has a regular childcare provider, this person is probably around children
all the time and understands her children's habits and sensitivities, causing her to wonder why Dad is so out of it. When you
are around children a lot you hone the habits that ensure a
smoother day, habits like pushing glasses to the center of the

table. People who are around a child many hours a day understand the penalty for disrupted routines. like a missed snack or nap. Since Dad may not be around kids as much, he tends to celebrate by letting them skip naps and stay up late. This can bring a rain of criticism.

Some clever fellows develop a charming cultivated incompetence, which both flatters Mom and avoids the work. "Oh you do the sunscreen so much better than I do!" ("Sunscream," as some harried parents call it.) The sad result is that he both excludes himself from a connection with his child and burdens his wife. Don't fall for it. Have a sense of humor and dish it right back: "You are such a fast learner, I know you will catch on with a little practice!"

If Mom does all the childrearing herself, she is cutting her husband out of some important connections with his child and important sharing with her. This is the weakness of the traditional Mom-does-it-all model. If she does everything herself, career or no career, she will very likely not be able to raise her kids and stay in tune with her spouse. The 1950s and 1960s, as recalled in TV and in books, were times of functional, not intimate, marriages. This is precisely the period that spawned the women's movement. Many children raised in the 1950s and 1960s say they felt cut off from their fathers. Mothers and children became isolated in a world of other mothers and children. They became cut off from husbands, who were out in the larger world. Excluding Dad, by his choice or not, is everyone's loss.

Today some moms may be unable to let their husbands help because they need to justify staying at home. Others who felt neglected as kids themselves want so much to get their mothering right that they *can't* let Dad help. Mom feels compelled to do it herself, to make it just right for her children. She is trying to heal herself at the same time.

Better to let Dad spend time fathering and make some "mistakes." Even when Mom doesn't work outside the home, kids need time alone with Dad. Mom and Dad will feel more connected and share more experiences if they each take time caring for the kids. Consider laughing about how hard childrearing is together rather than living in two very separate worlds. Keep a list of best and worst moments in parenting. Pam, a mother of five, keeps this list and uses it as a basis for her hilarious Christmas letter. Deborah is saving hers to pass on to her kids. Sandy used her horror list as the basis for a baby shower game and gave points for the best solutions!

Big worlds and small worlds collide. Before the baby, Mom and Dad both view their lives in the context of the larger world. After the baby, Mom's world very much focuses on a small but precious world: her baby. The fact that she has a lot of expectations left from the larger world, the man's world if you will, creates conflict for her. This pull between two worlds may feel intense. Some jobs require women to make difficult choices. For example, a friend of mine had to choose between her law partnership and part-time work.

If a woman tries to establish reasonable limits at work, the people there may refuse to let her withdraw. People from work may call her at home with problems even though they told her to go home and enjoy her baby. Sometimes women experience a huge conflict between their own career and mothering expectations. Mom may have trouble realizing she can't do "everything" all at once.

Dad, on the other hand, remains a citizen of the larger world, and this feels right to him. In comparison to women, some men are given fairly wide latitude at work about how much they participate in their children's lives. Dad generally has less conflict, although he may feel some pull from Mom and the kids to be home more in their world. He may even push her to rejoin him in his world of work because he misses sharing that world with her as well as the money she earned. He may even miss the prestige of *her* career! A man's worldview doesn't help him understand Mom's conflict between the two worlds and her frustration.

Competing loyalties draw Mom away from the marriage. A woman's struggle between her small world and her big world stresses her marriage because those competing loyalties reduce her time for her spouse even more. Women often have a clear sense of what a good mother does for her kids and what an outstanding professional in her career is like. They have a less clear view of a great couple relationship. Gradually, the time she has for a marriage erodes as she lives up to the great mom and great professional roles.

We expect children to demand time. Yet we are quick to label husbands who want their wives' time as childish. Before the baby, a husband who wanted to spend time with his wife was seen as romantic. After the baby, the same behavior may be seen as childish or dependent. While both partners believed that a child would bring them closer, they find that they have little time and energy to devote to each other and are spending less time together.

Women often see men as simply not understanding what needs to be done and not helping enough. Men, missing their wives, try to rekindle romance and excitement, often before their partner is psychologically ready. Mom is trying to solve the balance between work and home and feels very involved in the small world. Dad visits the small world, but is missing her.

I remember when Neil surprised me with tickets for a fabulous ten-day vacation in Switzerland so we could attend a friend's wedding there. It sounds wonderful, right? Well, not exactly. It involved leaving my three- and four-year-old boys with Neil's mom, followed by lots of jumping on and off trains. Secondly, it fell during the first week of my teaching schedule at the university. Third, the tickets were nonrefundable. Instead of feeling rested and romantic, I felt like a tin can tied to the tail of a Labrador retriever. I would have loved this vacation pre-kids and I will probably love a vacation like this again when we have an empty nest. But I didn't love it then. I felt guilty about leaving work and my kids. I missed the kids badly. I needed some rest. Moreover, I felt misunderstood since he didn't share my guilt. I went and I complained a lot. Neil was great. He listened. At least we had plenty of time during that vacation to figure out what was so wrong for me. We decided while the kids were small we wouldn't have any more surprise vacations. Instead we would sort out our priorities and make plans together.

Many would see my reaction to the vacation as silly and ungrateful. Back then I wondered what was wrong with me since I was reacting so differently from the way I might have reacted five years earlier. Only as we talked, did I begin to understand how differently Neil and I were experiencing this time in our lives.

Most couples experience conflicts similar to the ones I have described even when Mom doesn't work outside the home. The husband wants to have fun and reconnect the way they used to and the wife is worried about the baby-sitter, her job, and the house. Sometimes, the reverse occurs: The wife is the one missing the fun and the husband, who is gone a lot, misses the kids and doesn't want to leave home. Usually, though, the husband is the one who is upset by this difference first. The danger to the marriage is that the wife begins to doubt her love for her partner because she is less excited about doing things together. The romantic husband feels unloved because the new mom always says no. Other moms would see her refusal as understandable. Quite often a mom fantasizes about getting away by herself without Dad or kids, something she never would have considered pre-kids. This also may make both of them wonder if the marriage is failing.

A typical romantic husband's response is to encourage the new mom to just do what they always did to have fun. Dad sees fun time as the only way to preserve the relationship. Mom feels overwhelmed because her life has already changed in so many ways she didn't expect. He feels they should not have to lose the fun they shared before just because they have kids. Both parties feel misunderstood and hurt. Both partners are normal and right but see the problem through very different lenses. To feel closer again, each needs to begin to understand how different their parenting experience is while both need to work together to set priorities.

The mommy dilemma: Stay home, go back to work or try to ride with one foot on each horse? The question of whether to work outside the home, and if so how much, is central to a new mother's identity. For the most part, a man's central identity is usually his work, not his parenting. This is not true for women. A woman's central identity may be "Mom" regardless of whether or not she works or how powerful or prestigious her career.

Indeed, it may be harder today to have a marriage and kids than a generation or two ago because so many more moms work. Most women with children under five now work at least part-time and the percentage of working mothers is rising. Full-time career moms obviously have a lot on their plate, and studies repeatedly indicate they tend to be chronically sleep-deprived. The part-time mom is trying to do some of everything and often feels the strongest pull between these two different worlds.

Full-time moms often are set up for exhaustion too. Full-time moms frequently set very high expectations, don't hire help, don't initially ask their partners for help and don't give themselves much-needed breaks. Twenty-four/seven has new meaning because routine time off and breaks are not scheduled. Reality doesn't match the expectations and Mom becomes depleted.

The perception (often on the part of both parents) that staying home with kids isn't "working" aggravates the problem of balancing the new workload between the two parents. Dad may

BABY BLUES By Rick Kirkman and Jerry Scott

come home and sit down to read the paper, not recognizing that Mom needs him to take the baby, NOW. He may not recognize how exhausting her day has been since she has "been home all day." He thinks she has had all those great moments of playing with the baby, which he missed while he was working hard for the family. She thinks he got adult conversation and lunch at a restaurant while she didn't get to shower until 3:00 P.M. She may become quite angry if he must work late or meet social obligations for work that interfere with his being home. Both partners are frustrated because they are doing hard jobs well and want sympathy, appreciation, and a break. Instead their partner envies their "freedom" and nobody gets a break.

If she worked at a career before becoming a full-time mom, she may also suffer keenly because of her isolation from adult conversation and miss the respect she normally received from other adults. Her husband may appear to her to retreat each day to a sanctuary of relative quiet and order.

Dad may have difficulty really understanding her conflict between work and home unless he is part of the special group of stay-at-home Dads. These choices are just not a parallel experience for men and women. Perhaps they should be, but that discussion is beyond the scope of this book.

Dads aren't expected to think much about these issues although more dads have begun to look at them. When a couple decides that Dad will commit heavily to the world of work and Mom will cover the home scene, they are often making a significant decision about what they will share as partners. This decision also raises the question of whether Dad will have more or less of a relationship with each child. When Dad can discuss with Mom what they can gain or lose as a couple and what their kids can miss or have during the career building years, they can make better decisions for themselves, their marriage and their family.

When men truly consider whether or not they would be willing to give up their job to take care of Junior and depend on Mom's income or consider how they would be treated at work if they worked half time, they might begin to appreciate the difficulty of the decision each mother makes. Often men who lose a job temporarily become paralyzed with depression. Women often expect or are expected to give up a job or career temporarily and sometimes repeatedly to accommodate the needs of her husband and children. This has very real economic consequences. One man said that his wife used to be his boss. Now, after staying home with their child, she makes a quarter of what he does.

This decision has significant financial and practical implications for the family. Mom's work life will affect the family considerably, how much they have in common, how they will relate to the community, how much flexibility they have in responding to a sick child, how much time and money is available for fun, sleep, sex, and dating Dad. I happen to agree with my favorite research, which says children do best when Mom is doing what makes her happy whether that is being a full-time mother, working in a career, working from home, or working part-time. How these career choices affect the couple has never been addressed.

As moms or couples make these decisions, an intense period of emotional conflict often begins for mothers. Whatever their decision, moms continue to worry for years about whether or not they have made the right decision for this time in their child's life, a conflict that dads don't experience in the same way.

Sometimes Dad says, "I will support you no matter what you decide." Although he feels he is being very supportive, this leaves Mom feeling lonely. She feels like she struggles and he doesn't. Dads have trouble understanding the depth of moms' conflict. The closest parallel for a man is often whether to miss work and go to the pediatrician appointments with Mom or whether to leave work early and take time to be a coach in Little League. This is not the same magnitude of struggle as whether or not to pursue a career.

If Dad insists that Mom work because of the money, Mom may feel ignored and not given a choice. Sometimes Mom just announces that she is staying home and Dad feels that he has no say. This is a hot-potato issue that some couples have strong feelings about but don't discuss because they fear open conflict. Not discussing their feelings leads to resentments that poison the relationship.

As the baby grows, couples make critical decisions very rapidly that affect the long-term health of the marriage. The consequences of these decisions that couples make about their new life with a child can serve either as a wedge that separates them or as a bond that fosters closeness. These decisions, made for the good of the child, often don't consider the health of the marriage as a critical factor for the child and the parents. At first new parents ignore their relationship because the baby is the clear priority and has many pressing needs. Parents focus on who is getting up at night and who is changing diapers rather than on their relationship.

Most important to the couple's friendship is *how* the couple decides issues not *what* they decide. If both feel listened to and included then Dad, for example, is less likely to feel he is just there to bring home money and Mom is less likely to feel taken for granted. Happy couples approach the decision about who works, where and how much very differently, yet the outcome works when each person feels considered and respected.

Tips to Stay in Touch and Grow Closer

- Spend an uninterrupted twenty minutes each day engaged in face-to-face talking (maybe cuddling) and, most important, listening to anything the other wants to say. Yes, when you are desperate, you can break it into two ten-minute chunks.

- Be curious, not furious, about differences. Don't try to persuade your partner to see differences logically, rationally, reasonably or your way. For ten minutes, just listen.

- Take turns talking about what your fantasies for life with kids would be like.

- Talk about what you want for your marriage.

- Share when you feel the most love and pride in your child. When do you each enjoy your child the most? What is the hardest for each of you?

- Share what you each want for your kids. Write it down and save it. It is fun to revisit these lists and see how they change in light of who your child becomes.

- Keep a list of best and worst moments in parenting to laugh about together.

- Take a parenting class together. Neil says you will love it and be the only guy there.

- Talk about the kind of parent you want to be. Parenting issues aren't romantic but they are much more fun when you feel like you are on the same team.

- Read the same parenting book.

- Create a calendar time once a week to sit down and iron out scheduling difficulties, resolve division of labor issues, review childcare, and make dates.

- Talk together about what a good couple relationship means to each of you and about what time and other commitments you each need to make to fulfill your dream.

- Celebrate what you have. Include compliments to your partner and good news about your kids and your day in every mini-planning or sharing session.

4

Separate and Equal

Fantasy 3: Equality. Couples today expect their relationship to be much more equal than their parents' marriage. Reality: Babies are the great *unequalizers*.

This expectation of equality is possibly the single greatest change in recent years. New moms and dads expect to participate more equally in childcare than their parents did, especially if both partners worked at equal status jobs before having children. Prepared childbirth classes spend several hours getting dads ready to help on the day of the birth. This preparation supports an expectation on the part of both Mom and Dad that there will be a lot of shared activity and involvement after the birth of the child. But, in most families, this just isn't so.

Several research studies on work distribution in the home show that although both partners do more work after the baby arrives, most men actually do a smaller share of the total workload. If a woman works outside the home, she typically comes home to 275 percent more of the childcare and 15 percent more of the housework than her partner. I know it looks like a misprint. But it isn't. Actually the latest statistics, depending on who collects them and how, vary by fifteen to thirty minutes or so from year to year. Men may be shifting a bit in the last few years but those numbers are not yet available.

As we know, statistics can be manipulated and are subject to vagaries of collection methods. I prefer to use questions from Elizabeth Rapoport in her chapter entitled, "How Many Working Fathers Does it Take to Screw in a Lightbulb?" in a clever book called *Mothers Who Think*. She proposes a "Superparent Achievement Test" to underscore the time and attention to detail that childcare requires. Here is a sample of a few items that she assigns points for:

- What are the names and numbers for the pediatrician, pharmacy and fastest pizza delivery?

- When is your child's next checkup? Dental appointment?

- What are the names and numbers of the kids' emergency backup playdates?

She gives bonus points if

- You noticed the rug had weird pink stains and arranged for the steam cleaners to come on your day at home.

- You called the nighttime sitter and reserved the restaurant. (Double credit if you know which baby-sitters tidy up.)

You get the idea. Whether you use the linear or nonlinear approach to calculating the work, your daily life changes dramatically with kids and as a couple, you need a way to get this stuff done and still have a good marriage.

If couples start out as equal career partners—as many do—both are used to thinking of being at home as a break from their career. Both are then likely to underestimate the work to keep the home going once children arrive. Once you have kids, coming home from work takes on a whole new meaning. This inequality often unfolds because initially women are eager to do a good job mothering and they take over the childcare enthusiastically. Men cooperate. Both perpetuate the roles they saw their parents assume. Neither partner thinks about the consequences of this unequal arrangement for the long-term happiness of the marriage.

Women and men start with different notions about what equal parenting is based on what their dads and moms did. Men look at their dads and say, "I am doing way more than he did if I do diapering once in a while." A new dad may feel that he is quite generous about what he is contributing. He may also be very proud of his wife's career. Meanwhile, a new mom is looking at her mom and thinking, "I am doing less than she did but way more than my husband is and way more than I can manage." If she also works, they may both enjoy and depend on the money she is making. So he encourages her to work; and she may not see leaving her job as an option. Sadly, moms who work more than 35 hours a week also get less sleep than men and moms who don't work outside the home, according to researchers. Mom and Dad both incorrectly assume that a little childcare and cleaning help will solve the overload and imbalance.

Another complication occurs when Dad is an experienced parent with a child from a previous marriage and only reluctantly agreed to have this child with Mom. This piece of history often prevents Mom from asking for help until she is so overwhelmed that she is suddenly demanding. Dad now feels even more unappreciated since he expressed his reluctance to take on the extra work from the outset.

Even when both parents work, the shelter of work can serve to divide the couple even more. For some parents, especially as the child moves out of infancy and into toddling and talking, work becomes a welcome relief from the constant demands of a two-year-old. Arlie Russell Hochschild, sociologist and author of three *New York Times* notable books on this subject, has thoroughly documented this phenomenon. Yet, retreat to the relative serenity of the office means more time away from the partner, family and kids. When both parents are absent from kids many hours a day, they may also be less skilled and easily slip into blaming each other for normal frustrations when they are with the children. Retreat into work makes the increased workload and the demands of kids at home seem even more overwhelming and more tempting to avoid. Gradually, they see less of each other and less of the kids.

To get back to comfortable and equitable, if not equal, ground that supports the growth of the marriage and the children, the couple needs to make some thoughtful decisions. Both partners must consider their expectations about what must be done, whether to get more help and negotiate compromises around issues of career and family. Yet faced with big decisions, their problem-solving styles are likely to be very different.

This inequality of time and work grows slowly at first and then escalates. If he is doing much more than he did before kids—and the family has childcare—he is convinced that he must be doing more than half of all the work now. But even with childcare, there is more than twice as much work to do, so a man is very rarely keeping up with close to half of all there is to do. I could do the math to show you how this works but it is more dramatic to use your own daily hours as an example.

To see how work is divided in your house, do a rough calculation of hours spent each day earning money and doing childcare, household chores, and errands. (See Partner and Parent Activities Worksheet.) Look at an average week. Precision isn't important. This framework helps focus on who does what. Then look more generally over the last six months or a year at exceptional time spent taking sick days, interviewing household help, and selecting childcare. Couples are often surprised at the outcome.

Partner and Parent Activities Worksheet

First, calculate your sleep in Part 1 and compare it to the sleep that you had before kids. Second, calculate how much time you spend at each of the other activities per week. If one of you travels a lot on a random schedule, you may want to use a longer time period, like a month or a year. Then, for fun, guesstimate your partner's activities and compare to see whether you each view time spent the same or differently.

Use the subtotals to help you consider how you are balancing your time. Notice whether you each include items like social activities, home decorating or car repair as personal, fun or family time. Include time spent finding, scheduling and supervising help. There are no right or wrong answers. Use this to focus your thoughts and discussion.

Notice whether you are each spending time where you most enjoy it and still having enough fun couple time. Express appreciation to each other for all you do. Is one of you overwhelmed with responsibilities? Consider where hired help or family help could lighten the load.

For an even more enlightening exercise, fill out a worksheet for yourself and your spouse. Have your spouse do the same. Then compare your *perceptions* of how you each spend time. Now take a look at your workloads and perceptions together and discuss them. The purpose is to figure out how to care for

---

PART 1   Mom   Dad   BK
Sleep

Record normal wake up time: _____
Record normal sleep time: _____
Hours up with child at night: _____

Calculate Sleep Hours   _____
Uninterrupted Sleep Hours _____

PART 2   Mom   Dad   Help
Work

Time at work, including commute time and travel: _____
Work-related calls, evening meetings, nighttime
    paperwork, etc: _____
Optional: (Calculate money earned per hour spent): _____

Subtotal Work Time   _____

Childcare   Mom   Dad   Help

Dressing and feeding children in the morning: _____
Putting children to bed: _____
Scheduling and going to pediatrician, doctor's
    appointments, and therapy appointments
    for children: _____
Diapering, bottle washing, homework help: _____
Researching schools, teachers, lessons, etc.,
    for kids: _____
Chauffeuring kids to lessons, play dates, etc.: _____
Staying home with sick child: _____
Preparing snacks and feeding the kids: _____
Spending one-on-one time with kids: _____

Subtotal Child Time   _____

Household Maintenance   Mom   Dad   Help

Handling household finances, bill paying,
   preparing taxes, loan applications,
   filing insurance, etc.:   _____
Picking up after kids, housecleaning and
   organizing: _____
Drop off and pick up laundry or dry cleaning: _____
Washing, folding, sorting, and putting
   away laundry: _____
Handling home maintenance and repair: _____
Handling car repairs: _____
Scheduling and supervising or doing yard work: _____
Preparing meals and snacks; cleaning up
   after meals: _____
Grocery shopping: _____
Eating meals and relaxing: _____
Emptying dishwasher and taking out trash: _____

       Subtotal Household Time _____

Fun and Social Arrangements   Mom   Dad   Help

Gift and card shopping: _____
Traveling, vacationing, fun together as a family: _____
Researching vacations, making reservations: _____
Making social plans, play dates, and the like: _____
Social time, church time, etc., with kids: _____
Charity and volunteer activities: _____

  Subtotal Social Activities and Arrangements _____

Couple time   Mom   Dad   Help

Date time, couple-only vacations, sex: _____
Staff planning, calendar, and touch-base time: _____

Therapy or attending a class together: _____
Watching TV, reading, or hobbies together: _____

Subtotal Couple Time _____

Personal Time	Mom	Dad	Help

Reading, haircuts, golf, shopping, computer surfing,
   personal therapy, solo activities outside family: _____
Exercising alone or with a friend: _____
Telephone social time, girls night out, parties
   alone, etc.: _____

Subtotal Personal Hours _____

TOTALS HOURS _____
(Compare hours reported and hours available.) _____

---

the kids, make money, do the things you each most enjoy, and
still find fun time together.

Neil, like most guys, says, "This is a loser for guys. They
don't do quizzes in chick magazines. How about an exercise
where you talk about the things that need to be done?" And he
is right. Many women feel centered working out a sheet like this.
Many men would rather be shown a list or have the problem
outlined and then figure out with their partner how to solve the
issue. Work together on who does what and what can be dele-
gated and/or eliminated. Try not to make it a contest to see who
does more. Instead use it to see if you need to delegate activities
or perhaps the more efficient person can take over more. Do you
each have personal time and couple time? Are you both getting
enough sleep? How much time do you spend together doing
these activities?

Negotiating and Cooperating

Men are taught to emphasize negotiation while women are trained in cooperation. A woman may say, "I need help with the kids. I am exhausted." She would like—perhaps expect—him to ask, "How can I help?" A man might think, "You want to share chores? Sure, let's negotiate." His point of view is "Why volunteer for trouble?" at the beginning of a negotiation. He says, cheerfully or defensively "I take out the trash and empty the dishwasher." He expects her to counter with a direct request like, "I know and I really appreciate that you do those things but I was thinking the kids would really like it if you put them to bed sometimes." Instead when he doesn't volunteer to help, Mom feels he doesn't really want to share and doesn't care about her. This puzzles him because he is negotiating and wants to do his part.

For men, a good bargaining session is a form of connection. Picture two guys hassling each other in a fun way before agreeing who drives on a fishing trip or picks up beer. They feel like buddies because they are close enough to tease, hassle, and negotiate. A woman, on the other hand, thinks the highest form of love is when Dad *volunteers* to put the kids to bed every other night or take over some duty that relieves her and will mean he spends more time with their child. In a few marriages, if the husband reminds her, she may vaguely remember when teasing, hassling, and negotiating could be fun occasionally. That stuff is not fun now when she is this tired and needs help, *now*.

Using the cooperation model, women often assume that if they do nice little extra things for anyone, but especially for their spouse, then that person will feel loved and reciprocate with nice or loving gestures. Women believe, "If I do this for you (and you care about me) you will remember and reciprocate. She expects—but normally doesn't get—the same in return. She can't believe they share the same house if he believes that emptying

BABY BLUES By Rick Kirkman and Jerry Scott

the dishwasher occasionally (and leaving half the things on the counter because he isn't sure where they go) covers his fair share of the new workload. She feels enraged when he doesn't volunteer to help more with the kids. She will often respond by saying, "You don't care about me or our child." The implied part of the sentence is "because you don't volunteer more, you don't care." He feels crushed by this criticism since he adores her and the child and doesn't know what she is responding to or talking about, because she has not asked for anything. He may actually want to be asked and included.

When women do speak up, and men try to negotiate, women perceive that approach as insensitive, self-centered, uncooperative, and unloving. A woman's strong negative reaction to negotiation strikes men as emotional or crazy. When kids arrive with their attendant laundry, toys, diapering, and other needs, skilled negotiating becomes a bigger factor in the relationship than ever before.

Men's negotiating rules differ from women's. Men negotiate hard. Then, win or lose, the fight is over. Generally, in the male world you play a game as hard as you can, but when it is over, it is over. Men have pet sayings like, "Let it go," "Move on," "Forget about it," or "Close it out." Women tend to look for a pattern of cooperation over time. Women expect that if they give in now, their partner (as would any sensitive and reasonable person from their point of view) will give in later. Since women are looking for a pattern, they recall what has occurred. To men, this feels like women are keeping a running score of their mistakes. Thus, men complain that women bring up irrelevant old history just to make a point. Men often believe the events recounted by their wives probably happened years before or were just invented as examples to torment them. Bringing up the pattern is a female response that men see as uncomfortable, emotional, irrational and unreasonable. Men also see it as not playing by the rules as they understand them. Women bring it up as they unconsciously or consciously strive to achieve equity over time, which is how they believe the game of life is played.

Since most new parents don't recognize these differences in male and female expectations and negotiating styles, women often assume a greater share of the responsibilities. She expects that if she is good enough, sweet enough and well loved, he will soon pick up one half of the load. This does not happen because men don't work that way. He expects to be asked and then to negotiate. He puts up resistance because he is negotiating. She gives in because she is cooperating, but assumes he owes her one. He assumes nothing of the sort because to him the game is over until the next round. As this continues, the woman grows more and more resentful and winds up feeling like a martyr.

Without conscious effort and understanding of their negoti-ating styles, and the importance of taking care of both their needs, couples gradually drift into an unequal relationship with a resentful wife and a husband who feels abused by her irritabil-ity and anger. Although women joke about men not doing their fair share, women and men don't easily recognize what each partner does to help create and support this situation.

Who decides what is on that to-do list anyway? In spite of all the advances in women's rights and the enlightenment of many modern males, some dads (and moms) still follow the rea-soning that if the baby is mostly the wife's responsibility, then the housework is her responsibility as well. Men are not to blame for taking comfort in this idea. Often the new mom sup-ports this idea, particularly if she is "only" working part-time at her job or staying home full-time and feels she needs to earn her right to work less by doing all the housework and childcare as well as making the social arrangements. Or she may just like to do things her way. She is soon swamped.

Parents, parents-in-law and/or coworkers may support that notion as well. Without careful examination of the work in-volved, the marriage is thrown out of balance. The wife is soon exhausted and resentful. Dad is feeling unappreciated, criticized, and resentful that she has no time for him and no interest in ro-mance. In fact marital troubles follow from a plan they both supported.

For the average woman, her mother and model often did not work outside the home. Or her mom may have worked outside the home at a defined job rather than having a career with ex-pectations about travel, speaking engagements, or deadlines. If she did work outside the home, she may have done so after the youngest was in school. So a new mom, expecting to have an equal relationship with her partner, may be doing less than her mother did at home, but a whole lot more with a career added to the mix. The career mom feels overwhelmed and guilty. She would often like to spend more time with her kids than she does and have a home fit for *Architectural Digest*. Even when she manages with household help that her mom didn't have, she may compare herself to the fewer than 6 percent of full-time at-home moms, and constantly feel like she isn't quite keeping up with her ideal standards. In fact, full-time moms, both then and now, often have household help.

She also has new burdens her mother didn't. For example, attending every one of your child's games (and practices and maybe coaching or being team mom) is a new requirement of parenthood that was not prevalent in the 1950s or even the 1960s or 1970s. (This is a new time-consuming task for some dads as well.) All these new time commitments, while possibly quite pleasant, add up to less time for the couple to share alone with each other.

We see our own childhood through a wavy mirror. As I indicated earlier, most people have a somewhat skewed picture of their parents' relationship, taken from when they were old enough to remember, usually at around age nine to twelve when kids are much easier to handle and live with than at age two to five. In most traditional relationships Mom didn't work when the kids were really little. Or another reliable person provided either significant household help or childcare. Or Dad or older family members helped them balance the workload. As any woman or man who has worked full-time and then stayed home full-time with small children will tell you, staying home is harder than working, if it weren't for missing the kids. Yet society defines it as easier, and it pays less.

If a mother stays at home, she is often seen in the community as someone who could lead scouts, run PTA, volunteer in the classroom, and pick up the friends of her children whose mothers work outside the home. As part of a rapidly dwindling minority, she is often expected to pick up more and more of the community activities. While it is wonderful to do these things, and many moms stay home so they can, moms sometimes get so caught up in these activities that the couple relationship suffers.

The woman who has a career and is fortunate enough to have paid help with both housework and childcare, often functions fine during the week. On the weekend however, her partner sees it as his time with the kids and she becomes the family maid. He says, "Why do you always complain? You have paid help and your mother didn't." The difference is obvious to her: He gets no housework and two days to play each week. She gets to work seven days a week, unless they consciously plan together to make it otherwise.

In addition, a mom typically has higher standards for housekeeping and childcare and thus sees more that needs to be done. She views herself as a good mother and wife only if she meets these standards. Often Dad doesn't define the workload in the same way. Thus Mom takes on too much and grows resentful. Dad tends to take on less and feel lonely, unappreciated and criticized. In some families partners reverse roles on this one, Dad likes neat and Mom doesn't care. Then she feels criticized and he feels resentful. Anyone who expects the house to be as neat as before kids is likely to be frustrated during the toddler years.

In any case, the wavy mirror of our childhood sets us up to be frustrated with the present. Expectations about what is necessary and what is equal are still miles apart. The contrast between the different perceptions of men and women about the workload at home leads to misunderstandings that could be interesting or amusing if the couple stopped and had enough perspective to consider them. More frequently couples blame each other for the stress they feel.

Good friends of ours cleared the work from their shared home desk one day by pitching stuff over the balcony together in a burlesque of accusations about having four children and no time. They howled with laughter when they told this story. As a semi-neatnik, I was horrified. But I realized it put them on the same side of the mess, making fun of their desire to blame each other and cleaning up together rather than fighting. Their sense of humor keeps them happily married.

Still, role differences can have value in a happy marriage with kids. The notion of equality and sharing seems like it should make things easier and fairer. It doesn't always. One perceptive and very tired mother of twins explained it to me like this:

> "Sometimes a nontraditional relationship means every little thing has to be decided. I just don't always want to discuss where the mustard should go in the refrigerator or whose turn it is to pick up the kids. My mom just knew her job and did it."

As her comment indicates, sharing tasks equally isn't for everyone. Interestingly, in the study that showed working women did 275 percent more childcare than their partners, some couples said they had very happy marriages while others said they had very unhappy marriages. Some people aren't comfortable sharing roles. Some may not perform roles equally well. Some have no patience for the negotiation. Some are unskilled at negotiating. Others fall into their parents' roles without planning or questioning.

Happy couples do, however, have a sense of respect and fairness rather than equality that is flexible and balanced. For example, I have known two different couples whose first child was colicky seventeen hours a day for the first seven weeks of life. (I would have shot myself!) One husband simply moved out because he felt the sleep disruption was a threat to his career. His wife eventually divorced him. I think I understand why. Another husband in a similar situation traveled a lot. He was gone from home more hours than the first. But when he came home he took the baby for a few hours right away. This gesture communicated that he understood her terrible predicament. He supported her seeking professional help for the child. The second couple is still very happily married. I think his wife felt that she and the baby were understood and supported, not judged.

Happy couples don't necessarily share childcare equally in the sense that they alternate each diaper change. But they do each have a sense of appreciation for what the other brings to the marriage and they communicate that appreciation. They don't keep track of every little thing. Tag team parenting isn't good or bad. Some cross-train for parenting responsibilities and feel closer. Others divide and conquer the work. However they manage it, happy couples achieve a balance that works for them. True fairness is flexible, balanced, and shows a deep appreciation for the contribution of the other. Couples need to make a conscious decision about their priorities and the division of labor in the marriage. These choices about the structure of the family and division of labor affect the future happiness of the whole family.

Fostering Fairness and Balance

- Step in and take the kids. Send your wife to the bath or out to lunch or let your husband take a nap or watch a game.

- Switch roles occasionally. Send your partner on a day or two away if you are the one who always travels.

- If your partner spends too much time on chores and not enough time having fun, ask how you can help so you can plan fun time together. This kind of person needs a plan to feel comfortable having fun. Don't call them a stick in the mud.

- Take the kids and do something your partner usually does with them. Fix a meal or go to the park.

- Check in monthly (put it on the calendar!) with each other about the decisions you've made about the division of the workload and time with your careers versus time for the kids. Are you comfortable with your own decision and with your partner's? Do you have second thoughts? Are your family needs changing in ways that require adjustment?

- Wash dishes, empty the dishwasher, or take out the garbage occasionally, even though it isn't your job.

- Adjust your expectations. It takes fifteen minutes to get kids in the car to go somewhere. The house will be messier than it used to be. Everything from grocery shopping to picking up clothes at the dry cleaners will take at least twice as long, sometimes more.

- Never criticize your partner for a messy house. Ask what you can do together to turn things around. You can make a new plan to deal with the mess together (although it probably won't work the first time). Joke about the mess together, but don't call your partner a slob or lazy.

- Partners who work outside the home and don't mind a mess, may need a more direct wake-up call. They need to know even if it doesn't matter to them, a clean house matters to you, and if neat matters to one of you, the other will often help. A friend told me that her husband has four areas—his desk, his closet, his sink, and the garage—that she doesn't touch and even the housekeeper can't manage. They talked it over and now once a month she says, "It's time—this weekend. I want your areas cleaned up," and he does!

- Trade jobs. Learn how your other half lives. Let the person who balances the checkbook "wrong" or who doesn't

clean as well do it his or her way. It is a brief experiment.
Talk about what it feels like.

- Sit down and make a list of all the household chores, how
  often they need to be done and the hours required. Include time spent on the job making money to pay bills as
  a chore. Discuss and divide the time in a way that seems
  equitable so you both get to do what you like most. Decide to skip some stuff or delegate what you don't like.
  Discuss what you like doing alone and what you really
  miss doing together. (See Partner and Parent Activities
  Worksheet, page 48.)

- Add up how much relaxed personal time each of you has
  whether it's jogging or TV watching. See if you can figure
  out how to have a bit more personal time without losing
  couple time.

- Work together on your budget, your goals, and your parenting. Happily married couples can say we decided to do
  it this way, so we both get some of what we want.

5

Support Networks: It Takes a Village to Shelter Your Marriage

Fantasy 4: We expect our partner is going to rescue us from the day-to-day rigors of life with kids. Reality: It takes a village to shelter a healthy marriage.

Hillary Clinton's borrowed African aphorism, "It takes a village to raise a child" is branded in the American consciousness, and for good reason. In reality, a happy marriage also needs a village of concerned parents and community members. Parents need good models to show them their options and to create supportive environments for themselves and their kids. Who is going to watch your children so that you can have time alone? Who is going to make you feel safe on your child's first sleepover? Where will you find a sounding board when you doubt your parenting decisions? Who is going to tell you how they resolved that perpetual conflict with a spouse?

In some magical places extended family live nearby supporting both children and parents. That is not the case in urban America today. Without a solid support system at hand, many women, especially if they previously enjoyed working outside the home, experience periods of intense loneliness and isolation staying home. However, a supportive village of nice families can help buffer the feared effects of violent movies, music and two-income families.

As for her relationship with her partner, a new mom often expects her spouse to be her main, and sometimes only, source for warmth and emotional support. In addition (and in contradiction to the expectation of support and talk time) the harried new mom may begin to see her partner as a quality childcare person who owes her break time from the kids rather than as a romantic partner.

Meanwhile, the new dad expects the new mom to be as attentive and supportive when he arrives home as she was before the baby. Dad loves his baby, but he'd like his wife back the way she was—paying attention to him. Each is unaware of how much of a toll the new workload is taking on their relationship. Occasionally couples reverse roles and Dad is gaga over the new baby and Mom misses the attention she once had.

A strong community of close friends or family is vital to helping with stress. This network helps both partners by providing concrete assistance and models for how to deal with new experiences. Having someone to watch your kids can be vital as a stress reducer at a critical time. In healthy families, aunts, uncles, reliable young cousins, old family friends, and grandparents who adore your children can be trusted caregivers when you need a break. They also can provide invaluable perspective when your child's and/or spouse's unique needs or temperaments are confusing to you.

My sister now chuckles about how her son sweated through his first three years because the books said to dress your child as warmly as you dress yourself, but he had his daddy's warmer metabolism. An understanding mother-in-law can help explain how she came to terms with a night-owl husband. A good friend can let you know how they coped with a partner who simply doesn't believe in recording checks. An outsider can notice that the supercompetitive athlete in your family is your daughter and not your son. In the midst of struggling with parenting and marital issues, my clients often ask in a desperate tone, "Is this normal?" Family and friends help you understand the variety of temperaments, conflicts, and issues that are normal.

When you live many miles from family and friends, it is important to create your own family of choice nearby. (See the box on page 64.) If you have a "special needs" child, your own relatives may not understand your child's needs. It may be harder to build your own couple network as well. But someone somewhere has successfully raised children very much like yours. They are in your community or can be found through the Internet. With the support and resources of this community, it will be possible to find the time and energy so you and your partner can support each other and your child.

For people who have parents and grandparents who are substance abusers or verbal abusers or otherwise unsuitable, it becomes even more critical to develop a family of choice. Even if a partner has one good parent, he or she may have not seen a model for how a good marriage works.

Often people from emotionally abusive family situations have a hard time seeing that such relationships with helpful people in the community are possible. They may have been isolated in a terrible childhood. They also may not know how to establish a family of choice or they may be afraid of being rejected it they try. If you feel completely alone in your community, seek help from your church or a professional to find the support you need.

A baby changes your village. Just as when you move or go off to college you lose friends and gain many new ones, so it

CREATING YOUR FAMILY VILLAGE

Few families are lucky enough to have all these roles filled by relatives and friends already in their lives. You can add village members of choice to fill in gaps. Whether you pay them for childcare, exchange baby-sitting or they volunteer, find people who share your values. Religious groups traditionally can be a good place to find community support. If you are not religious, participating in local school and community activities can provide a chance to meet people who are child friendly. Good support will feel good and enhance your marriage.

Don't expect to find these people all at once. These special people sometimes arrive in your life just when you need them. I am so grateful for people who have filled these roles in our lives. Here are some types of people to watch for when creating your village.

Old Souls: Wise grandmothers and grandfathers, widowed or not, who have or had a happy marriage are great. Though they may not be your kids' grandparents, they have solved the problem of staying together twenty-five years or more and raised caring competent kids in reasonable financial stability. It is best if they live nearby and feel lucky to have time to spend with your kids, maybe even when the kids are sick. Although some young moms find old souls intimidating and overly helpful, older women or couples can be the best baby-sitters.

"Older Siblings" to the Parents: Couple friends who are happily married and have a child one to four years older than your oldest can give you a heads-up about what's coming in school and what is ahead developmentally for your child (and your marriage).

Aunts and Uncles to the Kids: Responsible young adult figures, who find your kids adorable, and have lots of energy are a real blessing. This allows kids to have one-or-one uninterrupted time with an adult. Sometimes aunts or friends who have only girls adopt boys or vice versa so they can enjoy a different energy.

Godparents: Two people who support your values who can step in to raise your children if you were disabled or ill can also spend special time with your kids. Traditionally they attended your wedding and also oversaw your child's religious education. (My kids say it helps if they are rich and shower them with chocolate and wonderful presents.)

Cousins: Both older and younger kids who are being raised in homes that support your values can help your children learn to get along with kids at different developmental stages. Older children of close friends, teenage coaches, tutors, or baby-sitters can be great role models.

Nearby Family Friends and Neighbors: People who have kids about the same ages as yours are great for sharing a car pool or picking up the kids when your car breaks down.

Mates. *Most happily married couples have happily married friends.* Whether you choose to work out of the home, in the home, or be Mr. Mom, having friends who have made the same choice help your sanity. If your friends are competent, functioning adults with decent children and loving marriages, they can provide valuable perspective for those rough moments in your marriage. Besides they are fun.

Friends and family overlap in various roles but they can form a magical safety net to support you, your family and your marriage. The neat thing about a family of choice—unlike your relatives, who can be a mixed bag—is that *you choose them.*

goes when you have kids. Research suggests that women experience greater disruption in their social world after the arrival of kids than at any other time in their lives and they experience that disruption to a greater degree than men do. If a mom knows what to expect and can talk with old friends as the changes occur, she can deepen these relationships and not feel guilty or crazy as her friendships change. Mom may even keep some childless friends that she might otherwise have lost, if she can talk with them. She also won't wear herself out trying to meet their expectations or her own that no longer fit her new life.

Girlfriends without children have stronger social expectations about spending time together in adult conversation, exchanging gifts, talking on the phone and attending each other's events. A mother who routinely juggles multiple kids' birthday parties is less enamored of exchanging gifts. She definitely has a harder time talking on the phone now that her children demand and need her attention. Even within extended families, frustrations can arise between grown siblings who have children and those who don't.

My very patient younger sister, who had children earlier than I, struggled through buying gifts for each of the twenty people in our extended family for birthdays and the like. As time passed and I had my own kids, I began to realize why she had been gently suggesting we no longer exchange so many gifts. After a few Christmases with my own kids, I eagerly agreed to draw names for presents so each person bought for only one other.

Friends with kids, on the other hand, intuitively understand problems with time constraints and the art of making conversation between interruptions by little ones. Friends without kids may grow quickly impatient or judgmental about how Mom has "let" the children interfere. If relationships with childless couples don't end, some alterations in the couples' social life are inevitable.

BABY BLUES By Rick Kirkman and Jerry Scott

Mom is often the first to notice these changes and to suggest spending more time with people who have kids. If Dad notices this change in the couple's social relationships, and particularly if Mom insists he not hang with his "derelict" friends, he may feel this is a gross intrusion on his social life. This can lead to major conflict in the marriage. Or he simply may not notice a change in their social life because he expects her to manage that. While changing or ending these relationships can be sad, it opens the door to new relationships with people who will help you raise your kids.

This network is an antidote to loneliness for the new mom. Soon it will be a safe place for those first sleepovers. A good village supports your values so your kids accept your rules more easily. As kids grow, friends reassure one another that the crises of parenting are normal. Later, you can watch out for each other's kids as they gain independence. Friends also help each other broaden their horizons. From variations in traditions and lifestyles, parents and kids learn the different ways that people do things. Most importantly for the marriage, this network gives you healthy models for a strong couple relationship and, if they offer childcare, the time together to pursue your marriage.

Loneliness and the New Parent

Shortly after the birth of my first child, my friend Judy startled me by saying how lonely she had felt after the birth of her older son. Judy always seemed so outgoing and had a large circle of friends. What startled me was that, though I am less outgoing, I felt lonely, too. I soon learned that many new moms feel this way. A very happily married woman told me she felt so lonely for adult companionship when her kids were small that she would long to go to her husband's work dinners, which she previously avoided like the plague. My sister confessed she cross-country skied in the middle of a Vermont snowstorm with her baby on her back to make a planned mom's meeting!

Particularly if they used to work, loneliness is the number one complaint of new moms, possibly due to their isolation. Studies show that the risk for depression is highest in this period in a woman's life. If the new mom becomes mildly depressed, as there is some possibility she will, she may become even more removed from both her partner and her friends. Her withdrawal may cause the father to feel isolated, as well. Because she is inclined to stay home, Dad may feel isolated from the fun part of their social life such as dinners in fancy restaurants or extreme sports activities.

If the new mom leaves the workforce to stay home, the loneliness can be intense. This isolation is softened if the mom is part

BABY BLUES

Although a very small number of women experience full depression during pregnancy, studies published by the American Psychological Association suggest that 50 to 80 percent of women experience "baby blues," a mild postpartum drop in mood. This occurs about the third or fourth day after delivery and lasts from one to fourteen days. Postpartum depression, on the other hand, is much more serious, occurs for some women from six weeks to four months after delivery, and may last six months to a year. About 16 percent of women experience this more serious problem.

Depression occurs most frequently among women who have marital difficulties, are depressed during the pregnancy, and/or experience significant anxiety and life stress before the birth of the baby. Thus, in one of those tricky circles of life, sometimes depression is caused by marital difficulties, and sometimes marital difficulties may result from a biologically based depression. This circular relationship can spiral up or down, depending on whether the marriage relationship aggravates the depression or supports the person through the depression.

If you are depressed, a professional can help you and your partner eliminate the depression and save your marriage. If both of you aren't at least a little more hopeful after four weeks of therapy, find a new professional. Depression is a serious threat to your marriage, but in most cases effective treatments are available.

of a close-knit community of friends who are having children at the same time. The feeling may also be less intense with the birth of later children because the mom now has an active, talkative child already at home, has more girlfriends with children, and has resolved loneliness issues with her spouse. On the other hand, the second-time mom may be so busy meeting the needs of two children that she may feel lonelier because she has even less time for her friends and her spouse.

Not too surprisingly, many men also feel this loneliness, though they rarely say so because loneliness isn't a macho word. Yet many men feel cut off because the new mom is freshly enamored with someone else: the new baby. Many men will say they feel abandoned or that they miss the romance. They may blame the new mom but they rarely call it loneliness. If they go off to work each day and interact with people, the loss of intimacy may not seem so bad, so they may be puzzled by a wife's discomfort. If she says she is lonely, he is likely to feel she is saying it is his fault.

A woman's realization that she is deeply ambivalent about or just dislikes being a mom can be frightening and disorienting. Many moms feel, "Why don't I love this being with kids stuff as much as other mothers seem to?" Many recently published books explore this experience and give voice to this frustration. Naomi Wolf's *Misconceptions*, Rachel Cusk's *Life's Work*, Nina Barrett's *I Wish Someone Had Told Me: A Realistic Guide to Early Motherhood*, and Ann Crittenden's *The Price of Motherhood: Why the Most Important Job in the World is Still Least Valued* all address aspects of why becoming a mother is not the pastel and sentimental experience of a Mother's Day card. *What our Mother's Didn't Tell us: Why Happiness Eludes the Modern Woman*, by Danielle Crittenden, faults the feminism of the 1960s and 1970s for devaluing motherhood. Whatever the reason, the loneliness, loss of freedom, and radical change in status common to motherhood takes many women by surprise. Like

Ms. Cusk, some women rebel at "sliding into a feudal relation-ship" with a spouse where she does not work and depends on her husband for financial support. Many women find it refreshing to hear another mother say that she is not required to be deliriously happy about all aspects of mothering.

Fulfilling marriages have room for the partner to be disillu-sioned after the birth of the baby and to talk about how the dramatic changes feel. What is vital is that the new parents take time to share feelings with each other, so they have a connection beyond the baby. Many couples, who thrive in this period of new parenthood, bond by joining together in their love of the child. They enthuse together about the magic of the baby. Many of the tips and hints throughout this book are designed to foster this couple connection.

However, most couples still feel a sense of loneliness because the structure of their relationship shifts so profoundly. You need to talk about that shift and accept that one or both of you may be less than ecstatically happy about aspects of the experience. As a couple and as individuals, both partners will need to re-solve how to handle feelings of loneliness and abrupt change of identity from adult to Mom or Dad.

Moms' Night Out: The comic Rob Becker, in his perfor-mance called "Defending the Caveman," suggests that men speak only two thousand words a day (to a woman's seven thousand) and by the time they get home they have used them up. To a bored and lonely new mom at home all day with a demanding but non-English speaking infant, this is frustrating. She's ready to talk but Dad has little to talk about. What a new mom needs is time with other moms so that when she is with Dad she can concentrate on their mutual interests other than the children. If she gets this friend time, she will be a more interesting and hap-pier partner.

Unfortunately, sometimes neither of them understands the need for this and both feel adrift. Both partners need to recognize the importance of balancing Mom's new desire to get out and connect with someone besides Dad as healthy for the relationship. But rather than support her, too often Dad feels more neglected or threatened that she needs time with someone other than him. When they understand the problem is normal, they can more easily resolve it.

Finally, another shift may occur when she rejoins the workforce, as many women do sometime before their child turns six. Her needs may shift again from needing to get out to wanting to be home. Meanwhile, if Dad's daily routine remains relatively stable, he may find the shifts in Mom's social needs confusing and uncomfortable. If the new mom looks to the new dad to respond and fill all these rapidly shifting needs, he is bound to fall short and be frustrated. He is also likely to try to enforce an old solution like: "Let's just go away for the weekend and do the things we used to do." But the new mom has a hard time separating from the child to carry out that solution.

Although new dads don't usually notice that they need new friends, couples are generally happier when Dad gets to know other dads with kids near the same age. Socializing occasionally with other contented couples with kids serves as a kind of marriage insurance. Dads enjoy the contact with other parents as well, even though they don't generally recognize they might like this until they experience it. As a general rule, they are more likely to get involved with other parents later than Mom does. Often moms who don't work outside the home are more successful at setting this up because they tend to meet people with kids their age through various child-centered activities. Gradually, as the families get acquainted and the kids reach the age of five to seven, the dads can do occasional outings like sporting events, or camping with the kids and other dads.

Overall, if you two, as a couple, recognize that the new mom's shifting feelings of loneliness are normal and work to adapt, you will grow closer. If you also note that Dad might benefit from new friends who are fathers, your relationship will have a healthy flow that a good social support system can provide.

When the Village Intrudes

While new parents need the support of a village they also need to avoid being overwhelmed by the village. Gracefully setting boundaries on your village is an important skill. A newly married couple has to solve the issue of how much time they are going to spend socially with friends and family. When a new baby arrives, this issue has to be resolved again. Right after the baby is born, drop-in visits may occur when Mom can least handle them. Advice and family folklore may come raining down, inundating both Mom and Dad.

Both the new mom and dad need to support each other in making sure they are comfortable with village members. Mom and Dad will feel closer when they make decisions together about when to include others. Many a mom and dad have to learn how to uninvite members of the village as well as include them. Telling another parent that their child bites, and resolving how to handle it, is a difficult but important skill.

Setting limits and building your village together can help you both know that your feelings and values as a couple come first. Otherwise the cocoon will be invaded. The sense of family will be diluted. The feeling that you know each other intimately and can play and have fun will be diluted, too, so that soon you may feel like strangers. The sense that you are a couple together in this world will be enhanced if you share relaxed time together alone as a couple at times and with great friends at other times.

Creating an Intimate Friendship Circle

- Set a routine that gets Mom out of the house every day if she is home full-time.

- Join a church or religious group or a Mommy-and-Me group. Invite people to your house afterward.

- Plan a family camping trip or short vacation with another family.

- Start a monthly book club of mothers and dads and take your kids. It is chaotic at first, but people say it works because the book is a shared experience.

- Get a walking partner/exercise partner for regular walks, with or without the kids.

- Make park dates or play dates and let the dads take the kids occasionally.

- Your list of obligatory social engagements may need to shrink to allow time for yourselves and for the new little person in your schedule.

- One couple does Calendar Night about once a month or so and looks at their weekend and vacation plans several months ahead. They plan who they want to spend time with instead of making passive choices as they respond to invitations.

- If you are lucky enough to have a grandparent or friend who wants to be close to your child, set up a time for them to take the baby out regularly. Then have a mini-date with your spouse. This works best if you start when the child is very small and keep the outings brief to avoid grandparent shock and child meltdowns. Gradually extend the time so they get used to having a special time with Granddad or Aunt Suzy.

- If you don't have a willing grandparent (and even if you do), scout out an experienced childcare person who will be available to baby-sit for your "parent alone" time and for emergencies. Grandma may leave town to be with her dying sister for six weeks, or go on a trip to the Caribbean with a new boyfriend. Some grandmas have more exciting lives than we do right now.

- Consider a computer support group of other parents to share ideas, especially if your child has special needs.

- Likewise, as your kids get older, hire the nice neighborhood kids you admire as help around the house. They will work for almost nothing and they will be great baby-sitters in a few years. Your kids will love them and may even copy some good habits along the way. You will have more time for your relationship.

- Take time to talk about your village. Discuss whether the village is feeling like a support or a drain on you and your marriage. Take action together to keep it in balance.

- Thank helpful people in your village warmly and often.

6

Chance for a New Start

Fantasy 5: Babies are a chance for a new start. Reality: Ghosts from our past take over when we are tired and stressed.

A new baby is like New Year's Day for some people, a signal for resolutions. "I'll never say, because I said so!"; "I won't lose my temper"; and "I'm not going to shout at my husband especially in front of the kids," are common resolutions.

What most well-intentioned couples fail to factor in, is that their own parents provided a potent learning experience that lasted twenty-some years. Even though you swear you will be different from your parents, inadvertently and when you least expect it, you open your mouth and your parents' words jump out. Unless your parents were blissfully happy while you were growing up those things that pop out aren't usually good for your marriage.

Ghosts from the past are experiences with your family of origin, your first family, which persist in the present and make you behave in these surprising ways. In a crisis we often do what we have seen done and not what we have planned. For example, untrained people who see a drowning person will often act from the heart, jump in the icy waters and drown with the victim. A trained lifeguard throws the life ring or extends a pole first. But it takes practice to learn to do that. The stress of raising kids makes us all the untrained lifeguards of our children and of our marriage. In moments of stress we may do what we saw done most. These reactions can be good or bad, depending on our own experiences. Kids bring out the best and worst in us. If you were married before, the early marriage may also influence you in surprising, often negative, ways.

Most couples get along reasonably well until they have kids. One partner may be emotional and the other reserved. Or one may be a caretaker and the other loves attention. While the couple may not be perfectly suited, they are engaged in a smooth marital dance. The stress of having kids disrupts that dance. Any stress can throw off a couple's routine and stir up ghosts from the past. Kids, however, are a bigger than usual stress. Being thrown off balance and feeling overwhelmed makes couples feel desperate to resolve the current issue or crisis and return to their former comfort zone. The problem is that once you have kids you can't go back. The issues, conflicts, and work keep coming. This prolonged stress leads people to try desperate measures— the things we thought we would never do or say.

For most people, the ghosts from their past are startling and frustrating. "What am I doing? I sound just like my mother." For others this sort of self-awareness is rare. Or they may see it when talking to their children and miss it when they talk to their spouse. However, most of us quickly recognize similarities in our mates and in-laws. "Oh, no! He is becoming just like his father." Or "I don't want to spend my life like his mother. No way." Or worse, "She is going to be just like my mother. I know how to handle this. I will be gone a lot."

In-laws teach us about our partner's ghosts. Just as your parents influenced you, your in-laws influenced your partner. By watching your in-laws, you may have some warning about the ghost behaviors that may be appearing in your marriage. Instead of critically judging what you see, think about what positive outcome the behavior has for them. Perhaps acting jealous makes your mother-in-law feel cared about. Maybe those fishing trips are a substitute for fighting and give your parents-in-law a breather. Ask the members of your village how they handle behavior that you anticipate will make you upset. With good planning you can work together with your partner to practice different routines to avoid problems.

Unfortunately, in-laws become the focus of frustration and anger in many marriages. Instead of agreeing together as a couple about those things that make you both crazy and making a determined effort to deal with them, partners often disparage their in-laws. Try watching your in-laws and your spouse to gain insight into your partner's sensitivities. Then, you can think about how to tread lightly so you two get along better instead of focusing your anger on your in-laws.

Focusing on changing yourself and on how to work with your partner is better than trying to fix your partner or your in-laws. Here's how. Think about three unproductive, embarrassing, or annoying things that your own parents do with each other that make you uncomfortable. Now write them down. Then write down three things that you wish they'd do instead. Tape those three positive things to your mirror to remind *yourself* to do them. Most people have trouble with the three positives. It's not cheating to ask another happily married person what they might do in a difficult situation. While many of these basic skills work for a couple without children, you will need these teamwork skills more often once you have kids.

To help you get started, here is a list of things that people do that don't work in a marriage and a sample fix for each:

THE LIST:
THINGS THAT DON'T WORK FOR A HAPPY MARRIAGE
(and Sample Fixes)

Expecting your partner to know what you are feeling.
Tell them how you feel.

Expecting your partner to know what you like and dislike.
Tell them what you want/expect calmly *before* the situation occurs.

Expecting help without asking for it.
Ask for help as politely as if you were asking a stranger.

Criticizing or ridiculing a spouse for their taste, preferences, or behavior.
Act the way you would like your children to treat a visiting aunt.

Withdrawing into silence when conflict comes up.
Warn your partner you need quiet time to reflect on this and that you will come back to talk about it at a specific time.

Keeping track of mistakes.
Remind your partner of something they do well when they goof. Better yet, remind them of *your* last blooper.

Blaming the partner.
Look at your contribution first. Then try to understand their behavior and why it may have occurred. Assume good intentions on their part. They may respond by now regretting or being embarrassed about what they did.

Yelling to make someone listen.
Be curious why they didn't hear you the first time. "This is the third time you asked me to tell you when we are going to

the Joneses'. Are you unhappy about going?" "This is the second time I asked you to fix the sink, and you agreed. Is there a problem getting in the way?"

Keeping score of who does what.

Strive to always do 60 percent of the load and ask for help when you need it *before* you get hostile.

Saying I told you so.

Don't. (If you can't help yourself, ask if they are surprised that you were right.)

Never saying what you want for presents and being very disappointed.

Act delighted with what you get or get over it and make a wish list for your partner to choose from.

Always coming up with the ideas about what to do and resenting it or getting sabotaged.

When your spouse asks what you want to do, switch roles and say, "I want to do what my wonderful honey wants to do." Or "I'd like to focus on what you want to do today." *Then* do it!

Never being happy with what you have.

Say five things you like about your life before voicing a complaint. I say five to my clients because it is a challenge and distracts them and they may never get back to the complaint. In real life, two or three will do.

Making suggestions about how your partner might improve.

Notice five positive or appealing things they have improved lately before you make a suggestion.

Criticizing everything around you.

Say five things you are grateful for before you criticize.

Always noting the negative.

Teach yourself to state the positive in every negative. (e.g., Your husband never helps so you always get to do things your way.)

Refusing to compromise.

Get over yourself or you are going to be lonely. Seriously. Think of three other things that you have compromised about recently before you refuse. Ask yourself why it is important that you win on everything.

Blowing up loudly when frustrated.

Learn to count to ten. Really. Tell your partner you would like to stop blowing up. Get help learning what makes you blow up and what you could do instead. Plan a ritual cooling-off signal with your partner or yourself. (This should probably not be your middle finger.)

Swearing all the time at a partner.

Stop or get professional help.

Drinking too much.

Go to AA and get professional help.

Threatening violence or caving in because you feel threatened.

Get professional help. If your partner won't go, go by yourself.

Doing violence.

Get professional help.

This list can go on and on. Do you recognize any of these habits in yourself? Start any marriage improvement program as a self-improvement program. Changing yourself changes your partner.

Unfortunately people sometimes have such severe traumas in their past, like sexual molestation, severe verbal or physical abuse, or alcoholic parents that being in any close intimate parenting/partnering relationship is very uncomfortable. Though they love their partners, they have trouble with sex or simply being close. Fortunately a well-researched and gentle treatment, EMDR, Eye Movement Desensitization and Reprocessing, an accelerated information processing method discovered by Francine Shapiro allows couples to resolve these issues and rapidly feel much closer and more comfortable.

Tips for Handling Ghosts from the Past

- *Always* work on your own ghosts first. If you must analyze, analyze yourself first. Ask yourself why your partner's behavior bothers you so much. Answer the question with an "I" statement not a "he" statement. For example: "When Jim comes home and watches TV instead of offering to help, it reminds me of my parents, and *I* feel angry. Not "When Jim comes home and reads *he* is so selfish and inconsiderate." Dig deeper and figure out what ghosts in your past are stirring. Then work on how you can change, like learning to ask cheerfully and directly for help. (If it is a big problem like domestic violence, substance abuse, or infidelity, get time away and get help for yourself first so you can make good decisions. It is not your fault, and no one thinks well under stress.)

- Ask yourself if there is something that you do that encourages your partner's undesired behavior. Consider asking your spouse or a friend the same question.

- Before you request a big change from your spouse, get an independent opinion from a happily married person you trust, who knows and likes your spouse.

- If you would like your partner to change something, do not describe what you hate. *Ask for what you would like to see* instead, tell him/her why and how good it would make you feel. Then reward your partner enthusiastically when he/she does it.

- Write your change request down and read it carefully before you give it to your partner. How would you feel if you were receiving it? Are you asking your partner to do something or not do something? Asking for something positive works better than asking to eliminate something.

- *Never* talk badly about your in-laws. If you need to sort out your feelings about your in-laws, talk to a friend or a counselor who will never talk to your spouse or your in-laws about your concerns. This is true even if your partner often complains about his or her parents or siblings. Remember this simple rule: I can criticize my parents, but not my partner's parents and vice versa.

- Listen sympathetically or be gently curious when your partner complains about his or her family. Ask him how it makes him feel. Avoid joining in enthusiastically with the complaints. This increases negativity and doesn't help either of you move on.

- Be curious rather than critical about why your in-laws do something unusual. Encourage them to tell you stories about their past and their relationship. They have ghosts, too. Things that seem strange at first will seem less mysterious. Your interest will make you more popular.

- If your in-laws do something that really makes you crazy, tell your spouse that his or her parents' behavior makes you uncomfortable, doesn't work for you, or hurts your feelings. Do not expect your spouse to understand why it makes you uncomfortable, although she/he may understand perfectly. Just ask for what you would like instead. Be careful that it is something you really need.

- If you are both at a loss about how to better manage your in-laws, ask an objective outsider in your village for suggestions.

- Do not criticize or compare your spouse or children to your in-laws, except regarding things that show them in a favorable light.

- Think of things that you genuinely admire about each of your in-laws and relatives. Be specific and genuine. Have a goal of five things. My favorite line was "My husband has a wonderful family. No one gets drunk or fights at family gatherings and they like kids."

- Be ready to mention your five positive things before you suggest changes in the way you as a couple deal with the relatives. Easier still, choose to marry someone whose family is great.

- Take parenting classes together and set goals for your parenting, not achievement goals to pressure your kids.

- Set people skills goals together with your spouse for your own family. Practicing social skills like making positive requests of your kids will polish your skills and your partner's skills with each other. Teaching your kids will help you change habits. Working together makes being married fun and you are less likely to do automatic things from the past.

- Set goals for your marriage together. Revise them regularly. Planning and talking about what you want rather than what you are unhappy about creates a positive atmosphere where good habits develop.

Summary of Part 1

As you can see from the last five chapters, equality, sharing, support and cocooning are *not* normal predictable consequences of having a baby. Some couples achieve these ideals, but most do not. Once a baby arrives, partners go through rapid changes in their relationship, but often Mom and Dad move in different directions. These changes happen while the couple is excited, sleep deprived, exhausted, and overwhelmed. They have little time to reflect on what is happening. As the pace quickens, these changes snowball. Home life, social life, sex life, and living environments change dramatically. Mom may stop her career. Dad may intensify his. The division of labor in the house shifts. By the time the child is three or four, the parents' relationship may have become something neither wanted nor expected. If a second child arrives, their couple relationship may go on permanent hold and be lost. If the issues go unresolved too long, efforts to salvage the marriage or create the marriage that you both dreamed of creating together come too late.

On the other hand, creating a few good habits that support your relationship can dramatically improve your marriage in a very short time. I have seen a marriage turn around when the husband first called to make a therapy appointment on the way to the divorce settlement conference. Usually things don't change that late, but this man was very motivated. A sincere desire to change can produce dramatic results.

No matter how bad your past is, you can have a good relationship if you work on it together. In fact, some of my couples with the most painful and abusive pasts develop the best relationships by working together in therapy. They feel a genuine and profound gratitude for what they have created in their own marriage in contrast to the serious problems of their own childhood and parents. They become even more deeply committed to each other and grateful for their time together than couples without such scary, problematic pasts.

Over time, good habits can lead to genuine sharing, a sense of comfort and solace that feels

> Equality, sharing, support, and cocooning are *not* normal, predictable consequences of having a baby. They take conscious effort.

miraculous. Such work and understanding leads to a sense of equality. Each partner feels equally valued, equally important, and equally respected. Working together makes it possible.

These equally valued partners in happy, thriving couples divide the responsibilities of marriage in many different ways. There are no cookie-cutter solutions. Certain general rules are the same in happy marriages. In thriving marriages:

- Both partners make time for each other alone, without kids.

- Couples spend at least twenty minutes a day communicating eyeball to eyeball, e-mail to e-mail, phone to phone, or some combination of these.

- Both partners express appreciation and fondness frequently in ways their partner recognizes.

- Both partners really get to know their partner's friends, interests, aspirations, and worries.

- Both partners actively contribute to the marriage. Neither feels put upon or used.

- Both partners have a good time doing little things together.

- Both partners express genuine appreciation for what the other contributes.

- Both partners influence each other.

- Both can work together to solve problems.

- Both can constructively complain without blame.

- Both expect to put in more than 50 percent of the work. Some contribute in similar ways, as when both work outside the home, trade meals and laundry, and spend similar amounts of time with the baby. Others take very different roles. Whether their contributions are similar or different, both feel that each contributes either monetarily or by household chores or childcare. Each feels they contribute what is right for them.

- Both sense that the division of labor is fair, if not precisely equal. They come up with a plan, however loosely patched together, that works for them so that they are not constantly upset when their expectations are not met.

- Most importantly, both have a shared vision of their marriage and what is important to them.

Expectations are critical. Quietly unhappy, resigned couples know what they expect and are chronically disappointed. Eventually the couple comes to a resolution that doesn't work well for either spouse. They don't feel close. But at least the relationship is predictable and keeps a kind of peace, so that they are not constantly upset. The marriage functions, but neither partner is very happy.

Happy couples, on the other hand, work together to understand each other's expectations. Each partner has adjusted his or her own expectations to fit their spouse's contribution. Both have adjusted their expectations to fit the reality of children. Together they have created a uniquely satisfying relationship. Happy couples work harder to have more.

Part Two

Normal Marriages—Real Solutions

7

Who *Is* This Person I Married?

As I work with young couples, I get a sense that the normal rage and tendency to withdraw they feel fits nicely into the big picture of how long-term, happy marriages work. Sometimes I draw them a picture like the one on page 93 to give them a sense of the continuity of a marriage *before* having children, during the kid crisis, while raising their family, and *after* the kids are grown and gone. I adapted it from the excellent work of Bader and Pierson and their book *In Quest of a Mythical Mate.* They feel all couples go through these stages, with or without children, but having children tends to push couples out of blissful stage one and into, and through, the difficult stages two and three.

Stage 1, the Bliss Stage is at the bottom of the drawing. Couples feel *made for each other.* No matter how different your backgrounds are, you bask in the things that you both like. You seem destined to be together because you like the same music and movies, you may share the same religious beliefs, you like the same car or truck, and, more important, you enjoy a powerful sexual attraction. I always ask couples what first attracted them to each other. Remember and savor those early romantic times to get you through the more difficult times ahead. In Stage 1, the Bliss Stage, couples count all the ways they are perfectly matched and simply ignore the ways that they don't quite see eye to eye. Sometimes the biggest attraction was that the other person seemed to genuinely like you just the way you were. This feeling of oneness and belonging together is the underlying and important foundation that supports the marriage through tough times.

John Gottman, of the Seattle Love Lab, calls this connection a couple's fondness and admiration system. My clients love the exercises in his book *The Seven Principles for Making Marriage Work* for helping them reconnect to the positive aspects of their marriage no matter what stage they are in or what crises have befallen them.

Most people remember this Bliss Stage fondly. If they don't have these warm memories or they tell me they married their spouse to leave a bad home or because all their friends were getting married, I find their problems are less likely to be resolved.

Some couples like this stage so much they just want to stay stuck here in a blissful romance. This sounds like heaven but doesn't work so well for the kids, because they may be neglected. Also in this type of romance, one partner frequently does all the compromising so that the relationship goes smoothly but loses its spark. Eventually it may collapse anyway, as we discussed in the rage chapter, because of all that is left unsaid. The nightmare version of this stage is the couple that fights endlessly but cannot separate. They make love *and* war constantly. Their children are usually quite disturbed because open warfare is so detrimental to kids.

But most couples advance after a few years to a new stage, which though frustrating, is healthy and necessary to survive

The Five Stages of Couples

Stage 5 Bonded: Mutual Respect and Affection
We share a strong bond *and* admire each other as individuals.

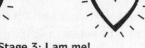

Stage 4: Friends Again

Stage 3: I am me!
Separate Identities

Stage 2: Who are you? Discovery of Differences

Stage 1 Bliss: We are One; Made For Each Other

kids and develop a stronger, more rewarding relationship. Although couples with and without children move on to this stage. Unfortunately the beginning of this difficult second stage often coincides with the crisis of the arrival of the first child.

In **Stage 2, the Differences Stage,** we draw back and say: "Who *is* this person I married?" Having children often triggers this stage and the question becomes: "Who is this person and why did I choose them to be the parent of my child?" Each partner begins to notice annoying differences. Lots of them. They also begin to realize that some differences are not likely to be resolved without compromise, and that compromise means that they will be giving up something, possibly for the rest of this life on earth. Not a comfortable feeling.

People react to this in a number of ways, depending on their personal style. Usually they feel heartbroken and disappointed that the marriage isn't turning out the way they fantasized it would. I call this the valley of the shadow of death for the marriage. In this period, each person fantasizes the end of the marriage. Some fantasize that their partner gets hit by a truck, a fairly normal image that still shocks them. Some daydream about divorce or simply being with other people. Each decides to stay or not. Some people don't ever fantasize about the end of the marriage but merely grieve the marriage that might have been.

Children often force us prematurely into this stage because we come face to face with what we want for ourselves and our children and whether we are living the way we want our kids to emulate. Children expose our values to us. Many things we accepted as okay for ourselves, aren't okay for our kids.

This is the stage when people decide to get a divorce, even if they linger here ten or more years getting the courage to take the step. Instead, with insight, openness, and perseverance, you can move out of this stage to something better. I have seen many couples stuck for twenty years or, sadly, until the end of their lives because they wouldn't confront this stage nor would they move on. This stage has no normal time limit but seems to last until couples figure it out or divorce.

Most couples enter this stage with a face-off that goes something like: "If only you would change, this marriage would be just fine!" The changes requested vary from the ridiculous to the sublime. But they tend to be preceded by *"If you would just learn to . . .* put the toilet seat down, ask me for a date, help around the house, get your parents not to smoke around the kids, listen to me when I need to talk, or ask me about *my* day." Issues surrounding helping with the kids and the house most frequently trigger this stage with new parents. "They are your kids, too!" Sometimes the issues are more difficult and personal like just stop smoking for our kid's sake or just lose the weight you gained in pregnancy. Some people are upset about these issues but never mention them and grow distant.

If you married this person because he or she liked you, these requests are experienced as a deep, stinging rejection. When people feel criticized, most become less motivated to change rather than more motivated. Some feel afraid that they can't change and give up without trying. Because they don't want to disappoint or be rejected further by their spouse, they counter-attack with their own list. Often the delivery isn't very artful. Partners tend to be too harsh when they do criticize or suggest change, or they simply don't ask. Others ask so tentatively that their partner easily ignores their request. Some try to change but end up feeling that no amount of changes will be enough to please their partner.

This is the stage during which an affair is most likely. Faced with the hard work of compromise and reconciling differences, many people opt out. A romance with a new, understanding person is just more appealing than dealing with the same issues with someone who has smelled your breath at 4 A.M. and knows you sneak off to take naps when you should be helping with the kids. Couples are at greater risk for affairs when one partner travels a lot or the family has moved a long distance from a familiar village of family and friends. Affairs are particularly appealing because they are usually conducted in a private adult's-only environment where talking in whole sentences, listening attentively, and dressing attractively are encouraged.

If step-kids are involved, this stage is even more intense. Both parents usually harbor a strong romantic fantasy that, this time, they will get the marriage right. Unfortunately, the opportunities to disagree multiply with each additional person in the mix and the differences in their backgrounds. The step-wife crisis that ensues has been amply documented in a great book entitled *Step-Wives: Ten Steps to Help Ex-Wives and Stepmothers End the Struggle and Put the Kids First* by Lynne Oxhorn-Ringwood, Louise Oxhorn, and Marjorie Vego-Krausz, (two step-wives and a therapist).

Most people seek counseling at this stage to try to get the therapist to fix the other person. The therapist must gently and firmly shift the focus from fixing your partner to what *you* can do to improve your life and your relationship yourself. A good therapist moves you to the *"Who am I?"* identity of Stage 3, if possible. She teaches you to focus on yourself, on your wants, needs and desires, on how to ask for the support you need and on how to take action in ways that are most likely to get results.

Stage 3, the Identity Stage is the "Who am I?" stage. In Stage 3, if you decide not to have an affair, or you have ended an affair and decide to make your marriage work, then you step back and ask yourself what is really important to you. This is when you look at the conflicts and disagreements between the two of you. This stage is critical for yourself, your relationship, and the development of your family. Although the self-examination is difficult, and to some it seems to be a lifelong pursuit, most members of a couple move through it rather rapidly in a year or two—maybe four at the most, if they can get past Stage 2, the Differences Stage. Some people get lost in this stage if they focus only on their own self-development and cannot address how the independent self fits in a relationship or a family. However people with enough emotional maturity to consider these questions of personal identity often move on from the Identity Stage and begin to figure out how each of their differences fit in to a good relationship.

In this stage, you develop an awareness of how each person in the family has separate and very different needs, how they get their needs met and how the family shelters and supports individuals. If you are successful at understanding that you both have different needs and each of you need support, you begin to choose your battles carefully and your accommodations thoughtfully. Compromises are seen as a gift to the partner rather than as a request to change your core personality.

You ask yourself, "Can I begin to change myself and my attitudes if it means peace in the house?" You consider what kinds of activities get you into a calm, patient, or self-reflective mode. You ask yourself, "Is there something personal like gym time or writing time or going back to school that I put on hold for the kids and the relationship? What helps me to be a sane and safe (nonhostile) companion?" You may need counseling by yourself to sort things out. You may learn what you are doing, thinking, or feeling that gets in the way of compromise.

However, if your marriage has serious problems, you may address the issue of whether you and the kids are better off in the marriage or out of the marriage. Sometimes the situation is critical and very difficult and you must move on to divorce because the differences are too great. You may have to ask yourself if you and your kids can live with an alcoholic or a rage-aholic. Certainly, if you live with someone violent, you probably need to separate and not live together while you sort out your life. Fortunately battered women's shelters exist across the United States to make this possible.

Civility is greatly underrated in romantic movies, but critical

to happy marriages. If your marriage is relatively sound, you begin to address how two people with very separate identities can live comfortably in the same relationship. This moves you to the next stage. If they have not been uncivil, one partner may make a big gesture of independence like a separate vacation or start an independent creative project that marks the independent identity stage before moving on to Stage 4.

Stage 4, Friends Stage, is when we decide to be friends. Many couples tell me that they just decide to stop fighting and to be civil. They may still feel a bit distant and mistrustful, if they have been very uncivil in Stage 2, the Differences Stage, or Stage 3, the Identity Stage, but they decide to try. One woman announced that her husband had decided to like her. He had always been madly in love with her but he decided to treat her as well as he treated his friends. He wanted to get along. Another woman announced to her husband that she would love him no matter how much "he screwed up."

Another long-married woman who had been discussing separations with a friend for months said, "I can't expect Gino to be my everything. He scores well on the important things," (meaning he works hard, doesn't hit her, or use drugs). She never brought up leaving again. But she made it clear that for other needs she had friends. As declarations of affection, these seem underwhelming, yet, they signal the beginning of a new stage. Each of these early declarations, though quite guarded, marked a movement in the marriage toward the last stage of respect and mutual affection

Each partner began to use the information they gained about themselves in the period of self-examination to compromise in ways that didn't ignore their needs and yet honored the needs of their partner and the children. They began to ask for compromises in ways that promote cooperation rather than competition. One partner may return to school or start a creative project with the full support of the other. They may more comfortably accommodate their partner's need for friends that are not couple friends.

Many people worry when they hit this stage that they lose their passion and spontaneity. At first, they feel more respect than passion for their partners. They miss Stage 1, the Bliss Stage. The task in this stage is to move beyond mere civility to a deep appreciation and understanding of their partner. As couples work through their conflicts their connection grows and leads them to a new stage.

This last stage, the Bonded Stage has a sense of oneness and brings a new sense that each partner really understands the other. They feel a deeply gratifying sense of supporting each other. This sense of connection feels more real, valuable and important than anything in their lives. Romance gradually pales in comparison to this deeper love.

Stage 5, the Bonded Stage is a stage of Mutual Respect and Affection for someone very different from ourselves, a true couple stage. And I believe it is the best. I encourage couples to struggle through the earlier stages because the end is worth it. In this stage the partners both experience a deeper kind of love. Lucky couples reach this stage by the time their kids are five, but most reach it much later, hopefully by their kids' teen years. Unfortunately, many couples don't make it. I rarely see couples in therapy at this stage because they have developed a mutual understanding of who they are as individuals, who they are as a couple and as a family, and what they share in common. They have created a space for each of them and each of the children to have private time and develop personal interests and pursuits. Thus, they can joyously share family time. Yet the family protects, accepts, and cheerfully encourages each family member's individual interests and pursuits.

When I meet families like this it feels as if they are sailing in a large and solid ship that has a direction and sails on calm waters. Their ship is a home base and they can each leave it to have fun but they will always return to their base and safe harbor.

If you look at the drawing at the bottom and top of the figure, what is shared and what is separate are clear in Stage 5. There is a clear sense of what is his, hers, and ours. In Stage 1, couples see only what they each have in common and don't appreciate the individual's uniqueness. Much is shared, but the individual is lost, indistinguishable. Likewise, the couple's values in Stage 1, the Bliss Stage, are often vague and general, while in the Bonded Stage, they are well articulated. In a Stage 2, Differences stage marriage, a partner compares the spouse to their own standards for a perfect marriage and thinks, "How do you fit into my dream?" Unlike a Stage 2 marriage in which a partner focuses on how the partner falls short of a personal fantasy of marriage, in Stage 5 each partner can see the other's good intention to support them rather than seeing how they fail to meet a certain preset standard. Couples work together to develop a vision of what a good relationship means to both of them.

The love you feel in the later stage acknowledges that you can see that the other person has different needs, desires, and interests from your own and that you love the other person and enjoy watching and helping them grow into who they are best suited to be. Think of a parent who encourages his child to be a doctor, just like he was, versus the parent who is curious and supports the child's interest in becoming what he wants to be.

How does understanding these stages help your marriage? Knowing that you are going through predictable pain is reassuring, especially if the pain has a payoff. It's comforting to know that other people have been through this and survived and thrived. Second, figuring out what stage you are in now gives you perspective. People rarely have trouble knowing what stage they are in most of the time. Your friends or a good counselor can help if you aren't sure what stage fits. Finally, knowing the stages and how you work through them can help make the process easier.

If you think you are in Stage 5 and your partner thinks you are in Stage 2, you are probably more stuck in Stage 2 yourself than you realize. In Stage 2, you each spend all your time figuring out what is wrong with your partner.

While the stages are mostly sequential, people can move around a bit and sometimes go back and visit Stage 1 to remind them why they want the relationship. Some people slip back into Stage 2, Differences stage when under stress or when they aren't feeling well. However, once you have experienced a better stage it is hard to go back for long.

Remind yourself when your marriage is difficult that this is a stage. Unless we have significant trauma in our background, we are programmed to grow through these stages just as the kids will grow through their predictable developmental stages. We can make that process easier or harder for ourselves by how we understand and work in each stage.

Getting Through the Stages Gracefully

- Try the next stage for size. If you are stuck fixing your partner, do something for yourself.

- Talk about your relationship on an ongoing basis, including what makes you happy about it.

- Share small moments and use them to remind each other why you believe you belong together.

- Talk about your commitment to make the marriage work and what you do to act on that commitment every day.

- Aim for three to five nurturing gestures a day such as calling, e-mailing, picking up dry cleaning, or thanking him for filling the gas tank or paying the bills.

- Hug, kiss, and hold hands . . . a lot. Look into each other's eyes. Let your partner catch you looking at them. The busier you are, the more important it is to make contact.

- Take a walk together daily, with the kids in a carrier at first; create family rituals that support communication.

- Don't pretend everything is perfect. You have small children. Things probably are not perfect. Tell each other every day what makes you grateful that day.

- Be there when it matters: to celebrate successes, encourage risk taking, and offering support when times are tough. One husband charted his wife's moods during a difficult job search to give her perspective. Another reminded his wife that, even though their daughter had to undergo five surgeries, their little girl was lucky because she would always be loved and not all kids have that.

- Share your deepest thoughts. Write them down if you aren't awake at the same moment, but share them.

- Embrace your differences. Enjoy how they contribute to the relationship. Does your calmness balance his anxiety?

- Don't bury your relationship under the demands of the children. Put your time and heart into taking care of your marriage, and your family's happiness will follow. When your relationship gets buried anyway, notice that, laugh about it, and talk about how you miss each other.

8

Rage as a Signal

Although he thought their argument had
been settled at breakfast, Jim sensed that
Sally had some unresolved issues.

Everybody loves this cartoon. At first I wondered why even those who professed to have no anger in their marriage loved this cartoon. I began to realize that rage, whether you call it rage, anger, or falling out of love, is a common experience for couples after the birth of a child. Ironically, the arrival of the first baby is often the time that couples begin to feel a much deeper commitment to the marriage and much less like they will divorce. Before the birth of a baby people feel that while divorce would not be a good thing, they *could* leave if things got too bad. "After all" they justify, "50 to 60 percent of couples do split." Once children arrive, they feel differently. Now they tell themselves: "I won't leave now that there is a baby." Or "I couldn't do that (divorce) to Juliette, (our tiny, defenseless baby)."

The problem is that with a greater sense of commitment comes a greater sense of entrapment. Each parent feels stuck as the frustrations of the new baby increase and the realities of what they have gotten themselves into start to become obvious. Soon they feel crazy because they feel *so* angry. They have never felt like this before. They assume either that it is the other person's fault they are getting this upset or that they themselves are not meant for marriage. Each parent independently decides they must be crazy or that their partner must be making them crazy. Neither is true, of course.

Calling this normal frustration "rage" seems too strong to some people. As I started writing this chapter, I realized that about a third of my readers would hate the chapter, a third would love it, and the rest would find it interesting but uncomfortable. Reactions to the first draft were as I expected. People who didn't like conflict asked me, "Why write about rage at all?" and "Isn't rage an awfully strong word?" and "What does it mean anyway?" Those who recognize and experience their anger and frustration responded YESSSSS. The rest were in the vaguely uncomfortable middle.

It's important to talk about this feeling of rage because too
many people interpret their normal feelings of anger and frus-
tration to mean their marriage can't, shouldn't, or won't work.
In fact, if couples understand these normal feelings and handle
them together, they are likely to go on to have strong, passion-
ate, and happy marriages. Discussing rage is very different than
merely venting rage.

Frustration, the root of rage, begins with the familiar violated expectations: increases in workload, difficulties negotiating endless chores, the partner's sudden changes, sacrifices in
careers, friendships and social life, sleep deprivation, and irritability, all the things we have talked about. The resulting disil-
lusionment can feel like a vague uneasiness, but more often it is
intense and profound. Some of us respond to uneasiness and
frustration with anger. Although this anger isn't a *necessary* part
of having children, it is certainly a *normal* part of having children. Not everyone feels angry and upset after they have kids.
Certainly more people feel frustrated than do not. In studies,
33 percent of couples report they are happier after the birth of
the child and 67 percent report they are much more unhappy. So
if you're in the unhappy group, you have lots of company—
miserable company—but company nonetheless. The good news
is you don't have to stay miserable or ruin your marriage if you
understand what is happening and take steps to deal with your
unhappiness.

Partners deal with this frustration and anger in different
ways. Women are more likely to feel a profound anger first and
most strongly because they generally recognize their unhappiness first. Men are more likely to try to pretend it isn't happening at first, and then become more upset as the frustration
continues.

Each couple manages their frustration and anger differently.
Many partners dance around typical conflicts they feel about
their baby and their partner and try to talk themselves out of

feeling so negative. Some withdraw and avoid their partner when they are upset. Some yell. Some placate and pretend to be happy, hoping that if they are nice enough their spouse will shape up. But I know several women (and men) who have just packed up and moved out, sometimes leaving the children.

I also know one woman whose five kids were ages three to twelve when she snapped. She stopped abruptly in the middle of fixing dinner and just walked out the door and started walking down the center of her neighborhood street. Her whole family of grown children quietly refers to this as her nervous break-down. I think she was contemplating murdering her husband and possibly her children and decided to take a break. Fortu-nately, after an hour of wandering, she figured out what had up-set her so much and returned to mothering and housewifery.

She never could quite explain this walking out to her part-ner. She decided not to try because she realized that he became much more cautious and attentive after that. Twenty-five years later, she seems perfectly sane and chuckles with me about how everyone misinterpreted her sudden departure.

A mother of a two-year-old and a proper English woman liv-ing in the United States, Jane had worked as a successful com-munications trainer before having kids. One night she kicked her husband in the bottom because she was so frustrated he couldn't remember something she had requested many times. Admittedly, she had her bedroom slippers on but she had more access to her rage than to her communication skills that night.

Another woman, Barbara, had helped found her husband's multimillion-dollar business. Her husband, Fred, acknowledged that she had helped him land most of his biggest clients. When they had kids, however, he began excluding her from the busi-ness with fits of anger. Puzzled by this change, she started stay-ing home with the kids to keep the peace. Gradually, Barbara did all the housework and took care of the kids to avoid his anger. She liked bonding with the kids. Both were relatively comfortable with the decision. But she began pleading with her husband that they needed more time together to talk.

Eventually, she had an affair with the man next door, who would come over and talk to her and help out around the house just to spend time with her. She filed for divorce. Fred panicked and called me for marriage counseling. When we met, Barbara told me she loved her husband and thought he was much more handsome than the other fellow but she got tired of trying to get her husband's attention now that she was at home and he was at work. She was hoping that if she were sweet and helpful enough her husband would want to spend time with her, help around the house and talk with her.

In therapy when Fred reflected on this period in their marriage, he said that he remembered deciding one day when he was washing dishes as a teenager that he would never wash dishes or do housework when he grew up. Kids meant housework, so he had started working more at the office to escape. He could see that his wife was great with the kids. Fred thought she managed everything so beautifully that he was living out his teenage dream. He felt free not to talk with her except to get the still much-appreciated business advice, which he called for many times a day.

When she began therapy she would say she wasn't angry with her husband. But, as we began to address the issues, her voice rose to a high-pitched, angry shriek. Soon she became aware of her anger and her frustration. Eventually, as they talked in therapy, they resolved some of the issues. He even did some dishes, just to demonstrate how important she was to him. She gave up the lover. The marriage healed and became stronger and better for both of them.

They were lucky. More often, the wife will become so burned out that by the time she leaves she is what Michelle Weiner-

Davis, author of *Divorce Busting* and excellent related books, calls a *walk-away wife*. She gives up and walks away, too burned out to try therapy.

If couples come to therapy as a last-ditch attempt to save a walk-away situation, one partner, usually the one being left, will state at the beginning of counseling that marriage is a form of suffering and commitment that one must endure. He or she often believes that people can't or don't change. The existing partner feels that they have constantly been trying to repair or improve the marriage. Those repeated attempts at improvement were ignored as pointless because the other spouse was more comfortable with the status quo and may not believe change was possible. Finally, feeling they had tried everything, the frustrated partner walked away. The committed partner was left feeling often shocked, stunned, and that whatever precipitated the separation was too trivial to lead to divorce. They want to know why the divorce is happening at all.

To me these stories sound like different versions of rage. Unexpressed rage is still rage. Better to deal with the rage and "minor irritations" than to face a surprise divorce or a coronary event from unresolved issues. So how can you resolve your anger and get back on track as a couple?

Decode your anger signals. When couples flare up in anger they are showing (or being shown) a big, beautiful red flag. This is a great opportunity to notice and address a problem. Anger is a signal that the marriage is suffering. But it is a *disguised* signal. Instead of seeing an opportunity to adjust their expectations, the common mistake frustrated partners make is to think that something is wrong with their partner and not that something has violated their own expectations. Rather than looking at themselves, they demonize their disappointed partner as a bad person who doesn't really know how to be a good partner or a good family person.

To recognize our anger as a signal, we need first to understand that the one who is upset is the one with a problem. That's right, if you are mad, you are the one with the problem. That doesn't mean that you are wrong about what you see or want. You are probably right. You are also the very best one to resolve the problem because you are both more upset and more motivated than your partner.

With my clients, I often use the example of the bad driver who cuts you off in traffic but goes merrily on his way. If you swear, scream and become upset, who has the problem? You do. You may be the good driver but you are the one who is upset and giving yourself a heart attack over his bad driving and having trouble paying attention to the road now because you are so angry. You are the one who is embarrassed about swearing in front of the baby, even if the baby doesn't understand language yet.

If you knew that the person who cut you off was rushing his wife to the hospital to have a baby, would you be as upset? If it were your beloved, gray-haired granny, would you be upset or would you be worried that she wasn't going to make it home? Or let's imagine your husband calls and says you have to pick up the kids and skip your trip to the gym. You do it reluctantly, muttering dark words about his character the whole way. When you arrive home he and your best friend have arranged a surprise party but didn't want you to arrive looking post-gym. You make a great beginning when you understand what exactly is frustrating *you*, not what is wrong with your partner. That is the first step to positive change. Bryon Katie is the master of investigating your own thinking. She filled her book *Loving What Is* with terrific examples of turning your own thinking around to enjoy your life more.

Our road rage and our spousal rage both have to do with our definitions of the situation. Rage or anger signals that our expectations for the situation have been violated and that we need to adjust *our* actions or *our* expectations. When we understand our expectations—and possibly even why the other person is doing whatever he is doing—then we may deal with any situation more calmly.

The person who is upset is also the person who has the energy to make the change. Sometimes we waste this energy trying to get our partners to change by nagging, scolding, pleading, criticizing, using the silent treatment, or many other unattractive strategies that we think might work. These strategies, which are the offshoots of rage, are terrible models for our kids and are better used as a signal to ourselves that we need to shift our approach.

If you are the one who is upset because your spouse won't change a diaper, then you have the problem. The dirty diaper motivates you, not your spouse. If you want your spouse to do something about diaper changing, you need to find a way to approach it that avoids name calling, blaming, and nagging. If you see him as the chauvinist pig who *ought* to change diapers and tell him so, then little progress is likely to occur. If you accept that he may not like changing diapers or may not see it as part of his role, and try a different, calmer approach, your life will be easier. If you tell him how sexy you think men are who change diapers, how amazing he is at helping and so forth, you may get a different response. Or you may agree to do all the diaper changing in exchange for having him do something you hate to do.

Often a wife drags her husband into therapy with her list of grievances in the hope that I can get him to change. I can't. I can motivate her partner to make a few small changes, but for the relationship to change in a lasting way, *she* needs to learn how to influence her husband, and he needs to learn to yield to her influence and vice versa. Even though I may be quite persuasive and her husband may change a little, he will change back when he stops seeing me if she doesn't learn how to support and maintain his changes. Of course if they both learn to influence and support each other, they both will be happier. (More on that in chapters ahead.) They will have also laid good groundwork for difficult co-parenting issues to come.

At first partners get upset when I say that a problem belongs to the unhappy one and think I am a little crazy. One woman, threatening divorce, forced her husband to come to therapy without her. She would leave me little encouraging messages about how brilliant I was in the hope that I could change him when she could not and did not want to try. But, eventually she came to realize that for anything permanent to happen, the person who wants change must change him- or herself. Gradually, the message-leaving lady began to come to the sessions with her husband. At first she tried telling him what a rotten father and inattentive spouse he was in the sweetest possible way. As we learned about her past and what her fantasy hopes for the marriage had been, we began to get to work on a joint vision of what their marriage could be like that would be satisfying to both of them.

Often, however, our own personal histories and expectations combine to fuel the anger in ways that make no sense to us. This is why I encourage couples to stay calm in the heat of the moment and try to figure out what events upset them. In other words: *Be curious, not furious.* Let me give you an example.

Keith and June were a doctor and a nurse. June had come to therapy alone because she was surprised by a recent event. She had cut back her work significantly to stay home with their first son. When their son was eighteen months old, they decided together to move to a larger house in a nicer neighborhood. The escrow date shifted again and again. Their moving date finally landed in the middle of a ski trip that had been planned by Keith and his buddies for some time. Keith's friends asked if he was going to cancel. Keith asked if June wanted him to cancel the trip. She assured him more than once that it wasn't necessary.

Of course, moving with an eighteen-month-old and the help

of a couple of loyal friends didn't go as smoothly as June antici-
pated. When Keith called from the resort to see how she was doing, June was standing chest-high in boxes with three people
asking where things should go. "Don't bother to come home!"
she shrieked at him, in a fit of intense rage that shocked her.

They talked the situation over when Keith got home. Keith
apologized but June went on feeling resentful for days. She
didn't feel like having sex or being touched. This fight was on its
way to becoming the fight that is recorded in maternal memory
to be hauled out in all the wrong moments. "This is just like
when we moved . . ." The intensity of her anger and the uncomfortable fact that June had told Keith to go skiing when he had
asked made it harder to see him alone as the insensitive bad guy.
June realized in therapy that she often took over in her family as
the competent one while others skipped out on responsibilities.
She had wanted Keith to participate in their move but wasn't
really aware of that until he wasn't there.

Harville Hendrix in his book *Getting the Love You Want*
says it perfectly when he explains that our unconscious wish
when we marry our partners is to heal the injuries of our family
of origin. By marrying we want to do family—or love—over
right this time. If our partner isn't clued into what we need to
heal, and we don't know and can't ask directly for what we
want, we can become intensely and surprisingly angry at critical
points in our marriage.

Fortunately, our anger issues are clearly marked for us if we
can learn to read the intensity of our emotional reaction. Usually
our reaction will seem out of proportion to the issue. Luckily,
for Keith, June and little Michael, June was able to talk through
her emotions in therapy. She was then able to ask Keith to listen
to what had gone on for her internally. To help repair the damage and reconnect, she asked him to participate in other moving-
related projects like filing changes of address and working on
the landscaping. She continued to work hard to use her anger

constructively. When she began to get upset, she began to learn to use her reaction as a signal to recognize her own needs and then ask for what she wanted before—not after—she got upset.

So how do you explore rage and anger? Most people either want to duck for cover when their partner is upset, or fight back. This fight or flight response is programmed in our biology long before we have children. After kids, this program is activated more frequently because exhaustion and stress reduce our impulse control.

Intense anger is like a roller-coaster ride, fast and furious. If we really listen to what the person is saying and let them know we understand what they are feeling, the anger crests and drops off. We do not have to agree with them or share their opinion. Remember when a person is angry, giving advice of any kind interrupts and frustrates the speaker more and typically makes them angrier. When a partner is expressing anger, the best response is, again to: *Be curious, not furious.* This phrase is simple to say and very hard to do. Most people struggle mightily to be understanding when their partner is angry.

You don't have to wait until your marriage difficulties have progressed to serious fights and flare-ups or to complete boredom or avoidance. It's better if you don't. Rage and anger are a signal to explore the violations of your expectations to create the marriage that you want.

When I teach my clients to work with their anger, I sometimes say that both Martin Luther King and Mahatma Gandhi were angry men, but constructive and peaceful in their anger. Their anger lit the way for great social and political change without burning people. It got the job done.

Coaching Yourself to Use Anger Signals

So how do you use anger signals positively? First, recognize that there are several targets of anger: (1) Your partner can be mad at someone else; (2) Your partner can be mad at you; or (3) You can be angry with your partner or someone else. For most people listening to a spouse's work problem or problem with someone else is easier than listening to an attack on themselves.

When Anger First Comes Up

1. Take a minute, close your mouth and take a deep breath—or several—and identify who is upset and why. Were you sailing along happily when your partner said something harsh? Are you the one who fired the first shot? Whose expectations were violated? Are you upset with something your partner did or is something or someone else irritating you?

2. Identify the disappointment, frustration or hurt that is causing anger. Choose a strategy based on who is upset and why.

If the problem is really something outside the relationship, let your partner know that you want to learn more about his/her distress and move to the coaching sequence below: "Oh gosh, that is tough!"

When Your Partner Is Mad at Someone Else

The steps in coaching others through anger or upset are:

1. Recognize that your partner is upset.

2. Use feeling words so they know that you understand they are upset like "Gosh, that is so frustrating" or "Don't you just hate that?"

3. Encourage them to tell you all the details that they want to share: "Did he say anything else?"

4. Engage in some fun hostile fantasies together about the annoying other person if you are both comfortable with that: "Wouldn't you love it if he got caught doing that?" Or "Would you like me to go beat him up?"

5. *Do not give advice!* This is the hardest part for most people. We love to give advice. Men like to be the knight in shining armor rescuing the damsel in distress. Women like to be seen as nurturing and wise. But the emotionally intelligent spouse, when it gets to the final stage, asks, "Have you thought about what you want to do about it yet?" This question implies that whatever has the partner struggling is so annoying that he or she might not be ready to move on yet. This phrase also suggests that you would be happy to move to problem solving when your partner is ready but doesn't push the person to go faster than his or her own pace.

When Your Partner Is Mad at You

Remaining calm and listening when your partner is mad at you is much harder. But it is possible. Most men and many women find the steps for listening to an angry partner tedious. Slowing down and carefully choosing your words when you are angry or when your partner is angry with you will have a big payoff for resolving problems.

Usually when couples want to discuss a conflict, I ask each partner to repeat back what the other has just said before stating their own point. Frequently this leads to comical results. She says, "Let's talk about our relationship." He hears, "You think I have ruined your life."

If you can't listen right now, and in the beginning you may not be able to, then tell your partner you want to be able to *really* listen carefully and understand the issue. Then suggest a specific time when you can both focus.

BABY BLUES By Rick Kirkman and Jerry Scott

Neil says men need this on a flash card because no man he knows would think of it spontaneously. It is *very important* that you come back to the issue and bring it up at the time you suggested, so your partner will trust you.

> "Can we talk about this later tonight, so I can listen without being interrupted? I want to be able to really listen."

If your partner is upset because you did not fulfill their expectations, do not defend yourself no matter how reasonable your actions were. Just be curious. "What did you think I was going to do?" Or simply feed back the feeling they express: "You were really hoping that I would remember and it feels like I don't care about you because I forgot?" As you talk, try to get in these points too: "You are so important to me. I hate to see you so unhappy. What would you like me to do next time?"

You don't have to agree that you did anything wrong. Agreeing may feel dishonest to both of you. Just make sure you understand your partner's position and let your partner know you care.

When You Are Mad at Your Partner

Don't rush to respond. Take all the time you need, as long as your partner knows you're not ignoring them but cooling down and thinking. I have many constructive hints for expressing your anger in a way that you can be heard. I discuss this in Chapter 21, "Fight Like the Windows Are Open." Right now I would like to help you calm your rage with truce triggers before we start a constructive fight.

Learn Your Truce Triggers. When you are angry, what is it that makes you stop fighting and start over? Michele Weiner-Davis, best-selling author and solution-oriented therapist, first described truce triggers in her book, *Change Your Life and Everyone in It*. Most of us analyze to a gnat's eyelash what is causing a problem, but few of us figure out what gets us over our upset and back on track. Instead of analyzing what went wrong, take a look at your past fights. What made the argument end? How did you both get past it and move on? What worked?

For some people it is laughter. My husband once looked at me when I was ranting away on some subject and asked me if I had been reading *Totally Fascinating Womanhood,* a mismash of the titles of two books. We had just read a review saying the authors each recommended pouting, petulant arguments as a good way to keep your man. I burst out laughing because we both thought the review made the books sound so dumb. Then we started over.

Startling someone works. Neil once calmly poured a beer on himself to demonstrate that since I was so intent on dumping on him he may as well dump on himself.

A direct request to start over can be effective. Once, when I was a new mother, Neil came home to a torrent of pleasant but persistent verbal abuse about his lateness. Neil looked me square in the eye and said, "I am going back out and let's start over, please." He then backed out of the room. I started laughing and we started over.

Some couples signal a do-over more indirectly. Some choose a pet phrase to remind them they are on the same team. One couple used "I know we both have good intentions." Another

said, "Christmas tree lights," which recalled their all-time dumb-
est fight and roughly translated meant, "This argument is also
silly and we don't need to keep it up." Some couples just withdraw to a favorite place and start over later. Some couples start
over with a hug. That's my favorite, but some people can't be
hugged until they aren't mad anymore.

Michele Wiener-Davis points out that in most marriages
both partners don't necessarily have the same truce trigger. She
likes a hug and her husband likes to be alone to recharge himself. They each needed to learn to give each other the trigger that
worked. So her husband gives her a wooden hug, which makes
her feel that he at least wants to resolve the problem even if he
isn't ready yet, and she lets him leave to regroup by himself.
Learning to give what your partner needs rather than what you
think they should need is critical.

My favorite couple therapist, Ira Poll, Ph.D., happily married for twenty-five-plus years herself, says that normal partners
will disappoint each other. If you are pleasing your partner even
70 percent of the time, your marriage is doing very well. How
the couple recovers from those disappointments determines the
quality of the marriage. Learning to share your anger and frustration constructively is probably the best way to build your
marriage and protect it from boredom, affairs, and other destructive factors.

Tips for Using Rage (or Withdrawal) Constructively

- Discover your truce triggers and your partner's.

- Agree in advance on a signal to start over.

- Create a buffer zone, a time-out plan that either of you
  can use when you are too upset or angry.

- Consider how to fix a problem next time rather than dwell on what went wrong this time.

- Create a signal that means you know this conversation/ situation is going downhill and you would like to help it go better.

- Consider specific behavior on your part to *avoid* the problem next time.

- Notice fights that you stop or discussions that go well; congratulate yourselves and see if you can work on issues in the same way in the future.

- Give support to your partner. A foot (or head, neck, or back) massage for a temporarily distant or silent partner will often change the relationship in a hurry. Having the energy to give a foot massage when you have the small children is the hard part. Some people find that turning off the phone, putting the kids down, and doing nothing but the foot massage helps to restore both partners. If they then trade massages in their quiet time alone, things can get even better. *Giving* support is one of the best ways to receive it.

- Plan your life with a little leeway in it. Leave the kids with the baby-sitter or daycare, and head out to the party an hour early. Spend that time with your honey. The good-will from this prevents petty irritations from escalating into rage.

- Try to go one hour, one day or one week without criticizing anything. I once clipped and saved a Dear Ann letter by a woman who saved her marriage by not criticizing her spouse for thirty days. I thought the woman should be canonized for sainthood for making such an abrupt and complete change. Yet, I know her method works. A single day without criticism generates incredible peace in my house. Though I still find it hard to do. I have given this advice to many of my clients teetering on the brink of divorce. When a couple can refrain from criticizing, a "no complaints" day (or better a week!) quickly brings peace for them so they can resolve deeper issues.

9

Happily Ever After with Style: Models of Marriage

Our culture celebrates the happily-ever-after aspect of marriage, and most newlyweds have a fantasy that attracts them to marriage. For him, this might be as basic as a regular sexual partner and regular meals, or as superficial as the expression "arm candy" implies. For her, the fantasy might include great conversation, genuine understanding, and help with decisions and heavy lifting. Whatever the fantasy, the point that professionals and newlyweds often miss is this: *All good marriages are not alike.*

True, people have a stereotypical image of a good marriage. In this lovely marriage people disagree civilly, sometimes in front of the children (so they have good role models for the resolution of conflict), resolve their differences and generally get along harmoniously and companionably. Sometimes they even have fun. This is your basic *Leave It to Beaver, The Waltons,* or *Lit-*

tle House on the Prairie marriage of yesteryear, where conflicts are resolved in under forty-five minutes. Present-day reality TV paints a seamier version of marriage, laced with witty repartee. Real marriages aren't like either of those. To have a chance at a good marriage, you need to separate fantasy from reality and come up with a clear vision of what a good marriage looks like to both parents. A fantasy image of marriage can cause very real stress when the baby arrives.

Almost no one lives up to his or her own fantasy of marriage. Often your partner's and your unconscious image of the good marriage don't match. Before the baby, you compromise easily. After the baby, especially as he or she grows, the differences in your fantasies emerge. The added stress of children makes it harder to discuss these style differences calmly. Compromise is difficult. If the two of you together can envision and articulate what you want for your family, achieving a good marriage will be easier.

Before you read what I am going to say about good marriages, write down the five most important things that make a good marriage. You may have twenty but list your top five.

_____

_____

_____

Ask your partner what his or her five are.

_____

_____

_____

Now share them with your partner. I find these lists interesting. I have had several couples say that the reason their marriage
works is they both take a shower (not even together) before bed
each night. While this doesn't strike me as the most profound reason to stay married, I think the fact they have one shared item on
their list is important. Items they don't share need to be explored.

While these discussions are interesting, research suggests
that it really doesn't matter a great deal how different your goals
are or how many interests you have in common. What distin-
guishes long-term marriages is how partners discuss their differences. There are several different ways of discussing or fighting
that work.

Styles of Conflict in Long-Term Successful Marriages

For more than twenty-five years John Gottman, at the University of Washington, has been doing research on married couples
in his "Love Lab." He has found that there are several different
types of couples who stay together for a long period of time and
report being happy.

Fair Fighters: The first group he calls validators. When I
have them as clients or observe them as friends, I call them fair
fighters. These people fight as if they have read George Bach's
old book *The Intimate Enemy: How to Fight Fair in Love and
Marriage.* They are what therapists generally try to get their
clients to become. They are clear when they disagree. They use
"I" messages and not "You" messages. They generally follow
the rules of good fighting. (See inset of communication rules.)
When they start a discussion, one spouse validates or confirms
the other's description of the problem. "Yes, we *are* having a
problem saving money." "Yes, I miss feeling close to you lately,
too." Validation may also be as simple as nodding in agreement
and giving feedback. The fair fighters don't sound so much like

they are in agreement with each other as they sound like they are listening intently to their partner's feelings. A really sophisticated validator may even communicate that what the partner is feeling makes sense given their position or viewpoint, even though the listener sees it differently.

Two therapists married to each other sound like this. Two people who have had a lot of marital therapy can sound like this, at least in the first part of the conversation. Later in their conversation there may be a great deal of spirited arguing for their position, yet they stay focused on the problem and don't drag up unrelated or past problems. There is a strong sense in these couples that they are both working together on the same problem. Finally, they know how to hit the reset button and move on after an argument.

When the baby arrives, if they understand the issues, recognize the new stresses and talk about them, they tend to make a smoother, calmer transition. Even when they have no awareness of the issues, their usual communication style helps them weather the storm of a new baby more easily than most. Even so, their relationship is likely to be rocky, and they can be quite puzzled and frustrated by their partner's unexpected and inexplicable differences after the baby arrives. They find it discouraging when the frequency of their disagreements jumps.

Because they value intimacy and just being together, they ask about their partner's feelings before jumping to conclusions. They communicate clearly and warmly when they hand off the children to each other in toddlerhood and do even better after the kids are three. They can each apologize fully and completely. Although they make it as a couple, they remember those early years as really difficult.

Que Sera, Sera: The next group I like to call the "*Que Sera, Sera*" couples. For them, "What ever will be, will be." The researchers call them conflict avoiders. I experience them more as feeling as if what *is* was meant to be. They therefore have an internal tranquillity that many mystics have sought. These people don't express a lot of emotion, although they often feel quite deeply. From a child's point of view, these kinds of couples make wonderful parents for there is little open conflict. Problems "work themselves out" without a lot of deep or specific discussion. When they talk things out, they agree a lot. They talk about how similar they are. Differences and disagreements, although acknowledged, are seen as not very important in the larger scheme of things. They tend to see their children as "amazing."

One very happily married couple I know is comprised of a practicing Zen Buddhist, Jon, and an agnostic, Ally, who each see their values as similar. They have no need for the other to have similar religious views and are quite comfortable allowing their children to choose religions. They can have spirited discussions on issues, yet they keep their differences in perspective. They don't see themselves as avoiding conflict. They just see differences as normal and good. When asked if a glaring difference in their religion or relationship bothers them they are likely to say things like, "Why would I be upset about that? That is just how he is and I shouldn't, and wouldn't, want to change his basic personality."

Like most Zen couples, Ally and Jon handle conflict deftly. When persuasion occurs, Ally is a little more likely to initiate a very tentative, calm discussion. Jon may respond then or later. Proposed solutions are so vague they drive any therapist over the wall. She and Jon are often quite satisfied once they get a proposed direction. Ally can, however, be the master of the stinging funny one-liner, a trait common to the Que Sera, Sera couple. Not in the destructive sense of a hostile couple but more in the manner of, "I know you and I see you completely. Can you see yourself?"

Like most Que Sera, Sera couples they remember the early years with the babies as good ones. Ally stayed home as they both viewed that as the best start for the kids. Most of these couples tend to have traditional gender roles in their daily lives, even if the wife works. Typically Dad may assume additional family responsibilities to balance the load.

The biggest threat to this type of marriage occurs if the wife is forced to work for financial reasons, and does not want to. Often the husband steps in to help out, and balance is returned. This kind of couple fascinates me because they are so unlike anyone I might see in therapy. Their style would be hard to teach because it is more of a philosophy. Yet research suggests such a couple is usually very happy for many years.

If this type of marriage is disrupted, it is likely to be over something catastrophic like the loss of a child, although the couple's fatalism helps even in such a tragedy. While there are many pluses to this style, both partners must share the style and have about the same need to engage in contact and conversation.

Passionate Partners: The third group is the *Volatiles,* or Passionate Partners. If avoiders are TV couples, then passionate partners are the movie couples. They fight. Loudly and clearly, but not bitterly. They also smile more and laugh more. They are more affectionate. They each give lots of compliments. They are more likely to make a positive and clear statement of the problem and their feelings about it. They don't seem to be good listeners because they don't nod their heads and murmur uh-huh all the time. They do seem passionately engaged in their disagreements. Arguing seems to express their individuality and separateness. It is almost as if they need the arguing to feel intimately connected and real. They talk about "good" fights that help them clear up problems and understand their own issues. Others have characterized these partners as independent. They are less likely to have a schedule and are more likely to view themselves as egalitarian.

They each sense they can really be themselves and be heard in the marriage. One friend of mine in toasting his wife on her fortieth birthday said, "What I really like about our marriage is that each person gets to make his or her point and each can count on a full hearing, no matter how stupid that point may be." Spoken like a true passionate partner.

When kids arrive, passionate partners have some difficulty in adjusting and redistributing the new workload. They need the time to have fun and argue things out and have trouble finding time to do anything besides argue. They aren't used to coordinating schedules and aren't that crazy about having a schedule. They like their independence, thank you very much. They adore their children and try to divide the workload in a way that is fair but doesn't require a lot of interaction and joint decision making. This is difficult and doesn't leave much fun time together. They will often go to therapy, because they believe they can learn and change and so can their partner.

The 5-to-1 Ratio

The absolutely most important point to remember about Gottman's research and all three of these couple styles is that happy couples tend to maintain exactly the same ratio of positive to negative comments and gestures in conversations about their conflicts.

> Happy couples maintain a 5-to-1 ratio of positive gestures, facial expressions, touch, and eye contact to negative comments, gestures, or tone.

Probably the most surprising finding is that highly positive, happy husbands show "disgust" the most comfortably. Some psychologists have even speculated and preliminary data show that the ability to show disgust or dissatisfaction is necessary to a positive relationship. The gentle Zen couples give the least strokes and show the least dissatisfaction and disdain, yet they can show it quite effectively according to researchers, because both partners receive it and care.

DO YOU HAVE A 5-TO-1 MARITAL STYLE?

Most people recognize their own marital style just by reading the preceding descriptions. If you love those questionnaires that men usually hate, I am not including one here. Regardless of how different your styles are, remember that *the key ingredient is the way you treat your partner.* When each partner expresses five times as much appreciation as negativity, starts discussions gently, makes requests politely, and consistently looks for and perceives the partner's good intentions, your style can work regardless of its passion or patience.

Marital Poison—Four Signs that Spell Trouble: Many couples try to work themselves out of normal conflicts using strategies that don't work. They can feel the disaster happening but persist in the hopes that their behavior will resolve the problem. Howard J. Markman and his colleagues have done over thirty years of research with couples in Colorado and have developed the PREP program, a wonderful program for helping people develop positive skills before they marry. They have identified the "Four Horsemen of the Apocalypse" that guarantee a relationship is in trouble. Any one of them spells doom. If you can recognize these in your own marriage, you need to change your style and learn new ways to resolve the inevitable conflicts of marriage.

I don't even like to write about these deadly habits, and don't permit my therapy couples to engage in these interactions for more than a moment or so before I redirect them. If your relationship has repeated encounters of this kind it is important to start some new patterns right away.

- **Escalation** is when something clumsy is said like, "Why did you leave the door open?" and the partner responds with "Why do you always put me down?", "Why are you as rude as your mother?" or something else guaranteed to get the sparks flying. Clearly this doesn't get anywhere.

  - **Better:** Learning to address the issue differently, perhaps by saying, "Oh, the door is open. Can you get the door before Johnny makes a getaway?" is a better strategy. Most partners will respond by shutting the door and make a note not to do it again. As Johnny gets older and the couple's experience increases, a simple "The door!" in a gently concerned way may communicate the same thing. If you find yourselves escalating, notice that it's a danger signal and start exploring a new approach.

- **Painful Putdowns:** Name calling, labeling, or describing your partner's feelings as overreacting all make pretty sure that an issue won't get resolved. Any time the argument includes the phrase "You are so . . . (fill in the blank)," the discussion might as well end.

  - **Better:** If you think your partner is irresponsible, lazy, inconsiderate or any other negative label, consider talking that behavior over with someone who values your partner, who can help you reframe your unhappiness in a constructive way. Your opinion about your partner's laziness counts because you're unhappy and you may be accurate, but it won't help you resolve the issue until you can state it in a useful way.

    This is what changing yourself is about. Instead of nagging, learn to ask, "What do you see as your responsibility to the housework (or with the kids)?"

Then really listen. The answers may pleasantly surprise you. Then ask how the two of you can make it happen. Maybe you will cheerfully adjust your expectations and maybe your partner will step up to the plate.

- **Perceived Bad Intentions:** When you begin to believe that your partner has bad intentions, your marriage is in serious trouble. If you think your partner says or does things just to irritate you or because they don't care about you, then things are rapidly heading downhill. If you find yourself saying something just to irritate your spouse, that's a danger signal, too. When you assume the worst about what your partner is saying, the worst is already happening.

  - **Better:** I always ask partners to state their good intentions clearly when making a request. For example, "You are always so helpful with the kids and I hate to ask one more thing but would you mind . . ."

    To resolve this impasse, each partner needs to be sensitive to the other and learn how to talk in a soothing way. To begin to pull the marriage out of the hole of perceived bad intentions, both partners will usually need a therapist who can see and reflect any good intentions while giving them an opportunity for intensive practice in communicating under duress. (For more on this, see Chapter 21, "Fight Like the Windows Are Open" and Chapter 23, "Protecting Your Marriage with Warmth and Persuasion.")

- **Avoiding Big Issues:** While Neil would probably say I could benefit from learning *not* to say what is bothering me, couples in which one or both partners avoid talking about issues often end up unhappy and divorced. When one partner brings up a problem and the other won't agree that the issue is a problem or simply won't discuss an issue, both partners become angry, frustrated and estranged.

While this often leads to a superficially quiet and apparently conflict-free relationship, nothing gets resolved. Both of you often feel deadened and depressed. The marriage can survive for a long time but it often disintegrates into distance and unhappiness. Sometimes affairs begin in the silence.

- **Better:** The one exception is when both of you agree the best way to handle conflict is to separate and not talk, do something else and come back and start over doing something you enjoy. If you share this coping technique, you may be just fine. Likewise, if you *both* feel closer and better after a good argument, the marriage will be fine if you both feel better having your say, *and* have a way to feel close again. Use the tips for handling rage and withdrawal constructively in Chapters 8, 20, and 21.

More Marital Poison: Four Bad Habits Besides the Four Horsemen above, Gottman's Love Lab identified these negative predictors that indicate a troubled relationship. Watch for these as well:

- **Harsh Start-ups:** If you find yourself raising issues in a crabby, insulting tone or making an accusation that includes *always* or *never,* reconsider how you begin talking about problems. The harsh start-up is a marker that leads to flooding. Best friends don't use harsh start-ups. Neither do good marriages.

  - **Better:** Think about how you would ask a friend and try that.

- **Flooding:** When you feel blindsided and simply can't respond, you can't hear what your partner is saying. People usually shutdown or flee when this happens. Some explode with anger or change the subject with artful distraction. Most women and men don't realize that men flood faster than women do. When your partner slips away from discussions, either quietly or explosively, consider whether you make harsh start-ups and your partner is emotionally flooding.

  - **Better:** Try again gently later. If you don't know how, ask a happily married friend how she would bring it up.

- **Failed Repair Attempts:** When one partner attempts to joke, apologize, or make a plan to improve things and the other partner ignores these attempts to get on track or becomes angry, serious problems are afoot.

  - **Better:** Repair attempts signal good intentions. Recognize all attempts to repair feelings even if the effort feels a bit awkward or forced at first.

- **Bad Memories Are Bad News:** When you can't remember the good times in your marriage, and the marriage doesn't feel like fun anymore, you are in trouble. According to Gottman and his research team, couples report that the beginning of the marriage was difficult and bad even when earlier tapes from the study show they had made glowing remarks about the marriage. Couples unconsciously rewrote history to match their present feelings. So if you can only remember bad memories, take heed, and talk to your spouse or a counselor. We will talk more about some strategies in later chapters to help overcome a dysfunctional marital pattern.

- **Better:** Spend time talking about your great memories, certainly more time than you spend rehashing mistakes.

An optimist might argue that some negative events are good because they signal the couple that their marriage needs attention or that they are ready to move to a new stage. **Negative events can be a *signal*, but when these behaviors become a *style* you are deeply in trouble.** Couples need to recognize these behaviors as trouble, so they can adopt constructive strategies and styles that will allow them to progress more comfortably through the marital stages discussed in the last chapter.

Choosing a Style: Since three styles work—Validation, Zen, and Passionate—one could assume that it would be easy for a couple to adopt one of the three. Of course childrearing repeatedly raises sensitive issues for each partner. Under stress, partners tend to adopt a more extreme style that may vary markedly from their calm style. So if your conflict style is going to be a problem, it will be even more so with kids and the attendant sleep disruption, chaos, and clutter. When both partners push the mess off the table or balcony together, they're a team and have a laugh. When one person longs to unwind from conflict alone in a silent room while the other unwinds to the sounds of rock music, it takes some creativity to meet in the middle for discussion.

In crisis mode, partners often each drift toward a different style than the one they usually share. One partner may begin to act even more like their own parents did in their childhood, particularly if the family was happy. Or if the parents' marriage was unhappy, they may adopt an opposite style.

There is great pain and frustration when one partner has a

Zen approach and the other is passionate. The passionate partner feels that the relationship lacks excitement, honesty and
meaning or that they must walk on eggshells. The more Zen-like
partner may feel under constant, unreasonable pressure. Couples with mismatched styles must work hard to adopt a style
uniquely suited to each of them and to their marriage.

As style differences become apparent, knowing how you
each prefer to handle stress and resolve conflict becomes vitally
important. Kids add stress. People under stress just don't compromise or solve problems as easily. Many people can operate
under a variety of styles, or match another's style until they are
under stress.

When we are stressed and burned out, we become less
thoughtful and resolve conflict in more primitive ways. "What
the *#*#* were you thinking?" doesn't feel curious. It feels hostile. But when we are upset, this is what comes out. "I can't live
like this" may sound like a statement of fact to you. Yet your
partner may hear it as a threat to leave the marriage. The communication skills of both sender and receiver disintegrate rapidly in this kind of exchange. While you both may have great
communication skills at work, these skills may fall apart at
home. To thrive in this period, couples need to focus on what
works in their marriage to keep them out of the territory of the
terse, harsh remark. They need to reach for what helps them recover from these bad spots.

When your problem solving styles don't match, as they don't
for most couples under the stress of kids, real love and commitment become important. Ferreting out the best way to be soothing when your partner is upset, learning to recognize and state
good intentions and asking clearly for what you need are all critical skills for building a thriving marriage with small kids. All
are skills that we'll talk more about in future chapters. Meanwhile, working to resolve conflicts in this period creates a much
stronger, more satisfying marriage for the rest of your life.

When partners have extremely different styles, the marriage can be saved, but it is critical that the couple see a therapist who can value and support both partners' styles. Together with the therapist, the couple can begin to understand their different styles and learn concrete ways to support each other, especially when sensitive issues are triggered.

Gratitude is the glue of marriage. Reviewing all these styles of marriage shows that positive feedback and the genuine appreciation of the other person is the glue that binds marriages. Each type of successful marriage studied in research has more positive talk than negative talk. Gratitude and kind remarks make each partner feel safe to express their concerns and discomforts in a way that doesn't threaten the marriage. I have seen marriages saved when one partner sits down in the midst of ongoing conflict and writes a lengthy list of all they value about their partner. This list creates the setting in which the partners can safely discuss what needs to change in the way they are with each other.

Each spouse needs a safe way to share uncomfortable information and make new needs known to the partner. As children bring new needs for adult companionship, and add time demands, chaos and disorder to a relationship, the need to make simple requests, which may have been minimal before, will skyrocket. Identifying a unique couple style or a ritual that works for each of you to manage these new demands is a terrific investment in a long and happy marriage.

Creating a Conflict Style that Works for You Both:

- Learn to recognize your own style. Figure out whether your style helps your partner open up and be close. If it doesn't, try new approaches.

- Learn to recognize and accept your partner's style.

- Give five positives—touch, warm looks, gifts, extra favors or praise before every criticism. Count them on your fingers. At the very least it will reduce your critical remarks. If you aren't treating each other kindly, your marriage needs attention.

- Change your own style first to make sure you achieve a 5-to-1 ratio.

- Study your partner to learn how they show dissatisfaction. If your partner expresses dissatisfaction in a way that doesn't work for you, tell them clearly, with an example of what works better for you.

- If your partner responds poorly when you ask for help, listen to how they make the same kind of requests to you. Even if you find their way annoying, ask for help exactly the same way they do. If that doesn't work, then ask gently how they like to be asked to help.

- When your partner expresses dissatisfaction, try remaining calm and imagine that your partner is a new person you just met and she is complaining about her roommate. Be curious and sympathetic first and see what happens.

- Notice what other couples disagree about that you and your partner don't. Why? Gives yourselves a pat on the back.

- Notice conflicts that are resolved easily. Is there something you could do again to repeat that success? Comment on your success. "Wow! We got over that a lot faster than we did last time. How did we do that?"

- Ask yourself what works as a truce trigger for you and what works for your partner. Are the triggers the same or different? Do more of what works for your partner. Let your partner know how much it means to you when he or she tries your truce trigger.

- Ask your partner what helps them recover when they are upset. If neither of you knows the answer, ask parents or best friends. Although it seems spouses should know best, sometimes outsiders may have more objective ideas of their own.

- Create gratitude rituals for yourself and your family, times that you stop to tell each other regularly what you value about the relationship.

- When your style differences are really severe, you may require professional help. The good news is that when you have young children and your problems are fresh, therapy frequently works quickly and easily.

10

Good Moms (and Dads) Feel Guilty:
Balancing Work, Love, and Life

Parents feel guilty about an endless list of things. Not spending enough time with their kids. Letting them watch too many videos or DVDs. Exposing them to germs. Shrieking occasionally. Perhaps the most pervasive guilt feelings come from moms trying to juggle jobs and kids. "Mommy, why can't you be our nanny?" a precocious seven-year-old asked, leaving her hard-working mom momentarily speechless. If moms work for any reason—and especially if it is by choice rather than grinding financial necessity—they worry they aren't giving kids enough attention. If they stay home, moms feel guilty that they aren't earning enough or being a good model for their children, especially their girls, of all that one can accomplish. Women feel this conflict between work and home most acutely, and earlier, than most men do.

Feeling a little guilty is actually a sign of a good parent. Conscious parents have an acute sense that they are making choices that profoundly affect their children. Women typically begin to think and worry about these home vs. work conflicts before their children are born. In surveys, men don't report thinking about this until they are over forty. It's like men at fifty slap their foreheads and go, "Oh no, I forgot the kids!" Sometimes their wives slap their heads, verbally of course. By now their kids are teenagers and the parents are trying to forge a relationship with strangers.

The point is good parents realize the inherent conflict between time with work and time spent in personal pursuits or with their partner and kids. Good parents notice that conflict and make conscious choices that they discuss with each other about that conflict.

Models of Work-Family Priorities

Couples in happy marriages set priorities in several ways. The traditional approach was the wife stayed home and gave the kids plenty of attention. Dad went to work and brought home the money. But there are many other models. Couples today often both work and hire a nanny or take the child to daycare. Some couples try to share all tasks equally. Even rarer are Mr. Moms, the stay-at-home dads. Although couples can discuss these options in advance and will probably choose an approach before the kids are born, the reality is that people often change their minds once they have kids. They also often regret or second-guess their choices a lot! Dedicated career women suddenly quit; committed homemakers pine to go back to work or have a small escape. As one woman commented, "I want a job just so I can wave my hand cheerily and say, 'I have to go to work. Bye.'"

Couples that have the easiest time with this decision have a flexible model they agreed upon and were comfortable with in the beginning. This plan almost always changes somewhat with new responsibilities. When the husband takes the approach of

"It's up to you how much to work and how much to be home" and encourages his wife to make an independent decision, this approach can be easier, but still carries the seeds of potential conflict. The wife might feel abandoned because he isn't participating in such an important decision. Sometimes the husband says, "Choose whatever you like," then becomes resentful when she chooses not to work. Or he goes along but feels tense and worried under the financial burdens.

Men rarely discuss their conflicting desires to be the sole breadwinner, which can be an ego booster, versus the very tangible benefits of two incomes. Sole breadwinners often feel that they are left out from the family while Mom exerts, as one guy put it, "executive control over parenting." As more than one single-income family man has said to me, "She makes all the decisions. The kids know it. She only asks me when she isn't sure what she wants to do." She feels she decides because she is the one who is there.

The nature of the partners' work affects these choices. If one partner's work requires frequent travel, very long hours or disruptive, irregular scheduling, then the other partner is almost required to stay home or have a job with shorter hours and little travel. Otherwise, the children will have to be raised by a nanny or a boarding school.

Moms worry about these issues; dads rarely do. Mom often feels the need to talk (obsess endlessly) about her feelings about the daily choices regarding childcare, school and time for her work and herself. Most likely, Dad isn't going to get it. He will feel that these discussions are uninteresting and pointless. Even if he does get it, he wonders, "What am I supposed to *do*?" After all, he knows his role; he is supposed to go to work and make money like dads have been doing forever. She often envies the freedom society has allotted him and his guilt-free take on parenting. Often he seems clueless about her angst. The contrast is clear when he leaves for work while the kids kiss and hug and

CATHY By Cathy Guisewite

wave sweetly. She leaves for work and the children cling and cry. Or she lingers and feels melancholy after she drops them at day-care, wondering if she is doing the right thing.

Of course, some moms drop the kids off with relief so they can retreat to the relative quiet and calm of the office or the gym. It doesn't take long to realize that most jobs are cleaner, quieter, and neater than raising kids. Withdrawing into the relative comfort, safety, and quiet of work is tempting. Long hours at work usually mean that you miss time with your partner as well, cutting yourself off from the emotional support you once had from your partner. Work begins to seem like a haven, not only from the kids but also from the emotional issues brought up by trying to co-parent. Thus, if someone approaches you to flirt you are emotionally a bit hungry and needy.

But there is more: You are both likely to be in that stage (discussed in Chapter 7) of your marriage where you have begun to notice all the ways you're different, and to criticize and initiate change. You're bound to have more conflict in the marriage. If you have attained any level of success and comfort at your job, you will probably get much less criticism and conflict at work. Your spouse may be indicating that you really aren't such a good parent because you don't feel guilty and torn about how much time you spend away from the family. You may withdraw—feeling misunderstood and unappreciated—and refuse to discuss these issues. When you go out to dinner you may argue about who has the most responsibility. Soon work starts to feel like a better place to be. You begin to feel quite distant from your spouse.

So how do you start a conversation about these issues with your spouse? For women, the best initial conversations about these issues may be with girlfriends. Most women are going through these issues and will be inclined to discuss them at length without feeling they need to fix the problem.

Talking to sensible, happily married girlfriends can help you sort out your feelings before you approach your spouse. For example, after bouncing my feelings off my girlfriends, I realized I needed to work at least part-time. I am far too bossy and controlling. I would drive my kids crazy if I spent too much time around them. They would never learn to be independent. I reasoned that they need me distracted with work so that they could learn to deal with other people and fend for themselves. I always loved the Harvard research that indicated that the most successful adults could be identified at age three by the fact that they could ask another adult, besides a parent, appropriately for help. The other studies that reassured me were those that said the family does best when Mom is happy with her choice.

Once you have sorted out what you think is a good idea, it is easier to address this issue with your spouse. A good way to begin is by being curious about your partner's own family. My favorite questions come from *Finding Time for Fatherhood,* by Bruce Linton, Ph.D., therapist and founder of the Father's Forum website.

He starts with these kinds of questions:

- How do you spend most of your time between work and life and how did your father prioritize his time?

- What was most important to your father in his life?

He moves on to more difficult questions like:

- How did your father fail you in your life, and how was he there for you?

- What do you do or plan to do to let your children know you love them?

- Aside from your father, are there other "fathers" you would like to be more like?

For both women and men, I would repeat the questions about their mothers' lives as well, since frequently that dramatically affects both men's and women's views. These questions help you bring to light your own assumptions about parenting.

Linton encourages men to discuss these issues with other men, although men can usually find fewer buddies with whom to talk over these issues. Their wives will be quite eager to talk, but a little too quick and impatient for change. Finding a male support group of dedicated fathers can be more rewarding because the men will more likely be at a similar stage and less judgmental with each other. These groups were practically impossible to find ten years ago but are now more common. Still most guys would be reluctant to form such groups. They would more likely do as some couples do and team up with another couple or two to discuss the questions and get to know each other and themselves better.

If you wish to talk about these issues with your husband, you may need to change Linton's questions to make them less formal, more casual, and related to his immediate experience. "How do you handle your frustration when your child's needs must come before your needs?" might be better phrased as, "What do you think about and feel when the baby cries and we have to stop talking or kissing to deal with her?"

Of course, you can ask the same questions about your own childhood. Discussing these questions is an important part of co-parenting. More important, the talking itself bonds you to each other and helps create a closer marriage. Knowing your partner's frustrations and dreams around parenting helps you understand when they appear to you to be emotionally under- or overreacting to everyday events with the kids. (An extreme example would be if your spouse knew you had a sibling die on a family vacation, they would be more likely to understand what might otherwise seem like excessive concern about health and safety.)

Another milder example, might be if your mother became extremely upset and told you how selfish you were whenever you asked for something, then you would likely learn not to ask for anything. In marriage, you would try to be a good person so the other person would be good to you. You would expect your partner to ignore your needs, which would be easy since you'd never express them. On the other hand, if your father made you repeatedly ask over and over again and then discuss and "sell the need" before you got new shoes or a new backpack, you might be a fabulous salesperson, and you might also wear your partner out when you wanted something.

More important, ask each other questions about work and family that aren't directly about the kids:

- What made you feel the most loved as a child? Was it helpful gestures, chores done for you, praise, attention, gifts, hugging, and/or affection? What makes you feel most loved in the marriage?

- What things did your parents do that made you feel unloved? Ashamed? What most upsets you today?

- What things did your parents struggle with in their marriage or before their divorce, like drinking, drugs, infidelity, abusive arguments, or silent treatment that you fear and adamantly do not want to repeat?

- How important is it to have accomplishments? What accomplishments do you want when your kids are grown and you look back on your life? Is there something that you feel called to do? What have you done in your life that makes you proud?

- How do you want/expect your marriage to support your achievements? Do you need someone to share your excitement, attend functions, travel with you, work with you, listen, and plan with you?

When you understand each partner's dreams and frustrations you can begin to plan together to avoid both harmful emotional withdrawal and serious fights with each other. You can learn to ask in advance for what you want rather than criticize afterward. You can share signals for when no means no, rather than wearing one of you out or creating resistance with obnoxious persistence. You can learn when to discuss something and look for a solution together. In the process you will be teaching these useful skills to your children.

The form of this relationship doesn't matter as much as the *process* by which parents reach their decisions. What each member of the family needs will change dramatically over the course of the marriage. But a good process will help you respond more easily to those changes. Respect and affection in the way you resolve problems is critical to a happy marriage.

Your marriage is supposed to be the shelter that fosters your children, your marriage and your career for a lifetime. Both partners need to create an understanding of their separate individual strivings and the needs of their children so they can create and repeatedly remodel a structure that can last through a lifetime of changes. Working and struggling together you can create a great marriage, gently and playfully.

Tips for Becoming Comfortable with Parenting Choices

- Answer the questions on the previous page for yourself.

- Ask your partner the questions only one at a time rather than doing them all at once so you can really consider the answers and not flood your partner. You don't want it to seem like an oral exam.

- Compare the answers. Be sympathetic.

- Look for differences as well as similarities.

- Consider doing a journal or list of things that you both admire and things you both would rather not bring to your marriage.

- Save the information from this discussion to do the goal setting we discuss in Chapter 13, "Where Is this Train Headed?"

11

When and Why Benign Child Neglect Is Good

My mother always said that the best parents are lazy parents. Her theory, as I understood it, was that lazy parents don't jump up every time their kids need something so that children learn to entertain themselves, feed themselves, and otherwise plan ahead. In couples, lazy parents, theoretically, have more time for each other because their children learn, maybe by the time they are twenty-five, not to interrupt them when they are together. Of course a lazy parent is often too lazy to spend the time making the marriage work better. While I would never recommend neglecting a newborn in hopes of improving their character, I am going to talk about ways to support your marriage that may substitute for time with your child. This chapter is intended as an antidote to all the literature on how to be the perfect parent. The current high standards for parenting lead to low standards for marriage. The irony of these contrasting standards is that having a healthy marriage is a great gift for your children and yourself.

This chapter is devoted to the imperfect parent who creates time for the marriage by making the kids more independent and being a more relaxed partner. Benign child neglect involves discovering ways to help your children be more independent, without endangering their safety.

Perhaps the most articulate proponent of making time for your marriage is William J. Doherty, Ph.D., who wrote *Take Back Your Marriage*. I agree when he says that he rarely sees couples who are so involved with their marriage that they neglect their children. He says they do exist, but they are people who have other problems and shouldn't have had or didn't want children. The goal instead is to keep kids from completely overwhelming the little love rituals and routines you once shared with your mate.

Encouraging your child's independence to create time for yourself and your partner is an art that can start very early and evolves with the ages and stages of your child.

Finding Alone Time: Even though finding time is challenging, parents need to continue to find a way to "park the kids" safely and turn toward each other. No matter how established the marriage, talk time remains critical to long-term happiness in the marriage. Many women have very clear rituals around talking to their children after school or at dinner that they are loath to interrupt. They can see how the kids deteriorate without their contact. Yet they have no such connection to their spouse and may not see the immediate impact of missing time with their partner.

When I first read about couples needing daily fifteen-to-twenty-minute talk times I was astounded, as many of you probably are as well. I knew so few couples who actually could say when they talked routinely. The very idea of having time to chat together, uninterrupted, seemed like a fairy tale.

One not-too-happily-but-long-married friend of mine flatly told me regular talk time was impossible, given real people's hectic schedules. Although she could tell me when she talked to her own kids every day, she believed that real couples would need to find and agree on a new time every day. However, if you are too busy to make a regular time to talk, wouldn't you be much too busy to agree on a time every day?

When couples are courting, making time together to talk is given careful attention. Before you have children, the idea that you would lose your connection seems strange, even impossible. If you tell someone without kids that couples that actually talk fifteen minutes a day are rare and special, they will think you are unrealistically pessimistic. However, married people with kids think you are special if you *do* talk fifteen minutes regularly.

Yet, in truth, I have met couples that snuggle in bed for twenty minutes after the alarm goes off, or have a cup of coffee or tea together after dinner, or always talk before or after a late night show. Or call each other at lunch. They are a lot happier. Their kids see themselves as safe from divorce, whether or not their parents are passionate or Zen-like in their approach to normal disagreements. Couples who connect routinely see habitual time together as reassuring rather than rigid. They certainly feel something is missing if more than a few days go by without the connection. They then do something to restore it.

It's never too late. Instituting agreed-upon dates and rituals, times for talk, sex, and cuddling soon begins to change feelings of abandonment and erosion of love in a marriage. It also eliminates a withdrawer's guilt that they aren't doing enough and the sense of oppression that nothing would ever be enough. The parent who usually seeks contact starts to feel reassured.

As soon as your kids are old enough, ask them to help support you in this time by not interrupting. Explain that what is good for Mom and Dad is good for the whole family, and arrange one-on-one regular uninterrupted time with each parent for *them*. They will love it and that time is a great investment in your relationship with them, too.

Creating uninterrupted time for each family dyad, even if it is once a week and not daily, develops the communication bond. Like parents, kids who get this brief one-on-one attention are easier to live with and experience a healthy relationship and connection to family. They will also support your time with each other more readily.

My friend Marni commented: "My girls love to see me get all dressed up on date night. They help me pick out my shoes and lipstick. I think it is great that they see the romance of getting ready for the date—even when they sometimes whine a little that they would like to come, too. I like that they are fascinated by this other side of Mom and Dad that they don't share."

Likewise, I like that my kids know that Neil and I are going to talk over some family problem together before we set rules and consequences. Sometimes waiting to see the outcome of our meeting is nerve-racking for the kids but as they wait they get to think over for themselves what we might decide about the issue. They know if we disagree, Neil gets the last word on issues relating to their athletics, and I get the final vote on school matters. On money we use consensus decisions. Everybody has to say yes. We laugh because when we get in a heated exchange, one or the other child is likely to ask us to either go have a meeting or take a time-out, using our own advice on us. Watching us solve problems prepares them to participate in family meetings.

Kids' and Parents' Comfort with Parent Talk Time and Getaways

Over the years your children will vary in how comfortable they are with your absence. And each of you will differ in your comfort at various stages of your child's development. I have listened as many couples argued about what is normal when it comes to separation. There is no normal. Normal kids and normal parents vary in their comfort level with various separations. The critical thing is that each person in the marriage is respected for his or her wishes to be away from the kids and to have time as a couple. Recognize and accept that you won't always feel the same about these issues. Here are a few guideposts.

Infants to Twelve Months: Infants can often stay with either parent or a regular caregiver quite easily the first six to nine months. Although infants in the first six months need nearly constant attention, being slow to jump every time the baby cries but always reliably responding, creates a trust that you will arrive and they don't need to shriek to get you there. This is the best time to get the child acquainted with anyone who might become a long-term caregiver because there will be less protest later during the stranger anxiety period to anyone already familiar and comfortable. While the general wisdom is that the stranger anxiety period starts at nine months, assume that your child will be a genius and may have anxiety a bit earlier, as many children do.

This early period is a great time to introduce them to Grandma and Grandpa, Granny nanny, or a neighbor who is a weekend or daily caregiver. This is also a time when it is easy to take the baby with you, for long walks and talk relatively undisturbed. Some couples even take their first baby to the movies, if he is a good sleeper. Even if you don't go out as a couple without the baby, try to make time for each parent to have time alone and one on one time with the baby so that any small problems can begin to be sorted out now. Be mindful that breastfeeding can make Mom miserable if you go for an overnight, even if Mom pumps. Mom deserves a lot of support if she goes overnight.

One to Two Years: Kids are really hard to leave with anyone right now because they are so active. A child-safe environment is critical and even the most loving grandparent can be leery of chasing a toddler and have difficulty doing a good job. Because you will already have childproofed, it's usually better to have care at your home than elsewhere, particularly if the caregiver doesn't have small children. A baby-sitter who will come to the house so the child can fall asleep at home often works best. Because kids have little sense of continuity and are developing trust, it is better if they can have a caregiver that they already know and like.

Two to Five Years: Children often scream in protest when you leave and settle down shortly afterward. If they are sunny and happy to see you, and seem to forget that particular trauma by the time you return, you are doing fine.

By the time their kids reach two and a half or three, many people train them to wait a few minutes (about a minute for each year old) while the parent uses the bathroom or talks on the telephone. This is a good time also to make a point with kids that Mom and Dad have a particular talk time, perhaps just after the bedtime routine or early Saturday morning. They can learn to play quietly for a few minutes or fall asleep alone sometimes. They can also spend the late afternoon or evening in the care of a sitter, so you can have weekly dates.

By age three they can be quite upset about being left with someone other than their parents and will begin to verbalize their distress and remain angry about it longer. Familiar caregivers are an exception. (They are also gold!)

Five to Twelve Years: They usually begin to like games with rules at this age, so they may enjoy following rules that support your time alone. For example, they now will tell their friends that it is the rule that their mom and dad talk every Saturday morning so they must not bother them.

Most kids get more independent in these years and gradually get excited about sleepovers with friends. Our kids often begged us to have a night out so they could go spend time with friends or have friends over with a sitter at our place. This can be the easiest time to take trips together or away from your spouse because kids are more independent and interested in friends. With careful planning, you can arrange to trade sleep-over times with friends so that each couple gets a break while kids are having fun. Unfortunately, disruptions in the family routine mean that homework and the like may not be done. As the size of your family increases, the difficulty of such exchanges grows exponentially. Some happily married couples that I know with four and five kids hire college kids or couples to supervise.

Teen Years: Early teen years are in some ways the most difficult for parental outings and yet the easiest to find talk time. Some people feel if they have enough talk time they don't need to get away as much. Your teens will gladly leave you alone because they want you to respect their new independence. They have seen the consequences of divorce and appreciate that their parents talk together.

Teens can also make some meals for themselves or the family, and occasionally baby-sit, although most people recommend against making their duties so heavy that they interfere with study or normal social time. They still need some regular contact with a parent or adult, so be sure to maintain one-to-one parent time.

Most concerned parents find this the very hardest time to go away as a couple, because the kids view themselves as too old for baby-sitters. Making weekend plans around teen schedules is hard because they have a short-term view of plans, but like to make their own. It goes like this: The teen says, "I am going out." Mom says, "Where are you going, who are you going with and when will you get home?" The teen says, "You just ruined my plans again!" This teen testing, which stresses marriage solidarity, discourages parents from leaving, but makes couple trips even more important for some parents. Kids need a parent at home base to help them make last minute decisions about their own evening plans and to drive them when they are tempted to ride with other teenagers.

Leaving teens alone is hard. Even lovely, responsible, non-drug-using teens get into trouble because other teens know in a heartbeat (or a few cell phone calls) which home is not supervised. Many kids have trouble saying no to other kids. Learning to say no and set limits in difficult situations is a skill they must learn in the early teen years. Meanwhile, leaving your teenage kids alone can be frightening. I don't recommend it. These limitations can be quite difficult for a new mate without children in a blended family to understand.

Happy couples differ on how much they need to get away from the home at this point. Some couples are so committed to this routine talk time that they feel getting away is critical to feeling close, for setting goals and relating to each other without "help" and disruption. Some just like to go to socialize with other adults and see grown-up movies and plays. Other parents have grown accustomed to watching videos and revel in staying home alone together waiting for teens to return.

If you take a vacation during the school year, disruptions to their homework schedules may have a more negative long-term impact on grades, depending on their development and personality. When my husband and I are away, a beloved grandma just happens to want to visit. We encourage our boys to spend time with her instead of going out or having friends over. I know parents who have hired college kids to watch their teens when they were away only to discover the remains of an out-of-control party on their return. Damage ranged from zero to many thousands of dollars, with the young adult hired to supervise cringing in the closet until she got the nerve to call the police. Going over rules, expectations and worst-case scenarios with the caregiver and your kids helps ensure a peaceful time.

Parents' Separation Issues: Parents who work long hours

may hate to get away from kids because they rarely see them. Conversely, parents who work long hours may have difficulty readjusting to the child world and may desperately want to be away from the kids to have the adult conversations they are used to. Moms who spend a lot of time at home may desperately want to get out for a few hours, just as Dad may yearn to hang out at home because he has been away.

Most people have no real memory of their own childhood before school age so have no guideline good or bad from their own experience. Not knowing how much time they spent with a sitter, they can only guess what is appropriate baby-sitting time at the early stages of a child's development. Parents who were wild teenagers themselves may be either quite relaxed about their teenagers since they themselves survived, overly protective because they know all the possibilities, or they may be quite strict realizing they are lucky to be alive.

Partners need to recognize that their mates may have legitimate reasons to differ about baby-sitting and time away. Nonetheless, they need to create a plan together that balances the needs of the child and each parent.

With benefit of hindsight, I can see that it is easiest to plan trips without the kids as they age. Trips for the two of you without kids are more difficult when your kids are younger. There are, however, clear benefits for your marriage and your kids if you leave your children for a brief trip together. A separation that is comfortable and fun helps them become more independent and bonds them to important people in their lives. Spending time with other people makes them more flexible about dealing with a variety of individuals. Two or more siblings often grow a bit closer. I have the sweetest picture in my mind of my two boys, at three and four, holding hands as they marched into daycare together.

This, of course, presumes that you and your children are comfortable and familiar with the caretaking person. Aside from issues of having your child molested, things can go radically wrong. I have heard some horror stories. One single parent returned from England to learn that even though she had called her kids regularly, the caretaker, a friend who had eagerly volunteered but had not baby-sat these kids before, had decided the kids ate too much and was limiting their food intake. The boys, who were in fourth and seventh grade, didn't want to upset her, and so started hanging out at friends' houses in the neighborhood to eat. They avoided coming home until quite late at night. The frustrated caretaker started screaming abuse at them when they did come home. Fortunately, the trip was only a short visit to an ailing father. The mother reviewed the fiasco of the baby-sitter carefully with the kids and went over all the options they would have in the future. After that came more trips to her father's bedside, but she arranged childcare with sympathetic parents of friends who were more used to kids and their healthy appetites.

I don't want to discourage you from taking trips away from your children, just know the importance of planning those trips carefully. When your kids are old enough to discuss the trip and understand it, listen to any caregiver concerns they have and make sure you have a plan that is comfortable for your children. Plan together how often and when you will call. Plan some scenarios in advance to cover what they might do if things go awry. The safer the more active or attached parent thinks the children are, the more enjoyable the trip will be for both of you. Sometimes parents simply plan one trip away a year when the children are staying at a camp, just be sure they can always reach you. It can be unnerving enough for kids to be at sleep-away camp, but they sometimes feel even more insecure if they know no one's at home base.

Leaving your kids isn't a requirement. It can be great fun and a wonderful bonding experience with your partner. Plan these escapes carefully so they are relaxing and restorative for you and the kids.

Summary: By toddler time you will discover whether you can each relax and have sex with the kids in the house. To some extent this depends on the layout of the house. Some people find sex at home gets harder as the kids get older, because the kids are more aware. Other couples find it easier because they become more comfortable locking their bedroom door. However, whatever habit first develops often sets the tone for the rest of your married life, at least until kids are gone. Some people just can't have sex with kids in the house. Then weekends and overnights become much more important. Other couples never take overnights alone because they get plenty of intimacy at home. The critical issue is not how often you get away from home, but whether the two of you create time in your lives for each other. You need alone closed-door time so that you can have some intimacy and talk time.

The habits, love rituals, and positive experiences you create will either insulate your marriage from the problems discussed in this book or, if absent, they will leave your marriage vulnerable to the natural erosion that the stress of negotiating many new needs that kids bring. Fortunately, it is never too late to start your rituals even when the marriage feels dead or divorce looms.

Marriage Support Tips

At Home

- To keep in touch, write Dad little notes or e-mails if you can't talk together during the baby's nap.

- Talk about what is good for your marriage, just like you talk about what is good for your kids.

- Talk about what you each feel is appropriate marital getaway time.

- Talk about what you like about your marriage with your spouse, just like you talk about what you like about your kids.

- Talk about your values, standards, and beliefs for a good marriage just like you talk about your values, standards, and beliefs for your kids.

- Join community activities together. Think in terms of seasons of more outside activity and seasons in which you focus more on family time.

- Pick kid's sports in seasons and one at a time. When you are committed to their sports activity be committed and then, in the off-season, celebrate and enjoy unstructured time off.

- Find good friends who are happily married.

- As soon as your kids are old enough, like age three, create a couple time that they recognize, such as Saturday morning before eight, or a half hour after their nightly bedtime routine, or a half hour after dinner when they don't interrupt Mom and Dad's time. Let them know it is important and why.

- Schedule marital fun times once a week at least. Daily is better. It's never too late to start.

- Make sure you have regular locked-door parent alone time so that even if you are too tired to have sex, you know you could. Even if your kids sleep in your bed every night and you encourage them, the marriage needs parent alone time.

Getaway Tips

- Expect that at least one of you will be ambivalent about trips away from the kids.

- Make sure that each person is considered and the needs of the kids are discussed with lots of active reflective listening.

- The easiest escapes may be vacations at home or trips, stolen while the kids are at camp or otherwise fully engaged, but be available for the occasional broken arm.

- Use your community and other parents you know to drop in and check on your kids if another caregiver stays with them at home. You can return the favor.

- If you must take a trip during the school year and the athletic season, make arrangements for rides to the games with more than one family. This way no one is overwhelmed and everyone gets a break if the situation becomes uncomfortable.

- Prepare a medical consent-to-treat form, a list of where the kids are to be when, and telephone numbers of where they are staying and for emergencies. Make photocopies for anyone in contact with the kids while you are gone.

- Make sure that your child is comfortable with all aspects of the plan.

- Plan for emergencies. They will happen. Whatever doesn't kill your kids (or you) will make you stronger.

- Have a good time.

12

Finding Good Help: When Your Mother Lives in Mexico or Is Otherwise Unsuitable

Whenever I read those horrible and sensationalistic "Mother Kills Her Four Children" news articles, I always want to know whether the mother had childcare. Though I have never been able to establish consistently that the moms actually lacked childcare, I suspect this would be an interesting research project. Whether a mother works outside the home, has an office in her home or is a full-time mom, all parents need some childcare help. Most moms in happy marriages who don't have paid childcare have informal assistance from grandparents, relatives, and/or trade with other mothers.

Grannies are usually the first people that most moms will trust. However, many grannies live thousands of miles away, work, or are otherwise unavailable. Others could easily be stunt drivers (not with my kids in the car—thank you!), feed kids a steady diet of candy and videos, are hopelessly bossy, drive drunk, smoke around the grandchild or are highly critical, controlling, or generally not nice people. Even if relatives are available and great help during work hours, you may find you need more relief to make room for your marriage.

Women with home-based careers or careers outside the home quickly recognize the need for childcare. Both women and men are much slower to recognize the need for childcare to help support the marriage. The baby also benefits from becoming familiar with more than one caregiver. Everyone benefits if baby can learn to feel soothed and safe with someone besides Mommy. And as we have said repeatedly, the strongest marital relationships develop during childfree time. Before selecting childcare, first you and your partner must agree on what you both feel are your needs and the needs of the child. This may be the hardest part.

Childcare affects the couple relationship. We had friends who claimed they would be long divorced without their beloved nanny and housekeeper "to blame things on and do the messy jobs we both hate." Good childcare can mean valuable time together. However, often couples assign responsibility for hiring, training, and firing household help and childcare to the mother. Unfortunately, this can reinforce Dad's position as an outsider. Discussing childcare needs at different stages throughout the marriage means you are likely to be happier with each other and your decisions.

Childcare affects privacy. I had always assumed we would have a live-in nanny until I got ready to hire one, and my husband said he couldn't stand the idea of having another person in the house. I was glad he was so direct about his needs. That caused me to reorganize our plans and I have never regretted it.

Discuss childcare costs with your partner. The cost of childcare is a significant item in the family budget, and needs to be discussed in advance to avoid conflict. If one of you doesn't work outside the home you may assume you don't need childcare. Wrong. Skimping on childcare may be skimping on your couple relationship. If cost is an issue consider trying a baby-sitting co-op. We tried and it was great. If you want to read more about them I recommend *Smart Mom's Baby-Sitting Co-Op Handbook: How We Solved the Baby-Sitter Puzzle* by Gary Myers. This is an inexpensive solution and a great way to meet nice people. You will need the cooperation of your spouse if you want to use it for date night because you will have to reciprocate on other evenings.

If you can afford it, consider paying more than minimum wage. I had several friends who chose to pay the lowest rate and had numerous nannies per year. One friend who has five rowdy, outspoken kids and who has always paid the lowest going rate has had more nannies than I could count. They were always fleeing for calmer homes. Another client family with five even more rowdy kids has had the same nanny for the seven years I have known her, but pays a bit more.

Some parents feel if your nannies change often that your children will be more attached to you than any one caregiver but I think it just confuses kids and upsets the household. I generally hired nannies for the low going rate, with the promise to raise their salary at the end of the first month to a higher-than-average rate. If they couldn't grasp the advantage of that concept, we probably weren't going to get along anyway because I like a quick study. If we got along, I gave them a raise as promised. They remained loyal, and we suffered little disruption. I felt lucky that Neil supported this plan because many husbands or wives prefer hiring at the best price, and the wives were constantly searching, interviewing, hiring, and training. Still, even paying more, you can be left in the lurch due to the caregiver's family needs and, for some cultures, a norm against formal good-byes.

If you do decide to hire childcare, there are many thorny financial issues to address like how much to pay, who will file taxes, negotiate salary, check references, and so forth. There are also issues of where to find them: via word of mouth, agency, or by advertisement, and whether to hire teenagers, nannies, or au pairs.

Childcare and housekeeping require balancing. Because there are two main aspects to running the household—housekeeping and childcare—parents need to decide together if they want a nanny, a housekeeper, a nanny/housekeeper, or one nanny and one housekeeper. Some parents choose household help rather than childcare to support Mom at various stages because she is initially more comfortable with this.

I remember coming home one day when my kids were young and finding the childcare person relaxing in the backyard while I had been grocery shopping after work. That quickly convinced me that I wanted to do more of my own childcare and less of the housework so we rearranged her duties.

Childcare and housekeeping needs vary at different stages. The practical needs for childcare and housekeeping will change considerably as children grow, as careers resume and as schools and daycare change. Each couple must make many decisions about childcare over the course of the children's lives. Couples who openly discuss each of their desires and expectations for household support, as well as the child's needs, and work out the childcare plan together, avoid trouble. Mom may feel resentful if the plan is unappreciated or problematic to her partner. Dad may not understand the rationale, his role in the arrangement and resent the cost.

Whatever you decide, revisit and re-evaluate your decision together often. Expect that the arrangement that works today, may not work in a year. Kids' and family needs change.

Birth to Two and a Half: Many childcare experts feel that this is a time when the parent has the greatest impact on the child's personality and eventual IQ. Although many parents feel this means they must stay home, stimulation is the critical issue for IQ. Some research suggests that having Mom out of the home and away from the baby no more than about thirty hours a week is optimal.

In-home childcare means much less sleep disruption and exposure to fewer germs and illnesses for the whole family. Live out in-home care has similar advantages but can be less reliable especially if the person has small children herself. Decide together how important reliability is for each of you.

Some exposure to other kids at this age is entertaining for kids and makes them more comfortable socially, depending on their temperament. Granny nannies often like the calm and relative quiet of newborns and can be quite enthusiastic and responsive, but may feel like they can't keep up as well by age two and a half. Don't be surprised if at this stage of your child's development, everyone needs a change.

Three to Four: The benefits of at least part-time out-of-home childcare, or preschool, have been well documented. Preschool kids show greater independence, easier school adjustment, and better social adjustment. The downsides are more exposure to germs, which paradoxically also can build immunities and resistance, and exposure to forbidden words or bad habits from other kids who have older siblings or families with different values.

Children may be stressed by too many hours of group daycare. Depending on a child's temperament, she may need downtime and alone time that group settings can't provide. So you will need to strike a balance with a combination of parent time, baby-sitter time or parent trades and group time for play dates to provide wonderful opportunities to develop independence and social skills and still have quality family and couple time.

Working parents can find their marriage quite stressed when nannies encourage long naps during the day and the kids have lots of energy to stay up when parents need to sleep. The kids may be charming and rested when you pick them up, but then they are awake and awake and awake. I always suggest discussing naps with your childcare person. This usually quickly resolves the issue—or the need for new childcare becomes apparent.

Five to Twelve: Most kids are in school by this time and can tolerate some after-school daycare. However, they can still be stressed by too many hours in one highly structured place, depending on their individual temperaments. Their disciplinary needs change as freedom of expression grows. People who love adoring preschoolers may have a very hard time disciplining outspoken school kids. If you both want your kids to help around the house, your childcare choice needs to support your family values by being patient and expecting the kids to help.

The Early Teen Years: By their teens, kids may mostly need the company of someone when they get home from school. In many parts of the country, kids need a driver to run them from place to place. They can often pitch in and make a significant addition to housework by doing laundry and other regular chores. Part-time help, while not a necessity, is usually a good idea for working moms.

Summary: When you have an understanding of ages and stages, and of how your childcare and housekeeping needs will change over the years, you have a better idea of what to look for in choosing a person or people who can literally make or break the smooth running of your household. Obviously, unless you're very lucky, one person is very unlikely to be right for every age and stage.

Together you and your partner can figure out the best plan for childcare. There are many books as well as articles in parenting magazines and Web sites devoted to this subject. Books come and go at a great rate of speed but you may like *The ABCs of Hiring a Nanny, Expanded Version* by Frances Anne Hernan.

Choosing childcare is a very complex decision that has multiple implications for your marriage. Even though there are many ways to make the childcare arrangements so that you have time alone as a couple, the time spent working together on these plans is well worth the feeling of friendship and connection you are nurturing as a couple. Making childcare choices together and reevaluating them at various stages of your marriage means you are likely to be happier with each other and your decisions. And you can make time for fun.

Couple-Friendly Childcare Tips

- Discuss what makes good childcare for the age and stage of your child and your individual needs and needs as a couple.

- Consider your weekend or date night needs when you look for a nanny or daycare person.

- Join or start a baby-sitting club so you can arrange to trade with someone you know is equipped and experienced for caring for your child's age group and save money.

- When you find a good baby-sitter, consider paying a bit more than the going rate so that you have more loyalty. In some neighborhoods good nannies can be lost in bidding wars. Simply being caring, respectful, pleasant human beings, and arriving home as promised will go a long way to assuring loyalty.

- Be careful to hire full-time caregivers who have a history of loving and enjoying childcare. Check references carefully. Look for consistency and number of years in one job.

- Consider hiring/inviting someone to borrow your kids on a semi-regular basis for a walk or trip to the playground during the day so you can have quiet time at home together if you don't want to hire childcare. Then reciprocate.

- Ask what you can do to help find a baby-sitter for dates, if you aren't the one who usually does. Don't complain that your spouse won't find a baby-sitter because she/he doesn't want to go out with you because that may become the reality.

- Have lunch together while kids are in childcare to talk about goals and upcoming plans.

13

Where Is This Train Headed?
Goals, Roles, Rituals, Rules,
Routines, and Resolutions

When my kids were young, just getting through the list of have-to's, like getting groceries in the house, getting dressed and paying bills seemed an accomplishment. Our whole orderly life seemed to melt into a deep pool of urgent, yet trivial attention grabbers. Looking back, I wish that I had stopped to talk with my husband about where we were going. Neil and I had no vision together. We agreed about many things, most things. We both wanted children, but hadn't thought much about what we wanted to teach them or share with them.

Confronted with the inevitable myriad of choices for raising a family, we wanted to do it all. We found ourselves saying yes to every invitation for our kids. Then we got so booked that I began feeling like we never talked with each other. We just chauffeured the kids in different directions. It was too much. Our mistake was that we both assumed that the other wanted to do it all without discussing it. Our assumptions and missed time together left us both feeling frustrated and out of touch. When we looked back at our choices, we wondered where our weekends and our lives had gone.

As I reflected and read more about this, I began to see that many, more "together" people viewed life planning differently than we did. They operated from several levels of family organization that worked together. They had *mission statements,* or general shared beliefs; they had *rituals,* for warmth, fun, and identity; they had *roles, routines,* and *rules* to make life more comfortable and organized. All were useful depending on the scope of the issues they were facing. These people all had children and yet they managed to plan as well. This gave me hope that we could rediscover a semi-organized life. All we needed was a vision and some workable plans.

Goals, roles, and routines are also a positive way to get in tune with your partner. That way you don't need to argue, nag, and feel stressed to make snap decisions about what is important. Once agreed upon, each of these levels of structure gives a sense that you and your partner are working toward the same end. They give your family identity as well.

When I work with couples I start with their daydreams. Then we break that down to a small step for the week. For example, Kelly and Chris each wanted to return to school to pursue their dreams, but Chris felt trapped working for his father and Kelly felt trapped at home with two kids under six and another on the way. We mapped out a sketchy plan to get to their goals. The plan involved refinancing their debts and approaching the school goals sequentially. We kept the homework assignment simple. In the next two weeks, the goal was that Chris had to get Kelly out of the house one night to spend time on herself. They both knew that it would be hard for Kelly because she was a people pleaser, but that Chris would never feel safe taking his own time if she hadn't had a night out. He remembered well that she had been resentful about this in the past when he had taken

LEVELS OF VISION AND ORGANIZATION

VISION AND MISSION STATEMENTS

Short, focused on values and meaning like: Live, Love, Laugh, Learn

GOAL SETTING AND FAMILY MEETINGS

Plans for next week, month, or year for carrying out visions like:

Where do we want to go on vacation and how much will we spend?

Regular interests and hobbies

Saving money for college

A budget

ROLES

General job assignments like:

Who researches trips, who pays bills?

Who keeps the social calendar, who sends cards to friends?

Who watches the kids when, who does laundry?

Who makes dinners?

RITUALS

Reinforce sense of family, joy, and celebration on a daily, weekly, and special holiday basis:

Planning holidays we spend with the relatives and friends versus "just our family"

Singing a special song at bedtime

Family dinners

Friday night neighborhood potlucks

Going to church regularly

Going out every year on Valentine's Day

Tea after dinner together

Watching sunsets on Fridays

ROUTINES

Habits that help us get through the day or the week smoothly like:

Paying the bills on the first and fifteenth

Doing laundry one day a week

Changing the fire alarm battery on Halloween and April Fool's Day

Who drives the kids to preschool on a particular day?

Dad plays with Zoe while Mom makes dinner.

RULES AND CONSEQUENCES

Agreed upon discipline and self-discipline to support good habits:

If someone spends over budget, they get to do the bills.

Pick up before we go on an outing so the house is neat when we get back.

Taking a time-out, if you can't be with people.

If you hit, you sit.

Unkindness means losing fifteen minutes of a favorite activity.

time and she hadn't. Chris also decided he wouldn't swear out loud every morning as he got ready for work because Kelly took it personally, even though his frustration was about having to get up so early for work and not with her.

We laughed that the goals seemed so removed from the big picture, but they did get Kelly out for forty-five minutes alone, for a visit to the store by herself (no kids, yes!) and an ice cream. She savored it. Chris actually didn't succeed in not swearing, but started to giggle when he swore, so Kelly felt he was swearing at their overburdened life rather than her.

The second week's goal was that Kelly went out Tuesday and Chris got time alone Thursday. As they began setting little goals, they began moving toward the big goals. Chris used his time alone to find out what he needed to do to return to school for his dream job. Kelly felt so supported having brief time alone that she initiated the refinancing of their home, even though she was throwing up every day with her pregnancy! As they started accomplishing their goals they began to fight less and enjoy sharing their dreams. Because they fought less and were less resentful, they began actively helping each other more and expressing their appreciation more. A downward spiral started slowly and bumpily turning in an upward direction.

A year later they hardly recognized themselves. As they made their roles, rituals and routines more in line with their goals and values they began to see that they could reach their dreams. Goals, Roles, Rituals, and Routines help support your family mission and they also create a shared sense of purpose.

A *mission statement* is a brief, clear expression of exactly what your family finds meaningful, either a statement of purpose or a vision of your future and the future of your family. For some the mission is clear and simply stated. A strong religious base, like we will both serve God, is a clear mission but has few specifics. Some only have time to discover a joint purpose or create a mission statement when they are grandparents. But sooner is better. Although there is no right way to work these issues out, working them out helps couples survive these rough years.

As Steven Covey, author of many books about building a beautiful family culture, including *Seven Habits Of Highly Effective Families* and *How to Write a Family Mission Statement,* says, without a vision, we may climb the ladder of success while it is leaning against the wrong wall. He says that no one on his deathbed wishes he had worked more. *His central point is that if we work first with ourselves, then with our spouse and then with our whole family to develop a mission statement of what we are about, we are less likely to be torn with indecision and unhappiness about our lives.*

More important, we won't be blaming and guilt-tripping our spouse! This is particularly true at this critical stage in women's lives, when they are first faced with the consequences of their choices of whether to forgo a career for mothering, to work part-time or to work full-time. A really good mission statement can be invaluable for gaining perspective and avoiding unnecessary conflicts. You will have plenty of issues to resolve even with a mission statement in place.

My favorite mission statement is: Live, learn, love, laugh. When compared to that standard, a lot of family conflicts simply dissolve. A dear friend's husband died a slow and painful death from a chronic illness. Yet the couple stayed happy and active with their kids right up to his death. After his death, she and the kids knew how to enjoy life. When my cranky, critical self begins to emerge, I ask myself if I knew Neil were dying in three years would this issue matter? A lot of stuff doesn't matter then.

Goal setting is more involved and less lofty. Setting goals together goes a long way toward making your relationship strong and happy. If you try to impose goals on your spouse you really meet resistance. Like a "honey-do" list that is imposed, husbands end up feeling burdened and resentful, not connected and motivated to act. Just ask Neil.

Couples who set goals together regularly say that they feel more focused and have less conflict. They are sure that they get more of what they really want from life and each other. Goal setting reduces stress because clear goals reduce the number of decisions you must make. Some families set goals every year and review them every quarter or every week to become focused on what is important to them rather than get sidetracked by other people's plans and agendas. Some couples include their kids in setting family goals as soon as they are old enough.

Neil and I have tried to recover from total chaos and spontaneity by having family meetings once a week. We succeed in meeting about once every six weeks. For some people, goal setting is as natural as owning a Day Planner. For others, it is foreign and repugnant. I have heard it described as a "restricting destroyer of spontaneity and true love." However, even the most recalcitrant doubters, once seduced into trying out family meetings often become converts because of the peace and order goal setting brings.

I have outlined a method here for goal setting. Use it as an approximation. If you come away with a few tiny goals to start that is a major accomplishment. As you revisit the method it gets easier. Since Neil was so resistant to the process I asked for it as a birthday present the first time.

Getting started has always been the hard part for us. By the time my son was ten, he looked at me one day and said, "Mom how come we aren't like other families who just make a plan and do it?" His best friend's family was very organized. I didn't have an answer. Over time I have seduced my husband to do some measure of planning and goal setting by asking first that together we make plans for our vacations. Next, I started working on sharing calendars, so I knew when we all had days off. Eventually we graduated to family meetings.

Family meetings to go over the upcoming week and reset the family course can be a good forum for establishing rules and ex-

STEPS FOR GOAL SETTING

Set Aside Times and a Place. Plan three blocks of time *without the kids or other interruptions*. An evening, a morning and an afternoon spread over one weekend is great. Make sure you have some small breaks in the process. Here's how to proceed:

Create Two Lists Each: Make an **Appreciation List** of what you like about your partner, your marriage, and your life. Make it as long as possible. Expect your lists to be different lengths. **Problems/Opportunity List:** Write down your needs, wants and wishes. Then list them in order of importance. Try to state positively what you want to have or what you envision, not what is a problem or what is wrong. Use "I" messages: "I would like more meals at home." Not, "We never eat at home anymore." Instead of saying, "I hate the way our kids behave," try, "I'd like our kids to speak more respectfully to us." This makes for a more productive discussion. Attack problems, not each other.

These are problems that you want to solve with your partner. Add dreams, fun activities, and projects like: buy a house, vacation in Spain, new career, good manners for the kids, or less clutter. (Dream Big.)

Try to write your two lists before your first meeting or at least think about them. If you think about it while driving or in a spare (when?) minute you can jot down key words.

THE FIRST EVENING:
Start with positives. Read your appreciation lists to each other first, and then enjoy dinner and the evening together. While this sharing doesn't take long, the goodwill helps you through the next steps.

THE NEXT MORNING:

Share and combine P/O lists. Have a pleasant breakfast. Find a comfortable and private place where you will have no interruptions. Take turns reading your dreams, needs and wants to each other without interrupting. Combine your lists. This should take only 10-20 minutes if you listen well, write down each person's list and do not interrupt.

Use your best communication skills. Stay positive or at least neutral. Some couples think the P/O stands for something besides problems and opportunities especially if they are lost in rage. When you are making your list, imagine reading your list to a respected friend. Would they hear your wants and needs or a lot of anger? If you are too angry to talk about your wants or needs, consider counseling or working with a friend to reframe them more positively. *If your partner's ideas seem impossible, too expensive or ridiculous, just listen.* Reflect back what your partner is asking without judging or criticizing, even with your tone of voice. *Ask questions* only to understand and gain clarification.

Prioritize the master list. Agree on what you want to tackle first. If there are easy next steps for some items, agree who will carry it forward. Do only one goal or topic at a time.

Brainstorm solutions for tough issues. Start with the easiest issues and move to the more difficult. Try to think of five possible solutions together. Each person needs to contribute at least two of the five solutions. Be sure you give your partner's wishes the same attention you give your own. Come up with crazy ideas. Have fun with this. Focus on win-win solutions. Write down all ideas. If solutions come easily, move on to other topics. Table the tough issues.

Take a Fun Break. Think about what you have heard. This break serves as a clear marker between listening and resolving conflict. Go out for lunch or for the evening. Exercise and have dinner and a date.

FOLLOW-UP: THAT AFTERNOON
OR THE NEXT MORNING

Evaluate the solutions. Happy couples have very different styles at this stage. Try to look for solutions that are acceptable to both of you. Some couples decide to seek more information and reconvene at an appropriate time. One couple, happily married thirty-plus years, who wanted to please each other had "secret ballots." After they had discussed every option, they would then write down what they really wanted on a piece of paper, slip the answers in a paper bag, shake it up, and then look at the answers. (Neither was a logic or a math teacher, but it worked for them.) Sometimes couples just agree that they have very independent goals at this point. Others table the discussion. They need time to think so they simply agree to return, after they each have had time to meditate.

Set mutually agreed-upon next steps. Break the solutions down into real steps. Talk about which are the most important goals and which are the nice dreams for (maybe) later. Some goals will be primarily for one of you, with the other playing a supporting role.

Discuss how you can work together and support each other. What will happen first and in what order? How will you pay for it? How will you adjust your schedule to make it happen? Notice those items that are easy because you are already working toward them and congratulate yourselves.

Plan for follow-up. Set a specific time to check in and say, "Well, what do you think? How did we do with our goals?" Plan follow-up for each project. A couple may decide to check in once a week on the relationship, if it is in trouble or every two weeks on new habits for a child. Some put the goal list in the family meeting book and glance at it before family meetings.

Celebrate your hard work. Congratulate each other on trying the process and agreeing on any tiny step together. Just taking one step together is an important milestone. Drink a toast. Frame your goals list. Put them in a memory book. Make love.

---

pectations. When your kids are young, they can be brief, two-person meetings where you just set the plans for who is handling what that week. There are some great books on family meetings like Jane Nelsen's *Positive Discipline,* Amy Lew's *Raising Kids Who Can,* and *Positive Discipline for Preschoolers,* by Jane Nelsen, Roslyn Duffy, and Cheryl Erwin.

People who have researched family meetings find that regular family meetings and family dinners are correlated with better marriages and better outcomes for kids, like better grades, higher self-esteem, fewer disciplinary actions at school, reduced drug use, and so forth. Here are the guidelines I have gleaned for a good meeting. I break all these rules from time to time, but the kids enjoy family meetings when we do them this way. Although it is a struggle for us sometimes, we are excited to see their problem-solving skills develop. They may not get their way, but they do get their say. And Neil and the kids love to enforce the rules that make the meetings fun.

Roles define who does what in a family. Many couples discuss and some even write down their roles and their responsibilities, although they don't usually call them roles and responsibilities. *Roles* describes who is in charge of what to make things run smoothly. Sometimes, as children get a bit older, families divide up roles and responsibilities between parents and children. Peo-

BRIEF RULES FOR STAFF AND FAMILY MEETINGS

Start with praise.

Keep them short.

Raise two issues at most.

Make them regular, but have an extra meeting as needed.

Serve good food or snacks.

End with positive feedback.

Do something fun after business is done.

---

ple with clear roles are often comfortable with quite a bit of independent functioning. This is great for kids and couples. A couple may need to review their roles, especially if theirs is a nontraditional marriage and they haven't resolved who does what. Couples who have had a traditional marriage—except that the wife also works—may find that she is overwhelmed and that they are growing distant. Spending time redefining roles may help the distance.

Examining roles: Although sociologists have spent millions of pages discussing roles, I don't know of any good books that describe how to resolve these issues. Roles are general assignments like keeping the social calendar, overseeing investments, paying bills, planning menus, hiring and supervising household help, volunteering at school, and selecting schools for the kids. These roles can be shared or divided into routines. While both of you discuss these issues one may take the lead or have the deciding vote.

To define roles, it is a good idea to follow the format for the goal setting above with some modifications.

ROLE SETTING

Each makes two lists.

Appreciation list: Listing those activities your partner does to make the marriage work.

Problems/Goals list: What needs to be done that isn't getting done? What do you want to work on first?

Agree on a time and place to talk.

Share your lists, using your best communication skills.

Prioritize your joint list.

Brainstorm solutions: Focus on what is likely to be fun for each of you and what you like to do. Remember not all wives cook and clean. I know urban families that have healthy meals delivered. Housekeepers are cheaper than counselors by a factor of ten, and cheaper than divorce lawyers by a factor of twenty. Some jobs can be shared or alternated to help build empathy for the partner's role. Consider if there are skills you can trade with people outside the marriage.

Plan to switch roles for a while. Some couples take turns picking their jobs off the list.

Pick your favorite solutions to start. Come up with a plan that allows both of you to do what you like most.

Decide when to reevaluate how the plan is going. Reevaluate it in two weeks and then in a month or two. Some couples take another look every year or so.

Celebrate how well you work together.

Rituals are habits that are fun and meaningful. They're sometimes wacky and sometimes just practical. For couples, rituals can include dinner at the same place every Valentine's Day, a Christmastime date alone, a weekly date or an anniversary date. The ritual can be that one partner always plans a surprise date for even numbered months and the other partner does the same on odd months. Some couples include an activity to intensify the meaning of a ritual like lighting candles, rereading the same story, discussing favorite surprise dates, rereading their mission statement ("NOT romantic," says Neil), or reviewing their goals on New Year's Eve.

When you choose family rituals together, you grow closer as a couple. For families, a compliment ritual at dinner or an awards day once a week supports the family values that parents are developing in their children. Choosing family rituals together and supporting each other in following them up strengthens the couple. Eye contact, a kiss and a hug when you come home can be a family ritual. Doing family memory books for each vacation is another.

Teaching Your Children Values by Richard Eyre and Linda Eyre (in book or audiocassette) describes many rituals for teaching and supporting family values for children of various ages. Deepak Chopra's book *The Seven Spiritual Laws for Parents: Guiding Your Children to Success and Fulfillment* also lists many ritual questions for the family to explore regularly to reinforce values. Going to church or synagogue regularly is a family ritual that supports family values. I have had several wives who weren't particularly religious say that their spouses are calmer and closer to them when they go to church, so they just remind them how much better they feel when they go.

Routines are more mundane but may be essential to the serenity of the family. Routines typically involve a schedule of days for who takes the kids to school and who picks them up certain days, as opposed to the role of car pool chief who keeps track of who has to be where and when. Some families do a monthly coffee and all-nighter with classical music for paying bills together. Neil puts out the vitamins and the juice for all of us in the morning and packs vitamins for our trips. It is easy for me to forget and I feel taken care of when he does it. It doesn't matter what those routines are if they are comforting to you both. Those very personal routines can be a kind of comforting glue that holds a marriage together. If you don't or can't identify routines that make you both happy, then you may want to consider creating one new one and trying it out.

Rules and thoughtful consequences are important just to maintain calm and order in families and to make home a haven where kids (and parents) can count on what is going to happen and can avoid having parents' (or partners') anger intrude in a random, moody way. Families often begin developing rules as soon as children can begin to understand simple rules like "This car doesn't start until everyone's seat belt is fastened." Rules taught very early like this save a lot of nagging later. My kids are still better about putting on seat belts than either Neil or I.

While rules are a great childrearing device, rules are also marriage savers. If the two of you agree on the rules you won't be second-guessing each other and having needless fights about why the heck you did or didn't do something. You present a united front that builds a sense of security for kids and parents. You also won't be passive and distant because you are going along with rules that make no sense to you.

Couples whose backgrounds and expectations around children are very different need to spend time initially creating straightforward rules and routines. Stepfamilies, particularly, need rules and consequences in the beginning to keep a kind of peace and to sort through the many conflicting expectations each member has from their previous and present families. Research suggests that functional, happy stepfamilies have more explicitly stated rules than happy first families like: no one comes in the parents' bedroom before 7 A.M. or Dad and Stepmom have a date every Friday night.

Summary: You *can* start creating order out of the chaos of your life at any of these levels. As you try routines and rituals they will reinforce the bond that the two of you have. Your relationship will become stronger.

Tips for Creating Goals, Roles, Rules, and Routines

- Brainstorm all the things, both big and small, that the two of you want for your kids and your family. Usually you will have some goals, roles, and routines in place regarding these things.

- Notice visions, goals, routines, rules, and roles you already have in place first. Are they long-term goals or rules and routines? If you have lots of rules and no goals, consider doing goals. If you have a vision but no steps to get there, consider your roles and routines.

- Consider whether your routines support your values and vision. Do your spending habits and time commitments support your values?

- Take small steps. I like the couples who put a dollar in the jar every time they make love and then use the money for a trip to Hawaii. That's a good example of small steps leading to a large goal. With kids, it is especially hard to make large changes rapidly, so focus on the small steps.

- Post your goals or mission statements where you see them often or put them in your Palm Pilot or Day Runner.

- Get an attractive family journal and record the date and notes of your meetings. Use it to note the changes and progress you make.

- List rules and consequences in a family journal and watch how they evolve over time.

- Expect to have to review and revise new or complicated rules or consequences every two to six weeks to keep them fresh and working.

- Start with a plan that is fun so you are more likely to do it and keep it up.

14

It's Not Working . . .
Normal Sexual Dysfunction

Most couples are staggered by the rapid changes in their sex life as a result of pregnancy and the birth of the baby. When the baby is newborn, a few hours alone, when you and your partner are both awake, can seem either like heaven or an awkward meeting with a stranger. Pregnant women and new moms often experience little or no sex drive. Easy spontaneous sexual encounters disappear and sexual responses change dramatically.

Many wonderful pregnancy books discuss possible changes to expect in your sex life. All agree that there is little uniformity in how women and men react. Sex can stop, or sex can become more intimate and personal as each partner begins to recognize the individual reactions of their partner. Familiar sex may be replaced by a different kind of sex that is more deeply satisfying.

Pregnancy, with its unpredictability, provides the perfect excuse and opportunity to improve your sexual communication because neither partner can expect the other to already know what works. If you don't talk, and instead act as though nothing is happening, you will still have several more opportunities to discuss these issues throughout pregnancy and after the birth of the baby because your reactions will keep changing. Prospective parents can learn how the two of them can communicate and work out feeling close when sex is difficult or impossible. Coping with this problem is also a small opportunity to work out redistributing social and work commitments that the couple will be renegotiating after the baby arrives.

Talking about feelings often isn't normal for young males and young couples. Asking Dad to share his worries about the baby's safety during sex creates a more normal context to talk about sexual feelings. This can become a basis for improving all their talk about sex.

Affair Issues: Some women feel convinced that their partner will have an affair during their pregnancy. So they have sex with their partner to prevent an affair even when they don't feel like it. I have also known men to have affairs during pregnancy, believing it was a favor to their wife so she wouldn't have to have sex. Of course since awareness of AIDS and STDs has improved (thankfully), this behavior is less frequent. Verbal reassurance that Mom is attractive, cuddling, touching, and massage may substitute or lead to even better sexual encounters.

Weight Worries: Often women feel that they will never be slim again. I gave away a pair of my pre-pregnancy jeans because I was sure I had somehow gotten the wrong ones in my closet. I truly believed that I could never have been that small and certainly never would be again. But, miraculously, I returned to size and my wise friend, who had laughed at my craziness, simply returned them to me when I lost weight. Neil swore up and down I looked great even though I gained fifty pounds, bless his chicken (but prudent) heart. Only when I lost my pregnancy weight did he confess he had doubts I would ever get back to my old size. Many men have this fear.

BABY BLUES By Rick Kirkman and Jerry Scott

Women can have very different reactions to their own pregnant bodies. Some feel fat and lumpy and others revel in their own voluptuousness. They enjoy finally having cleavage in pregnancy and love to flaunt it. Dad's reaction can have a lot to do with how they respond to themselves and to sex.

Occasionally husbands have trouble being attracted to the post-pregnancy body and need to talk about that with a counselor or a friend. Even if this is the case, avoid negative comments about the woman's figure to her. I have seen marriages struggle for years, even after she had regained her figure because Dad had commented negatively on Mom's post-pregnancy body before she lost weight.

Although a self-confident woman can lure her husband back

WILL I (SHE) EVER BE THIN AGAIN?

Uh. Yes, no, maybe so. This question terrifies many a new mom in our size-obsessed society. Some dads are anxious as well. Many a new mom can't have sex simply because she feels she isn't thin enough to have sex. "I can't bear to have sex because I can see the wrinkles in my tummy." There is nothing as discouraging as stepping on the scales after pushing a watermelon out between your legs and finding you haven't lost a pound! But breast-feeding and nine months may do the trick.

Jumping up and down to take care of a baby burns more calories than most Americans do in their sedentary jobs. However, when either of you allow the new baby to completely disrupt your previous exercise routines, you will risk gaining weight.

I won't presume to give you diet advice. Too much has already been written on the subject. Remember, no one can make anyone lose weight. There are helpful and unhelpful ways to respond. My clients offered these suggestions:

- Do not ever use the word *fat*. Fat is one of those loaded words that people can say about themselves but no one else can. I can call myself fat. You can't.

- Do not comment on my weight even if I complain about it constantly.

- If you want me to lose weight, spend time with me taking walks, rather than making drinking and eating our only fun time.

- Do not make cookies or other "treats" as a reward.

- Regular sex is a form of exercise that burns calories. Seduce me with talk and massages.

- Support my efforts to go to the gym or walking with friends either financially or by offering to do chores so that I can go.

- Go on a diet with me and we can both eat healthy. Stick to the diet.

- Praise my attempts to exercise and go walking.

- Arrange some childcare and time to walk with me.

- Clean up the dishes after dinner so I don't eat the extra food off the kids' plates.

- If I gain weight, comment that I look down or a little unhappy (not fat!). Ask if there is some way you can help.

- Ignore my weight and tell me I have beautiful eyes, skin or hair.

- If I lose weight, tell me I look fabulous and that you love to see me so happy.

Note: If I obsess constantly about my weight and eat candy alone like an alcoholic or take medication to lose weight, I am probably really suffering and I need therapy. High sugar food and white bread can be an addiction just like alcohol.

One clever, loving husband, whose wife drove them both crazy with weight worries, told her in front of me in therapy that it never stopped him from wanting sex. She blushed and soon lost weight gradually on her own. Great answer. Take note.

by giving and receiving massages and with seductive touching, if she feels that she is no longer attractive, it is very hard on the marriage because she is unlikely to have the confidence to try.

Some new parents have trouble having sex with their partner because they now feel they are in bed with a mom or a dad instead of a lover. And they don't see moms or dads as sexy. Generally women have less trouble with this issue than men.

Other moms feel they have to give up wearing sexy clothes because they are now moms and other moms don't dress like that. This may be related to how other moms dress, practicalities of stain-proof clothes that work around kids, or simply a desire to pull back and adjust to their new image. They may feel less sexy because they aren't dressing in a way that is a turn-on to themselves—or to their husbands.

Husbands will say, "She never dresses up anymore! She looks like a mom not a woman." Wives will say, "It's like he doesn't even know we have a baby." Avoid these traps by sharing your fantasies and feelings, and developing a relationship that is a turn-on for both of you regardless of size. Some couples work out a signaling system with a special nightgown that means "I am interested tonight" and try new sexual experiences when they are rested up. But other couples grow resentful around this issue. Remember to take time to reconnect because the quality of your post-baby intimacy—more than sex—will determine the happiness of your marriage for the rest of your life.

I have observed more than one woman who said she refused to lose her last twenty pounds because her husband *ought* to love her no matter what. This word "ought" leads to a lot of unhappiness. This attitude also puts a strain on the marriage and may require counseling to break through the marital impasse.

Psychological Barriers: New fathers have their issues as well. Witnessing childbirth, although supposedly a joyful bonding experience, has rendered more than one new dad temporarily impotent or at least reluctant about having sex because the possibility of repeating their birth experience, fearing that all sex is unprotected to an extent. Overly graphic doctors' explanations of death and danger, even temporary injunctions against sex after birth can chill the ardor of many a male who is sincerely fond of his wife.

Couples can find leaky breast milk or a crying baby jolts them out of their lover mood and into their parent roles. Some couples experience these feelings together, but in some couples one partner feels the contrast more sharply than the other. As one mom put it, "When you have a baby and a two-year-old sucking and touching you all day long, even cuddling with your spouse at the end of the day can feel like an invasion." Sympathy, understanding, and some adult talk time without the baby help to dissipate this feeling of invasion and eventually sex becomes more appealing.

As indicated in the introduction, there is a real possibility of depression and blues, which are usually accompanied by a low sex drive. Fortunately good treatments are available.

Painful Intercourse: Many ordinary physical difficulties interfere with good sex. Pain should be promptly explored with your doctor. Do not continue to have sex that hurts. Practice will *not* improve the situation. You can very quickly develop an aversion reaction that will make you both avoid sex for years. Until you solve this, use alternate forms of pleasuring. Medical expertise in the area of painful intercourse is quite uneven. Seek a second opinion if the doctor:

- doesn't help in one or two visits;

- tells you to just go ahead and have intercourse and it will pass; or

- implies that it is all in your head.

Despite all these difficulties and insecurities, this can be a wonderful time to experiment with techniques you never had the time and patience for before. Share sex stories and fantasies, oral sex, and massage. Be careful that whatever you do is mutually satisfying. The partner performing oral sex, for example, can easily begin to feel resentful if it only goes one way. Talking about what is mutually satisfying can lead to an even richer sex life because it opens up the couple to communications that surround sex they may not have tried before.

Workload Issues and Sex: If the wife now expects Dad to share more of the workload and is constantly disappointed, the new dad may have trouble being attracted to someone who is frequently disappointed in him and constantly criticizing. He will be revived after a few days of absolutely no criticism or expectations and a bit of romance. Numerous books tell how to seduce your man, but my clients haven't needed them once they stop the criticizing and learn to resolve workload issues as a partner. If you can't go a few days without criticizing, you may need some outside help. Most men do not have issues with Mom's body after the baby, and anything that worked before to get them interested in sex will usually still work.

Sex and the Housekeeper: Do-it-all supermoms may feel that they have no interest in sex for long after the doctor's warnings have expired and the baby has passed the disruptive toddler and preschool stages. Regularly, in our group practice, we see couples in which the husband drags a reluctant and overworked mom into therapy because she has no interest in sex. If the couple enjoyed sex before the baby and there was no pain with intercourse, we often prescribe what we call "housekeeper therapy." We ask the husband and wife to hire a housekeeper for a month prior to continuing therapy. (Housekeepers by the week are cheaper than therapy in California.) Generally this resolves the "sexual problem" and reduces our waiting list.

The astounding thing to me was the number of couples who

after three months of a good sex life would decide they didn't need a housekeeper and return for marital therapy a few months later. Clearly they have an issue about how the house must run. In one couple, the traveling executive husband insisted his wife could live without a housekeeper because his mother had. She felt as a good wife she needed to live up to his expectations. Of course, his mother's life was nothing like theirs and his wife was nothing like his mother. I joked about this with the couple, but I finally made having a housekeeper a condition of coming to therapy. This reduced the need for therapy and greatly improved their sex life, as it does for many couples, because the wife was no longer too exhausted or resentful to have a sex drive.

One working mom who clearly understood this issue regularly told her husband, "I would give up our nice house, my car, private school for the kids, and clothing expenses before I would give up my daily help. It is a marriage saver."

Whether you need housekeeper therapy or not, making sure that each parent has adequate talk time, personal time, together time and fun dates (as described in Chapter 4) is often critical to reestablishing a nice solid sexual relationship. During their time together, couples sometimes talk about what is sexy to them now and what used to be sexy.

Sex with a Toddler Around: Even if you navigate these various normal challenges to your sexual relationship and keep close communication, your preschoolers' activity level and inquisitiveness can become another roadblock. You may find yourselves so horny that you are picturing where in the house there is a closet big enough that you could lock yourselves in for a few moments without the kids noticing you're gone. At least you will be checking out closets and trying to find a slice of time together and that is a good feeling.

The bottom line is that sex—more than any other area in a relationship—stirs up the most varied and unpredictable responses. Feelings change throughout the pregnancy and in the early years after a child is born. Some level of sexual problem, mainly reduced frequency and desire, is the norm rather than the exception in this period. Yet, couples can, and sometimes do, emerge with a sense of greater closeness and communicate better than before. They discover new things they consider sexy. They can enjoy each other in ways they never knew were possible.

If sex just seems impossible for one or both of you post-baby, check out Michele Weiner Davis's book, *The Sex-Starved Marriage*. Ms. Davis has terrific insight into all the many issues related to this problem. More importantly she outlines clear action plans for overcoming these issues.

Doing It with Dad: Rekindling Romance

When I told my husband in a burst of excitement that I had found a whole series of books entitled *Romantic Weekends in Southern California, Northern California, New England,* and points in between, he said, "Does it come with a baby-sitter?"

Romantic weekends are obviously best when both of you are excited about the place you go and about each other. A year or two after pregnancy and birth, most couples gradually discover that their marriage needs new spark. Enjoying each other sexually on command during a romantic weekend may be difficult due to the hassles and issues discussed in the last chapter. Young couples may not be able to afford the baby-sitter or the expensive weekends that are advertised in glossy magazines. But somehow you need to carve out time without the children to reestablish your sexual relationship.

If funds are short, consider, as the British say, "vacationing on the premises." In other words, stay at home and have your kids stay somewhere overnight or for the weekend with Granny or a friend. Use the time you would spend packing and traveling, to spiff up your place like a bed-and-breakfast. Do the laundry or hide it from sight. Line up some indulgent activities that you could never do with the kids around like good massage books or stimulating movies. Since you aren't paying for a hotel room, consider having two masseuses come at the same time and get joint massages.

Some people hire a baby-sitter so they can go camping or hiking or add a romantic overnight on the end of a required work trip. This is easiest early in the relationship and grows harder as the children grow more demanding of your time.

Think of reestablishing sex as a two-step process. Romance first, sex second. I have recommended the classic book *1001 Ways to Be Romantic* by Gregory J. P. Godek to guys who felt clueless. Another favorite is *The RoMANtic's Guide: Hundreds of Creative Tips for a Lifetime of Love* by Michael Webb. While these books offer interesting suggestions, most new moms are the easiest people on the planet to romance.

Almost *any* gesture that is complimentary or helpful toward the baby, the mom, or the housework is romantic to a new mom. Sometimes other men friends will try to gang up on the helpful husband, because the wives in the group keep saying, "Why can't you be more like Joe. He is so helpful!" Anything that is the least bit caring will help create a good mood. Great eye contact and treating her as a woman and a person rather than just a mom will do wonders.

Romantic guys know one other secret about women. Their sexual feelings are changing constantly. What feels good changes during the day, during their cycle, and during the stages in their life. Their body image changes dramatically. (Gain fifty pounds in nine months and you will understand this.) This most romantic guy knows how to create a yes-set (as they say in hypnosis) by asking a series of gentle positive inquiries and noticing positive responses. If you comment on the softness of a woman's skin, it focuses her attention away from her worries about her body size. Contrast questions or bald statements like:

"Why don't we ever have sex anymore?"

"I feel like I am last priority in your life!"

"Your boobs are sure flat now that you aren't pregnant."

With:

"Would you like to sit here and talk with me?"

"Do you like it better when I rub your neck this way or scratch your head?"

"Your hair is so silky."

It isn't hard to see who will have his wife in bed more often.

Many of the books available are primarily aimed at helping unromantic men become romantic. A new mom who has a lumpy body, and isn't feeling all that comfortable with sex, often doesn't feel very romantic. She needs help discovering that she still likes sex and her partner still likes her. She may avoid love-making because she is tired, but once she is lured into it, she often says to herself, "Hey, This is great! I wonder why we don't do it more often." But lured is the key word because she will often remember sex as a pleasant experience, yet wonder why she ever went to so much trouble.

Before the baby she may have been the one who remembered special dates or planned special evenings. But now, if she is too tired and distracted to do this the relationship drags, and the new dad feels dumped. If the new dad takes over generating some of the romantic opportunities in the relationship, his gestures can carry the couple through these rough initial months. Likewise, any words of appreciation go a long way toward helping the couple through this period.

I encourage both partners to try to make one romantic, appreciative gesture for their partner a day, even if it is only a touch on the cheek and full eye contact. When you are exhausted and frantically busy, even one gesture a *week* will help jump-start the action.

In the interest of efficiency, I encourage couples to focus on caring gestures that really mean love to their partner. Gary Chapman described five general ways people feel cared about in his book *The Five Love Language*. If you can identify what makes your partner feel loved, your caring and romantic gestures will hit the bull's-eye with greater frequency and ease. Chapman's five categories include:

- Positive verbal feedback

- Quality time spent together doing fun activities together or attentive listening

- Gifts, both random surprises and for dates like birthdays and anniversaries

- Help with parenting, housekeeping or errands

- Physical affection or simply sex

Start by asking your partner what makes them feel loved. People give astounding answers. Often partners will give their mates what they would like to get rather than what their mate longs for and responds best to. I remember one woman married to a highly educated medical professional. This fellow felt neglected if she hadn't opened and sorted his mail when he got home each day. That was love to him. She loved to chat and felt loved when he talked to her and thought the mail was irrelevant. But when she did the mail, he felt loved and ready to listen to her chat.

If a couple is in trouble emotionally in their relationship, partners often don't know and can't make even a good guess what pleases their mate. Sometimes I help couples make "caring lists" of things that make each of them feel loved. Often on the list they will discover that there are things they already do that the partner enjoys and hasn't mentioned. They enjoy receiving the appreciation and can focus on those things more. I then encourage them to try things from the caring list and discover what else works.

Some people are universal receivers who purr and feel happy for any kind gesture. Some people simply respond to the absence of anger and upset; others feel neglected without active gestures of love.

Just like pregnancy can be a period to explore a broader range of sexual responses, post-pregnancy is a good chance to explore what rings your partner's bell in terms of caring responses.

Better Post-Pregnancy Sex

The positive environment created by these caring gestures lays the groundwork for good, open, honest communication and good sex. While this seems like, and is, a slow and indirect way to approach regaining a great sex life, I encourage couples to see it as an investment in their future and the future of their kids.

When you feel ready to try sex again it may be best to start with whatever is familiar. Double-check that your partner is ready, and inquire more than usual about his or her comfort as you go along. Good sex leads to more good sex.

Birth Control: If there still seems to be a barrier to restarting your sex life, consider what might be going on between you and your partner. Perhaps, one of you may be fearful of having sex because the other wants more children. The reluctant partner may just be too overwhelmed by the child you have and all the change that has come with that to feel warmly toward intercourse and what that might produce. This is a common issue when couples have difficulty resuming sex after the birth of a baby. You may need to establish birth control boundaries that you both like so as to feel okay with having sex.

Variety: Another problem some couples find is that after the birth of the baby, or after years of familiarity, what used to be exciting just isn't as exciting anymore. In the process of moving through the stages of marriage, one of you may become more eager to try something new. It can be very hard to discuss the desire for more variety with your partner. Just saying that you would like to try something else implies that you aren't happy with what is. Not a good thing. Partners have better luck when they say something like, "I feel so safe and secure with you and I am grateful for that. Feeling safe makes me wonder if we are close enough to experiment a little more. I have read that there are things that you can try that sound like you might love them. What do you think?" Saying I have read or seen things on TV is important because many partners jump to the conclusion that you have been learning from a new teacher or talking with someone besides them. Also not a good thing.

Helping your partner feel better by exploring new ways to be together is a good thing. Estimates indicate that more than two-thirds of women do not have orgasm with intercourse alone. Regular old straightforward orgasm is the big deal for men, but not as often for women. This is a simple matter of anatomy. Traditional intercourse usually hits a man's hot spot and misses the woman's.

A while ago, *Redbook* magazine (January, 2001) invited twenty-seven happily married couples, many with kids, to try five steamy positions for intercourse that would hit the spot. Before trying these only four women said they reliably achieved orgasm with intercourse. After trying these positions twenty-one reported reliable orgasms with intercourse. One man in the study said, "when you are twenty you are one big undifferentiated hot spot." After kids and post-thirty is a different story. An opportunity to have sex in a more personal way that makes the earth move for both of you is a possibility *if* you want to experiment together.

Man-on-Top with Pillows: The standard missionary position with the woman on her back—with her knees raised or not—and man facedown is the most popular and least likely to hit a woman's hot spots. This position can be revised several ways using the pillow under the woman's hips. Arrange the pillows either higher or lower to change the tip of the pelvis steeply forward or back to hit either the G spot or the AFE spot across from it. Former gymnasts can accomplish the same thing by wrapping their legs around his waist or neck. Putting your feet on his shoulders accomplishes a steep tilt but might terrify some men. Pillows are easier.

Couples loved this enhancement. It takes some patience to make the adjustments. You might need to shift your weight and thrust into him but the effect is to feel both clitoral and G spot stimulation, which makes the penis feel larger. One thirty-eight-year-old man whose wife used to use her hand to achieve orgasm during intercourse, said, "Giving her an orgasm without her 'help' is powerful. I don't think any guy is so evolved that he can't appreciate the difference."

Fine-tune the woman on top. The woman is more likely to reach orgasm on top. The modifications, either leaning back and resting your hands on the bed behind you or leaning way forward in the jockey position or even with your hands above his head can improve the pelvic tilt and increase his stimulation as well. Even more men than women loved this position.

X marks the spot. This position isn't as complicated as it reads according to the couples who have tried it. He lies on his side facing you and you lie next to him on your back. Put your inner leg, the one between you, over his legs and your outer leg between his legs so that you end up facing away and snuggled into his chest, spoon position. A butterfly vibrator can easily fit over the clitoris to enhance this position more. One of the couples who chose this as their favorite position were parents of an infant and a toddler. She said, "I haven't been as rigorous about doing my Kegels as I should and this makes my vagina feel tighter." The husband added, "Often we are just so tired that starting out slowly (in a 'lazy' side-to-side position) is the only way to get there." A lot of women who are self-conscious about their post-pregnancy tummy can relax and reach orgasm faster in this position.

Connection Cuddle: This is the more exotic of the positions. Adapted from Tantric sex, it is good for prolonging the man's arousal. You don't have to be a yogi to do this, but that may make the position easier.

Sit facing your partner with your legs wrapped around each other, woman's legs on top. You can make it more relaxing with your knees up or pillows propped behind you. Put your right hands at the back of each other's neck and the left hands on each other's tailbones. Place his penis inside you so it exerts as much indirect pressure as possible on the clitoris. Rock slowly together while rubbing each other's back and maintaining deep eye contact. To increase contact with the hot spot, use pillows to raise her until the clitoris and G spots receive the most stimulation.

One couple reported that this position "opened an erotic door" in their relationship. The wife added, "We had twins six months after we were married. Sex was quick; with orgasms for me problematic. This forced us to slow down and really gives me an orgasm every time." Another variation is to try this on your sides.

And that is really the point. Let yourself play around. Experiment with massage, caring gestures, and sex. See what works best for each of you. This private playtime, away from kids and responsibilities, creates a unique connection that can get better and better. But you need to take the time.

Tips for Fostering Romance and Sexual Closeness

- Expect your sex life to change, because it will.

- Talk about your worst fears about sex during pregnancy like giving the baby brain damage with your enormous penis and laugh together. Then comfort yourself that it is impossible.

- Get a book on massage and try something new.

- Get massages together. (Tell your masseuse who is pregnant.)

- Talk about what it is like to feel fat and tired . . . and a father.

- Practice alternate forms of giving pleasure, like sharing fantasies, looking at pictures of voluptuous, nude pregnant women, oral sex, and massage.

- Try to keep the satisfaction mutual even if you drastically modify your routine.

- Ask around and see who actually thinks their sexual relationship is better since pregnancy and kids. (You will become interesting at dinner parties.)

- If sex hurts, see your doctor. If it doesn't get better, see another doctor.

- Give your wife a lot of reassurance about her looks during and post-pregnancy.

- Cuddle and stroke each other a lot.

- When you are reading baby books, take some time to read about sex and massage.

- When you are out to dinner, make lists of the ten most romantic weekends you can imagine.

- Ask your partner what you do that makes him or her feel most cared about and most loved.

- Ask what else might make them feel your care and concern.

- Try the positions above and pick the one that's best for you at this time.

- Take a revote each anniversary on your favorite caring gestures (and sexual positions)!

15

Affairs: Preventing Them and Healing the Marriage

Few events in life are more heartbreaking to an unsuspecting spouse than an affair. Sadly, after the birth of a child—or even during pregnancy—a time when couples hope and expect to draw closer, is a common time for a partner to consider an affair. The stress of raising kids leads partners to long for a break. Not surprisingly, they notice that their most relaxed times are away from home.

If the person you trust the most with your kids aside from yourself is your partner, then your most relaxed time to talk probably occurs when you are away from the kids and your partner is home. If your kids are in childcare during the day, you still may be more relaxed away from home and stressed at home with your partner. When the two of you are out, you may be a bit distracted about what is happening at home. Because this compromises the quality of your time together, you may start to feel more uplifted when you're out and your partner is home.

This creates an atmosphere conducive to an affair or to fears that your partner may have one. Certainly, the time away can seem like more fun than time at home with its constant interruptions and responsibilities.

I can remember laughing with my friends about our unnatural attraction to our repairmen who came to the house in the few quiet moments when our spouses and kids had left in a whirlwind of noise and demands. Accepting your desires to escape, laughing about it, and focusing on your relationship can help avoid affairs.

Too often, however, couples don't have this awareness. Instead, they focus on what is wrong and blame their partner, making it easy to rationalize an affair. The frustrated partner reasons that it is not good for the kids if the parents divorce, so perhaps an affair would keep the family together. They could also have sex and/or a romance and still preserve the marriage—they think. "Who would it hurt?" Any rationalization works.

Some women fear their mates are more likely to have an affair after they have children. "Since I am too tired and exhausted for sex, it is only a matter of time until he has an affair," she assumes. Or he assumes, "Belinda never wants sex. I wonder if she is having an affair." Neither fearing an affair nor rationalizing having one is really productive thinking.

Most women, and that includes women therapists, assume that people who have affairs are miserable in their marriages. This isn't necessarily so. In order to have an affair, women must first feel that their marriages aren't good or lack intimacy. Men, on the other hand, are more likely to say their marriages are happy while they are having an affair. Male therapists and writers also more often acknowledge that there are multiple reasons to have an affair. To add to this confusion, many men and women often decide their marriage was no good in retrospect, after they have an affair.

Who has affairs and when? Men are a little more likely to have affairs than women, but statistics on who has affairs are shaky. Some estimates say that in as many as half of all marriages one or both partners have affairs. These numbers vary dramatically, depending on who is asking the question (and in front of whom I suppose), how long the couples in the sample have been married, and the definition of an affair. Suffice it to say that any long-term relationship is at high risk for one or both partners to have an affair at some point in the marriage.

Not surprisingly, the sheer exhaustion and lack of sex drive make the period just after the birth of the baby an unlikely one for women to be the ones to have an affair. Men, on the other hand, if they are not involved with mother and baby in this period are more likely to have affairs during pregnancy and in the first two years after the birth of the baby. Women are more likely to stray when their kids reach preschool and are a bit more independent.

Differences and similarities in the way men and women see affairs: While the vast majority of men and women believe that fidelity is the best way to go in marriage, some practice serial monogamy. In serial monogamy, or serial marriage, one remains faithful until the going gets rough, then that person trades his or her partner in for a new model. These people feel moral if they don't sleep with someone else unless they have properly informed their spouse they are no longer happy. Truly moral people, in this model, have moved out or divorced before beginning to date again.

In *Take Back Your Marriage*, author William Doherty, Ph.D., calls this model the consumer marriage. He likens the consumer marriage to trading up to a newer model car. Instead of taking care of the marriage, when your marriage wears out, you trade up spouses, as you would a car that needs repair. An affair is like trying the next car before you make the trade. Both men and women adopt the trade-in mentality, regardless of what is behind the affair. Women often see the reason to trade as having a lack of love, emotional intimacy, and, to a lesser extent, sex in their marriage. Men see the reason to trade as not having enough sex and feeling too often criticized. Thus, some view affairs as a normal step in adult development. But people aren't cars. Kids and families often get emotionally dented or totaled this way.

Sadly, I often see couples waver for years, lost in indecision about whether to trade up without ever trying to make the little, or sometimes big, changes in themselves to be truly happy in their present relationships. I also often see couples who ignore their own issues, instead of resolving them, and trade in their spouse, only to repeat the same problems with the next spouse. While seductive, the trade-in model doesn't work well. Unless the safety and well-being of you or your children is threatened by violence or addiction, working on your marriage is a better investment. In these severe cases, making a clean (affair-free) break from your spouse is still more healing than an affair is likely to be.

The couples who are more likely to avoid having an affair are those where both partners have some moral or religious convictions that prohibit it. You are also less likely to have an affair if you talk frequently in the ways we describe in Part 4 because you will be close enough friends to notice that things are drifting, and you will do something before it is too late.

Types of Affairs: Stepping-stone affairs, which are part of a trading up process, are most common. These relationships assure the person that someone out there finds them attractive. This helps the straying partner take the steps to divorce while assuring them they won't face a lifetime of loneliness. This affair is likely when the couple is in the "Who *Is* This Person I Married?" stage discussed in Chapter 7. The affair may not continue after the divorce.

A "charmer" starts another type of affair. Charmers often feel unsuccessful in their career or life at the time they begin an affair. They need to feel better about themselves by making someone else feel special, witty, and like they need them. Both men and women are particularly vulnerable to this type of affair when they are in the "Who the Heck Have I Married?" stage. In this type of affair, women and men who have been seduced are those who are more likely to define the original marriage as happy if asked early in the affair, and to define the same marriage as unhappy later if the affair proceeds well.

The "Can't Say No" affair is closely related to the charmer. Men will often describe being unable to turn down a proposition as though they have been taught that gentlemen never say no to a lady. Availability of an affair partner is seen as an opportunity, like the lottery not to be missed. Availability holds the most attraction for someone who didn't see her or himself as attractive or popular in high school. One fellow described his high school experience with girls as: "Girls 1,000, me zero." This feeling lingers despite the fact that the man may later be quite successful and attractive. Others (including, less frequently, women) simply don't know a nice way to say no and assume that what the partner doesn't know won't hurt them. I have had men and women tell me that the sex wasn't even good but they just went along. Of course, such indiscretions usually hurt both partners and the marriage. Marriages often recover from this type of affair if it is discovered or disclosed fairly rapidly because neither affair partner has much emotional commitment to it.

The "Duck Hunter" affair is another type aptly described by Frank Pittman, in his classic book on affairs called *Private Lies*. Some men have a duck-hunting mentality. They make a sport of seducing as many women as they can. Women, on the other hand, more rarely have the belt-notching approach. To some men, affairs are a sport learned at their father's knee. They often were told by their father of his affairs or asked to cover up his affairs. Duck hunters learned from Dad that such affairs have nothing to do with Mom and, therefore, nothing to do with his attachment to his wife. Rather these men feel affairs affirm their masculinity.

When these men grow up and try this in their adult life, they are quite upset if the wife chooses to leave because of the affair. Contemporary women just aren't as forgiving. This is particularly sad, because these men often describe their marriages as happy. They have great difficulty understanding why their wife isn't more understanding, as his own mother was. The advent of AIDS and public awareness of other STDs (and perhaps the equality of the genders) have somewhat reduced this type of affair.

The only way to prevent this affair is to avoid marrying someone who has this attitude and a parent with a history of multiple affairs. Men, however, rarely confess to this history.

Finally, there is the emotional affair. I see this most often in people who were molested and maltreated as children. Often, particularly if someone they knew and trusted molested them, the victim doesn't enjoy couple sex after trust and love are established. Pressure to resume sex leads to emotional distance because the victim doesn't understand his or her own sudden disinterest in sex. The molested or abused partner may seek an outside safe (nonsexual) relationship that is intimate and emotional.

In these cases, the nonmolested partner (usually, but not always, the man) may be in love with a wife who doesn't like sex. This makes him feel both deprived and inadequate. He first struggles with establishing a relationship and then engages in a long-term affair with a woman who doesn't want an intimate relationship but does want sex. Neither partner wishes to leave the other, nor do they want the marriage to end. When either the spouse or the affair partner presses for a more permanent relationship, the marriage goes into crisis.

Professional intervention, especially with EMDR, can help

the couple to work out the problem. Molested and abused partners are often quite relieved to learn that their loss of interest in
sex is related to their childhood trauma. They then can work in
therapy more comfortably.

Avoiding Affairs: Although affairs can be fun in the beginning, people rarely anticipate the hurt and havoc they eventually
wreak on all parties, including the people who break them off.
Kids suffer because a parent can't be fully present when his or
her heart and mind are lost in an affair. Having watched the fall-
out of affairs for years in clinical practice, the best advice I can
offer is to try to avoid them if you want a long-term happy marriage. *This seems obvious, but won't seem obvious when it is
happening to you.*

Before affairs seem like a possibility, discuss the boundaries
that are comfortable for you both. Will you go out to lunch or
dinner with friends of the opposite sex? What about professional contacts? How close will you stay together at parties?
Will you go to parties, theater, or movies alone or with others of
the opposite sex? What are the comfortable boundaries of sexual talk and flirting? Which intimate things that you talk about
with each other will you share with others? How do you feel
about chatting on-line with the opposite sex? I don't feel it is
necessary to impose my boundaries on my clients. However, if
they choose very loose boundaries, like exchanging sexual partners, I point out that the people who wrote the book on open
marriage ended up divorced. Also, daily or almost daily contact
with a member of the opposite sex that isn't primarily work related can spell trouble.

Tell your partner that if they have an affair you will kill
them. Just kidding. People who are quite comfortable in their
marriages will often say something direct, simple, and to-the-
point like, "If you have an affair, I will hang your cajones on the
clothesline." Unfortunately, if your partner's nature is to avoid
conflict, this may discourage your spouse from talking to you

about his or her feelings on this topic. People rarely know what they will do in the case of an affair, even though they may express a strong opinion.

Try to notice signals that indicate you or your partner are especially interested in someone and do something about that interest. Some people just assume that because they would not have an affair, their partner won't either. But if one partner is quite unhappy and has trouble expressing this, or expresses it repeatedly and is ignored or shut down, an affair begins to feel like a logical alternative. The spouse just drifts to an affair partner to avoid conflict or criticism, instead of choosing to struggle in the relationship anymore. If you start seriously contemplating an affair and can't talk to your spouse about it, go to therapy and save yourself the grief.

The majority of people who engage in affairs, except for the duck hunters, are conflict-avoidant. That is, they just don't like to fight with the one they love. They are nice people and charming when you meet them. They are often communicative and self-disclosing. They can be quite articulate and even argumentative about a variety of topics. But they have trouble delivering bad news about the relationship to their partner.

They have trouble making comments like the following, which could send up a flare for help: "I am not feeling close to you." "Our relationship isn't working." "I am feeling attracted to other people." "I am lonely." "I am missing you." "Our sex life is boring." "Our relationship is boring." "Sex scares me." Or "Sex hurts." They do not want to hurt their partner's feelings. They may be afraid to drive them away by speaking the unpleasant truth. But all these comments are easier to say than to deliver the news that you are having an affair. If you feel these things, use them as a signal that your relationship is in trouble. Either talk to your partner or seek professional help to figure out how best to approach your partner.

Many couples with difficulty talking about differences and

conflict in the relationship act out in ways that destroy their marriage even when they agree on their values and have nearly everything else in common. Here are two examples that didn't end so well.

Judy and Jim were both gentle, devoted, fun parents. Each arranged their schedules to tag-team parent so that they had no nanny or childcare support person, which left them almost no time for each other. Both parents agreed on the rules and standards for their kids. Their three children were the center of their lives and possibly the most beautifully behaved preschoolers I had ever met.

Unfortunately Judy had an unacknowledged need to talk things out and avoid conflict. Before kids, they had plenty of time to talk, without Judy having to ask. Love to her meant sharing her day, each day, with her partner. Judy's father had abandoned her family in divorce when she was quite young. Her mother had met and eventually married a calm man who liked to talk things out, which was what she hoped for in her marriage.

Jim came from a deeply committed family in which actions spoke louder than words. The chores you did for the kids and one another and what you each provided financially communicated caring in Jim's family. Otherwise he didn't need to talk. He felt that Judy demonstrated love when she went along with what he wanted. He didn't take her need to talk seriously because it was *just talk*.

Jim was willing to argue any point until Judy finally saw it his way. She felt she just gave in to stop his unrelenting "hammering" to end conflict. After kids, Judy seldom acknowledged her need for time with Jim to just talk until she blew up in a rage. Then she let Jim know just how inadequate he was in the communications department. He politely ignored these blowups because he felt she just needed to "let off steam."

She was a prime candidate too for the attentions of an unhappily married man at work who loved to talk and listen. This man had had multiple affairs and many family difficulties, but he was a great listener. Sadly, she soon became involved in an intense affair. She felt terribly guilty because her affair was outside her own value system. With the extra guilt, she felt even more hopeless and paralyzed about asking for what she wanted in her marriage.

When her new man was hospitalized for drug and alcohol rehabilitation, she sought counseling. But it was too late. By the time she realized this new man was not Mr. Right, she was divorced and struggling with an angry and unhelpful ex-husband. Her children were learning to live in two separate houses. Although both these people were good parents, they handled conflict in a destructive way, alternating between polite over-compromise and hostile explosions.

Clearly Judy and Jim had very different expectations about compromise, love and connection. Each assumed that because they had so much agreement about their children that the other things would get better. Judy didn't realize how unhappy she was until someone started to listen. Jim didn't realize she was really unhappy until she asked for a divorce. Then he was ready to work on it, but Judy was already deeply involved in the affair. By the time she realized her affair partner was not the answer, Jim was finished trying and had angrily moved on. How much better it would have been if Judy had said she missed having fun talk time and Jim had learned to listen sooner.

In other couples neither partner ever blows up. When post-kid frustration triggers a fight or flight response, they flee into an affair. Anger and frustration are underneath a calm, disconnected exterior. I know a couple, Doug and Meli, who were the center of a large circle of friends. They organized great parties, outings and vacations for everyone. They were viewed as the perfect fun couple. At first, kids just added to the mix because they organized great things to do for families with kids. Both participated in caring for the kids and they had lots of help. But neither could ask well for what they wanted.

When conflict came up, it was smoothed over. Although they problem-solved little things, they didn't talk about the frustration and distance they felt after kids. They would sometimes have long, grinding, rational arguments that left them feeling empty. They began to avoid each other and those arguments. Neither understood what was happening. Both were polite and yet bored with each other. Being with other people became a welcome distraction from their constant low-grade conflict and unhappiness.

Meli began having emotional rather than sexual affairs with a series of people and eventually found someone. The marriage ended because they "fell out of love," although each will tell you how great the other was. They went to therapy briefly, but Meli was already so deeply involved with the next person that they didn't continue. The kids suffered less in the divorce because the parents were always polite to each other and great parents. Not surprisingly, their second marriages had similar problems.

When there is this much unrecognized unhappiness in a marriage, affairs often result. Marriages can survive affairs but it is difficult, especially when the affair is well hidden and long-lasting.

Both couples, Jim and Judy and Doug and Meli, blamed the affair for the breakup of their marriage. But actually, the unresolved conflict that led to the affairs was the real culprit, and all had little insight into that. I have seen marriages survive even after very serious affairs because both partners sought help and took some responsibility, not only for the affair, but also for their own needs and their marriage.

Tougher to help are the people who have affairs and assume that nothing they do will improve their marriage and that there is no point talking about it anymore, or people who feel they have tried to talk about it and just gave up because their partner got upset, angry, or unresponsive are a bit easier if the counselor can calm the angry partner. Sometimes people give up on a marriage because they love their spouse (or married lover?) and don't want to risk upsetting them or threatening the relationship. I have also seen people who spend months and years unable to decide between an affair partner and a marriage partner for fear of hurting either one, causing everyone misery. Affairs don't usually happen because you fall out of love, but because you aren't communicating and aren't close sexually.

The best way to prevent an affair and a number of marital problems is to learn good communication skills and use them on a regular, daily basis to maintain contact interest, excitement and a good sex life. Good sex without intimacy can lead to affairs just as excellent companionship and emotional intimacy without sex can. Beyond that, your character and the commitment you each have to the marriage are the most important deterrents.

Normal Attraction to Others: If both people decide not to have affairs, because that isn't what they want out of life, that doesn't mean they will not be attracted to other people at times. They will and they need to decide how to handle that. Some people talk about it openly with their mate and use it to enrich their fantasy life. Some just try to pretend it isn't happening. Neither way is better than the other. No one certain antidote to affairs exists, especially when one partner has suffered severe abuse. However, re-establishing your sexual relationship and connecting well to each other is the best prevention.

Recovering from an Affair: According to the statistics, many people will have affairs, regardless of how well they do or do not communicate and how enjoyable their sex life is. As to whether one should abandon a marriage after an affair is discovered depends on many factors. I agree with Dear Abby, who always says to sit down and decide whether you are better off with or without the person. People often ask if it is possible to recover from an affair. The answer is: Yes! Absolutely!

In my first year as an intern therapist a couple arrived in my office. Together they proceeded to tell me that the husband had walked in on his wife having sex with his father. I kept my face perfectly calm so that my eyes wouldn't pop and carefully repeated what they had said to make sure I had just heard what I had heard. Yep. They then told me rather matter-of-factly that his father was "pond scum," or words to that effect, and that he had tricked her. The husband relayed that he had been away a lot and felt partially at fault. They had two children they adored. They talked it over and decided to move 2,000 miles away from his father, to the city where I was learning to be a therapist. They felt they needed a referee to talk about some of the difficult feelings they hadn't talked about, and to save their marriage.

I took a big gulp after listening to this and told them I was unsure and more than a little doubtful that I could save their marriage but I would certainly do what I could. They came every week for about twelve weeks, and we talked. When they felt that they had covered all the issues and we had done a little prevention planning, identifying what signals should bring them back to therapy, I asked them to send me a postcard each year on their anniversary or Christmas. Every year I got a card thanking me, even though I felt I had done nothing. Eventually I changed addresses so much as my husband and I embarked on our careers that I stopped receiving the cards. I hope that someday I will meet them again, because they gave me a great gift: *the knowledge that I could never know who would survive an affair and who would not.*

Over my career I have had a string of very unlikely-to-succeed couples, who went on to have much-improved and very strong marriages. In one couple the wife had an abortion with her affair partner, which she confessed to her marital partner. In another couple, both had affairs and decided after many days of talking it over that they were both "trailer trash" and deserved each other. I tell these true stories to my clients so they know that whether they survive an affair has more to do with them than whether the marriage can survive.

I have come to believe that a marriage is more likely to survive when the husband or wife who did not have an affair wants to stay married, feels partially to blame for the problems in the marriage, and wishes to understand what motivated the partner to have an affair. If they work together to change so that it doesn't happen again, they can succeed. But in order to get on the right track—and for me to agree to see them in therapy—the partner having the affair must give up all contact with the affair partner completely. I also require this partner to be in individual therapy.

If you wish to prevent or recover from an affair in your marriage it helps to understand why that affair occurred at this time in your marriage. If you fantasize about having an affair, ask yourself, "Why?" And, "Why now?" Use that knowledge to improve your marriage. Several good books are available to those who want to save their marriage after an affair. Both Shirley Glass's *Not "Just Friends"* and Michele Weiner Davis's *The Divorce Remedy* give excellent advice. Another personal favorite for describing the motivation for affairs in nonjudgmental but clear terms is a classic book by Emily M. Brown, called *Patterns of Infidelity and Their Treatment,* which has been revised and updated many times.

Summary: No one knows of any surefire formulas for preventing affairs. Most people are tempted at some time. Marriages can recover from affairs, but avoiding them in the first place is much less painful. To recover from an affair, you must understand what happened, what the affair partner was thinking to allow the affair to occur, and what each of you can now bring to the marriage that will improve it and prevent this from occurring again.

Tips for Avoiding Affairs

- Discuss with your partner whether they would ever talk to you if they felt like having an affair. Tell them you would like to talk about it.

- Discuss and set guidelines together about what is appropriate and comfortable with regard to time with other people at work and socially.

- Openly discuss affairs, possible affairs, and your comfort with your partner's behavior with people outside the marriage.

- Nothing you can do absolutely guarantees that your partner won't have an affair, so don't worry, make a strong marriage and enjoy the life you have.

- MAD (Make a Date) regularly.

Part Three

Travel, Birthdays, Christmas,
and Other Crises

16

When One Parent Travels

If having a baby is like tossing a hand grenade in a marriage, as writer Nora Ephron once quipped, then frequent travel adds the land mines. Some parents claim to enjoy the independence of a temporarily absent spouse, eating when the kids are hungry, and, briefly acting as sole decision maker. But that can get old fast. Often the stay-at-home parent feels the responsibilities of a single parent, imagines the spouse basking in a quiet hotel room enjoying her fantasy life of peace and solitude. Even if your spouse claims to hate travel, it's hard to be sympathetic as you see the golf clubs getting packed and visualize him or her going out to nice dinners and having adult conversation for several days.

Most couples don't realize at first that travel can be a challenge for the marriage. Travel usually comes in the context of a raise and a promotion. The excitement of the new situation overshadows potential disadvantages. Other times, travel may have been a significant part of the job that they both enjoyed before kids, especially if one got to tag along to the more exciting venues (sigh). Only as the relationship includes children does the difficulty become apparent. On the other hand, if you learn to manage these separations in good spirits, you can enjoy the times alone, and perhaps enjoy the frequent flyer miles for vacations, and greet each return in good spirits.

Not all reunions, however, are blissful.

Our neighbors Carol and Roger had a new baby, a large dog, and a noisy, obnoxious parrot that Carol hated but tolerated because she loved Roger. Roger was away on a trip and Carol was looking forward to his return and a night out to eat together. She got hungry, as nursing mothers do, and popped a slice of bread in the toaster. Just then the phone rang and an old friend from work was calling with devastating news about the death of a mutual friend. Toast forgotten, she was listening intently to the grim details when she glanced up to see the toaster shooting flames on the cupboard above the counter. The fire alarm pierced the air. The dog began barking hysterically. The baby started hiccupping and sobbing. She dropped the phone and lunged to unplug the toaster. Because her house is surrounded by flammable wooden decks, she raced outside and set the toaster in the street. Then, she came in, leaped on a stool, and ripped the batteries out of the smoke alarm, which quieted the dog. She said a hasty good-bye to her friend. Since the baby was still crying and the bird squawking, she decided to nurse the baby in a warm bath because it was the only thing she was sure would calm the baby. By closing both the bedroom and bathroom doors she couldn't hear the still-shrieking parrot. Just as the baby quieted down, Roger walked in the door and inquired why the heck the toaster was in the middle of the street.

To me this story illustrates the perennial problem of the traveling and the stay-at-home spouse. Traveling spouses, even working spouses, rarely comprehend the chaos that can be going on at home. If you aren't there, you don't know what is happening and you are likely to show up at the wrong time—too late to be of much help. Most often your natural questions will be perceived as annoying, insensitive and critical. Of course, this is true any time one person is home and the other is away, but being several time zones apart and having a new baby complicate the picture.

Mom can grow resentful because she didn't sign up to be a single parent, and yet often it feels as though she is. Traveling spouses often feel lonely and left out of the family, as though they are just there to send a paycheck. They feel even more strongly than most husbands that their opinion doesn't seem to matter except perhaps in an advisory capacity. As one dad put it, "I have all the authority of a teenage baby-sitter!" Both kids and the other parent will say, "Stay out of it, because you are never here!" So the traveling spouse often doesn't feel like a real parent.

Frequently both kids and Mom, if she is the full-time parent, are cool and distant upon Dad's return. Not because he has done anything wrong, but they react unconsciously as if they can't count on him because he will be gone again soon.

If you are prone to jealousy, worries about flings loom large. Meanwhile, stay-behind parents feel that all the housework and childcare has been unceremoniously dumped on them. Women often feel they can't complain because of the money the travel provides, which allows her to be home with the kids, as she wanted to do. Both parents struggle with feelings of resentment. Both feel that they should be receiving more gratitude from the other mate.

Good discussions about the relationship, the workload, or anything of real substance seem impossible because neither parent wants to discuss anything heavy or even mildly problematic—like that burning toaster—in the little time they have together. But you need to stay connected and avoid these resentments. Whether you choose to check in by phone or connect some other way, making sure you both feel connected is important to the long-term health of the marriage.

Planned Telephone Time: A common, unpleasant experience in families with a frequently traveling spouse is the phone call home at precisely the wrong time. Junior is in the bath, or it's story time, or you are trying to mediate a dispute. Although telephone interruptions seem trivial and annoying, solving this problem is the first step to creating a feeling of connection.

Schedule regular couple telephone times to call each day, like in the morning before the kids are up or evenings after they are asleep. Use that time to share about your day and to iron out any difficulties or plans that need to be made. Scheduling calls for a specific time creates a routine that is comfortable for stay-behind parents so they are less likely to be cool and distant. Often one or both members of the couple want to save money by not checking in, but do not realize the potential problems over the long haul. I remind them that time on the phone is much cheaper than counseling or a divorce and encourage them to choose some methods of supporting their relationship that feel right for them.

At the end of your call, confirm the next one. Depending on the number of time zones crossed, and unavailability of a phone in flight, you may have trouble keeping your regular time. These calls also allow the absent parent to participate more in decisions regarding the kids.

Call at another time to speak with the kids or use one of the other methods to keep your connection with them. Their time is important and is hard to share with the adult issues. Kids' ability to relate on the phone develops as they grow. Don't expect much in the beginning.

Traveling/Absent Parent Tips

Relationship Support Rituals for Parents: These fun reminders help keep you focused on each other, rather than letting resentments build.

- Attach some meaning or phrase to the wedding ring like "Every time I look at my wedding ring I think of you and what you are doing for us and our kids." This works both for the person out earning money and the one working with the kids.

- One couple has "back-up" date night. If travel or work interferes with their regular date, Dad schedules a date on designated back-up night and lets Mom know the change.

- Have a special item of jewelry, or clothing that you each wear as a reminder to feel close during your absence.

- One couple used the phrase "nos casa," which means we are doing this travel only until we can afford the house we are saving for.

- Leave behind a card or tuck one in a suitcase to say I am thinking of you.

- One husband I knew would call his wife on the cell phone when he got in late after a business meeting so he didn't wake her because she fell asleep early. When she woke up and listened to his message, she could hear the time he called and know he was safe and how he was feeling. Then they could talk together when he woke up.

- Plan separate child and parent telephone check-ins for quality couple time.

- Another couple said planning the next vacation months in advance gives them something special to look forward to and helps bridge the frustration of a heavy travel schedule.

Softening the Separation for Kids: Very young children quite often miss the traveling parent and complain to the stay-home parent, creating additional stress for the parent and the relationship. At a very early age, the child sometimes can't even understand that the traveling parent will be back.

Contented children help the home parent better tolerate the traveling parent's absences. Parents use an endless number of truly creative ways to overcome this separation anxiety for their child. Some of my favorites are:

- One dad calls home every night to read his kids a story from a copy of their favorite books, which they are holding at home. As the kids get older, longer, serialized stories work.

- A mom made a laminated photo of Dad and son together for the son to carry, sleep with, and talk to, as he needed.

- A traveling mom put a recorded message and a comforting favorite song on a play-back tape in a stuffed toy.

- One dad made a video of himself before a month-long trip to Paris.

- One family uses a calendar to cross off the days until Mom returns, as part of the bedtime routine.

- One daddy fills a special huggy bear with his hugs and kisses so they can go hug the bear when they miss him.

- Another mom gives her son a big lipstick kiss to carry in the palm of his hand.

- One mom videotaped Daddy reading, singing and talking to his daughter so she could watch it at bedtime until he returned.

- Another family has "Just Dad time" when he returns so that they can go do something special together, helping to create a bond for when he is away.

- One dad and son wore copycat shirts together at home on the weekend because it made them feel close and made Mom smile.

- Two little girls picked out the ties Daddy would pack for his trip. When he called, they would ask which one he was wearing.

These are all great things for your child, and your spouse will probably feel great that you made the effort to keep that link alive with your child.

17

Kids, Couples, and Vacations: Taking the Kids

Trudy and Tim, clients of mine, described the vacation from hell with their kids and Trudy's mother. In three short days of record-breaking heat on Labor Day weekend, they learned that their son could crack his head open twice on the same coffee table. The "suite" they booked at a resort was one room and so tiny that they needed an extra, expensive room. They learned too late that Trudy's mother didn't like to leave the hotel and pool, and that their infant son, overtired from an eleven-hour day the first day, could indeed whine and cry for four hours straight. The oldest child, age six, was deeply disappointed because Granny and baby limited so much of their activity. When all this became apparent, Tim, used to traveling with a backpack and no itinerary, announced he would never go on another family vacation again.

While I sympathized with them, I also giggled even though I don't generally laugh at my clients' troubles. I laughed because I had heard that so many vacations with kids turn out this way. I told them about a trip another couple took with two grandmothers and two kids to Costa Rica. Both grandmothers adored their grandchildren but preferred sight-seeing to watching them. The grannies wondered why they weren't invited on the next trip, despite dropping a lot of hints.

I suggested to Trudy and Tim that they were lucky they had only spent three days learning these lessons. Most couples take more trips and endure longer trials. Fortunately, Tim had been on many fun family vacations as a child, which helped put this disaster into perspective. He knew that trips are the stuff of lifelong memories. Even if children are too young to remember the trip themselves, they see the photos years later, and sense their place in the family's history. But the reality is that traveling with kids is a trip, but hardly a vacation. Making it enjoyable for everyone takes creativity and planning. In counseling, Trudy, Tim, and I started to plan their next experience.

I began by sharing some of what Neil and I had learned the hard way. We began flying with our kids before they were one, making our biennial trek to visit family. My only rule was to travel where the doctors spoke English, so I could communicate my hysteria should the need arise. Fortunately, our calamities weren't health related, but calamities we had. A porter once accidentally kept one of our boarding passes, so we were denied access to the plane at Christmas and spent an extra thirteen hours in various airports before arriving at our destination. On another trip, Clark's carefully packed formula didn't make a connection, and we arrived in Alaska at 11 P.M. with no formula. Good thing our taxi driver knew just where to get formula in the middle of the night.

I soon learned that traveling with kids can be both a time for great bonding with your partner and a time for marital trauma. The bonding occurs because the two of you are working as a team to get the kids through security, on the plane, and to a fun destination and home again where you will coo over pictures in a memory book. Trauma sets in along with the unanticipated realities. When planning a trip, it's hard to foresee it will be harried and awful, a microcosm of all the clutter, chaos, conflicts, and lack of spontaneity that you hoped to escape.

Couples who enjoy travel see it as the two of them against the elements; frustrated couples see it as the two of them against each other. While I have included some hints about how to make travel easier, the real challenge is to make the trip a joint effort and joint fun rather than a joint disaster.

Some couples fantasize that they will have a romantic getaway with the kids in tow. Not likely. If you expect to relax when you take the kids, you will be greatly disappointed. If you plan ahead, you can find a little downtime. For example, if you travel with friends or family, you can trade fixing meals. If you choose an all-inclusive-type vacation with meals and childcare provided, you may sneak in some relaxation if not romance. Some realistic (and experienced) couples take family vacations and don't expect to have romance until they take their private weekend, or later, when the kids are older, a private week when the kids are off with grandparents or at camp.

Others take grandparents on vacation. This can be great if your expectations match. Consider your agenda first: do you just want their company or do you want them to help? Are they healthy enough to truly enjoy the action or are they likely to slow you down? Are they good travelers and used to adjusting to what may happen? Will they need or want naps or free time away? If you expect help, the trip can be a significant disappointment if the grandparents just want to go along and vacation as well.

Vacation planning can be the toughest when children are infants. At young ages, Mom may be reluctant to separate from the baby even if you bring a nanny. She may also be reluctant to leave the child with a stranger at a resort that provides childcare.

Dad may not see the point of taking a nanny, and the nanny can be a problem. One couple I knew took a nanny to Hawaii. She was such a fish out of water that she wanted to take care of the baby 100 percent of the time. They had to struggle to get time with their baby! Very awkward. Other nannies want to party every night just when Mom and Dad want alone time.

As you can see from these examples, the parents need to talk both with each other and with the nanny or granny, if they decide to take them. They need to be particularly clear about what they hope will happen on vacation and how much relaxing they can reasonably expect.

Kids' Ages and Stages for Trips

Babies are the easiest to take on trips. They sleep a lot. Their food is portable and easy to deliver. Anything is a toy to an infant. Sucking either breast milk or water bottle reduces dehydration and, more importantly, takes away the ear pain on landing, which is usually the main cause of crying. Most airports and many planes have diaper-changing tables, but it helps to bring your own Velcro safety belt to strap in baby snugly in case the safety belt is missing.

The best strollers are those that accept the baby seat so you don't have to wake the baby to move from seat to stroller. If you can afford it, buy an airplane seat for the baby or ask when the planes are most empty, and fly then. Airlines are happy to inform you of those times. Be warned, however, that those are the most likely planes to be canceled because they are underbooked, although the airline will usually tell you that it is a mechanical problem. So be sure you have a back-up plan like there is another flight scheduled in an hour or so.

Arrive early if you can. I liked to get on the plane when they announced early boarding for those with small children so that I could stash all the goodies that I brought, including my overstuffed stroller. I traveled like a beleaguered Bedouin with all the comforts of home packed in the stroller. My husband is a career frequent flyer who likes to board at the last possible moment. He would frequently disappear just before boarding ostensibly to get a newspaper, but I think really to avoid the scene he knew I was about to make boarding with our kids and paraphernalia. When I tried waiting for him, I missed the early boarding call. While at first I contemplated murder and attempted useless persuasion, I eventually learned to just give him his boarding pass and climb aboard by myself with the kids. I often got sympathetic assistance from strangers and we didn't start the trip annoyed with each other.

Bring along a light blanket. You'd be amazed at the uses. I was given a thin open-weave, airy white blanket that worked as a breast-feeding shield, an extra layer on a cold plane and could wipe up spills in an emergency. Usually though, I draped it over the stroller or car seat handle when Clark slept. This blanket discouraged strangers from reaching out, touching him, and kissing him while he slept. When Clark woke up he could see out through it and would let me know he wanted to be uncovered, without screaming. I fantasized that it reduced the spray of viruses from sneezing strangers as well. Two years later, Xander and I happily used the blanket as well and it has been passed on to cousins.

Breast-feeding makes it easy to fly with a baby. Although I think breast-feeding is great and always give a smile of support to any woman I see breast-feeding, some people can be quite hysterical on the subject of breast-feeding in public. I developed a couple of tricks that made breast-feeding easy and private. I often wore light semi-loose fitting sweaters with another cardigan sweater or soft jacket over the top. Xander could happily bury his head under that combo and my breasts offended no one. He seemed to like the solitude. I also had the loosely knit blanky that allowed the kids to peer out while others couldn't see in. Xander loved the privacy. He would come and snuggle for comfort under my sweatshirt against my blouse long after breast-feeding was over.

I also used a crafty idea propounded by the La Leche League. They suggested teaching your child that breast-feeding was called "MAMA." No one blinks or suspects the nature of the request when an eighteen-month-old bellows out, "I want Mama" even when you are standing right there.

If you have a child prone to airsickness in the family, bring an airtight plastic bag. A large Ziploc bag proved invaluable for dirty baby clothes, bibs and anything else that I needed to carry off the plane but didn't want to smell. Also take one extra outfit to change the baby.

Our very understanding pediatrician's nurse recommended chewable Dramamine, a medication that helps prevent motion sickness, which proved to be a lifesaver for us. I hated drugging my child but I also wanted to go to our large, fun family gatherings. Be sure to use your pediatrician's advice on the dose. Fortunately, most kids recover from this tendency toward motion sickness as they grow older.

I have met parents whose children slept soundly through daytime cross-country flights. They reported giving all their kids cold and allergy medication. I was horrified. I could barely justify Dramamine. But it clearly worked for them. Again, ask your pediatrician, as not all children react the same way to cold medicine.

Another trick for traveling with babies is a large sturdy fanny pack with a flat top. This can hold water and formula bottles in the side pockets and can have an extra supply of pacifiers, diapers, your money, ID, tickets, lipstick, comb, and other necessities, while leaving your hands free to tend to the baby.

Best of all, the flat surface on a big fanny pack acts as a shelf or small seat if you slide it around in front of you, and distributes the baby's weight from your back to your hips while you are standing in line or walking. I think the hormones and distraction of having children made me witless and I was prone to leaving my purse on the top of my car and in public places. The fanny pack proved to be my best memory aid. I didn't leave behind what was attached to me.

Nine months to two or three years is the worst time to travel by plane or car. Kids this age hate to sit still. They don't understand why they should. Active children are especially challenging. Their feeding habits are usually disgusting to other passengers and for you. Toddlers don't really understand how to inhibit their actions at that age and think "no" means "look, quick, Mom is going to turn purple." Of course, it helps if you follow the parenting advice in most books for this age and teach your child that "no" is a signal that Mom or Dad are going to stop this activity. This requires teamwork, and kids this age need constant supervision, which doesn't translate to a relaxing vacation for you.

A dear friend and veteran of cross-country flights swears by flying the red-eye. The plane may be nearly empty and your child may sleep the whole way. If the child is prone to airsickness and you feed them well early in the evening, they may have nothing to throw up during the flight. There is rarely a need for any messy feeding since it is their sleep time. The red-eye flight is rarely canceled, and you can stay in a motel if it is. This works best if you tolerate sleep disruption, which I can't. I end up looking like yesterday's newspaper and feeling worse, so I developed daytime flying strategies.

With kids this age, bring your own food. The airlines will never feed you when the kids are hungry, and the kids won't eat what they offer anyway. I once spent two hours strapped in my seat with a baby and a toddler on the Denver runway waiting for take-off. This is not an uncommon occurrence and having your own food is a lifesaver. Breast-feeding several years eliminates some of the feeding issues.

I used a clever bottle-shaped device that allowed me to feed a young child strained baby food, which was great for occasional airplane or car use. Orthodontists panned this device because they thought excessive use contributed to crooked teeth, so it may be hard to locate. However, as an occasional treat, in a restaurant, on the airplane or a long car trip, we found the sipping bottle very handy.

Out of desperation, I also found the best travel foods for tots. Good travel food is bite-size, reasonably healthy, and doesn't spoil. Mini-bagels, with or without cream cheese, cut in halves or quarters depending on the size of the consumer, Cheerios and other bite-size non-sugar cereals, tiny peanut butter crackers, and string cheese were all popular. Eating any of them one at a time entertained for valuable minutes and wasn't too messy.

At this age kids love presents, and they don't even have to be new. Just wrap anything they haven't seen in a while. They also love to trade little toys with others. We would let them pack a tiny backpack with older, inexpensive toys on the trip so we didn't worry about losing things.

Older kids are easier again. Kids ages four to twelve may still have considerable difficulty sitting still for long but can be distracted with new books, games, and toys. If your child has unusual difficulty sitting still, traveling in the early morning hours or late at night while they sleep may still be your best bet. While we ordinarily avoided wholesale use of electronics, we found long car trips and airline rides could be vastly improved with electronic games, movies in the car, and other quiet, engaging pursuits as long as each kid had his or her own game or activity. We also loved travel versions of two-person games like Mancala, as long as we were prepared to use what Neil called the man-to-man defense: each of us watching and interacting with one kid. As they got older, a miracle occurred, and they actually began playing with each other so we could talk.

Alternate the group and individual games to break up the tedium. Good group games break up the tedium and become the family rituals that make memories. We have a certain card game, "I Doubt It," that we always play while waiting to board a plane. Many books are available to recommend games for car travel at this age. Kids enjoy games like "Once Upon a Time," for weaving wacky stories; The Alphabet Game, which involves spotting things out the window that start with letters of the alphabet, and "Are We There Yet?" where you use a stopwatch to see who comes closest to guessing when you will be at an upcoming landmark.

Work as a team when you travel with kids. My husband and I were clearly in the Who-the-Heck-Have-I-Married stage when we began flying with kids, as you are likely to be. Here are a few tips—learned in the trenches—to preserve your marriage. Even if it is while you are waiting to board, talk together about who is going to watch the kids and when and who is going to sit where so that you have a strategy. Most likely, at least one of you will need to be on duty all the time after a child begins to walk and talk.

Everyone develops a style when doing this. Divide-and-conquer strategies meant we each took a kid and managed them during the flight. Later one of us would sit between the kids and the other would get to sit across the aisle and have quiet time. Then we would change spots. Later when sibling conflicts started in earnest, we used the threat of sitting across the aisle as an incentive for good behavior.

Try new types of vacations. The good and bad aspects of kids are that they induce you to try new vacations, vacations that you never would have dreamed of going on before kids. But heads-up: deciding what constitutes the perfect family vacation is often a source of marital conflict. Each partner has his or her own vision—sometimes based on childhood reality and sometimes on unfulfilled fantasies. Dragging a city girl to family camp or a dude ranch can be a tough sell. Make sure you listen carefully to each person's dreams and fears and compromise if the visions are vastly different. Some couples alternate: a camping vacation followed by room-service luxury vacation. I have even known couples to combine them: Death Valley camping followed by Las Vegas resort in a single trip.

We've tried cruises, all-inclusive resorts, family camp, trading houses with a family in Europe (divine), living as the guest of another family in a foreign country (interesting and less divine), and camping with groups of families.

During one phase we rented a mobile home (christened the "noble" home by Clark) on a family trip. The noble home actually was a big hit when the kids were very little. The cousins were older and into staying up late. With a noble home parked in their yard we looked like Okies, but could retreat to quiet for naps and nighttime rituals. We were already packed and ready to go with extra towels, beach toys, snacks, and shade for sudden trips to the beach.

We even bought a "dream" vacation home only to learn it wasn't our style because it involved too much housework, and we like to go many different places. A timeshare purchased at a garage sale worked better and replaced the noble home and the dream home. The timeshare had maid service, laundry facilities and the right to trade freely around the world. Most vacations had their special charms with kids at different ages and stages.

Club Med all-inclusive vacations with built-in childcare can be appealing at early ages until kids demonstrate strong stranger anxiety, but I wouldn't trust my baby to a stranger. We found as a family we liked these vacations best when the kids were older and more excited about all the recreational activities.

Vacationing to see family can be relaxing if cooking and housekeeping duties are shared with other family members. For Mom to have a "vacation," it is nice not to have to do everything and still have access to laundry facilities for emergencies.

Some couples do great "family" vacations with friends who have kids, and can share some of the chores and childcare. We have taken car trips with other families and let the kids decide who rides in which car. Even toddlers loved this arrangement and were on better behavior with their buddies in other parents' cars.

Some people visit old family friends or aunts and uncles so that they can go to a child-friendly house where their kids are welcome. Just be sure you are truly welcome. Friends of ours brought a toddler to our house three years after ours were out of that stage. As I caught their son climbing a fence at the edge of a twenty-foot drop, I realized what great friends they were to have entertained us when our kids were that age.

Sometimes vacationing with other couples or at popular family camps with mixed age groups when kids are a bit older is fun. Your kids find the staff exciting and both parents and kids may be more willing to separate, so parents can have couple time.

Be sure to talk to someone who has been to the place you plan to visit, don't rely on the brochure. I once arrived at a destination to learn that "laundry included" meant once a week if it didn't rain. Another time, we thought a trip to the Galapagos would be fabulous because our young children loved animals. A phone call to the tour guide quashed this idea because children under eight weren't welcome. Before kids, traveling off the beaten path was an adventure. After kids, adventure can lead to frayed nerves and testiness rather than excitement.

Include the kids in plans. As soon as my kids could walk, I gave them little backpacks and let them begin packing whatever would fit that they wanted to take. (Remember you will end up carrying these when they are asleep, so keep them light.) Limiting toys to one backpack that they packed had many advantages. They learned at a very early age to pack their own stuff and could make great suggestions for what to take to help the time pass. By age eight, they were wearing their backpacks and helping me with my rolling suitcase, so I was empty-handed as we strolled through the airport. Quite a change from pushing a double stroller with two car seats in it!

Kids grow more vocal in the voting as they grow. One family treasures the memory of when their kids announced "Too many monuments!" and began participating in family vacation plans in self-defense.

Share your plans and expectations for car, plane, and restaurant behavior with your child before the trip. Library voices and good restaurant behavior are much easier to explain beforehand than later with a growing line of angry people behind you. Likewise for car rides, clearly stated rules that parents and kids agree upon in advance work best. Families adopt various rules like alternating the favored seat or assigning seats, and so forth.

Sometimes we have the kids make the rules for the trip. When the kids help articulate the rules, they are more likely to cooperate and they will be phrased in a more interesting manner. Almost any plan works, as long as Mom and Dad agree with it. But a plan is a must. In the old days, when just the two of you traveled, you could wander about making spontaneous decisions. Not anymore. Though some couples feel a plan ruins their vacation relaxation, some plans improve the traveling part. You can enjoy some spontaneity after you arrive.

Summary: Even with a plan, travel never goes quite as expected and is often frustrating. Working together as a team is essential when confronted with canceled planes, lost luggage and the normal travel disruptions. Parents who help each other find a solution when a howling two-year-old loses a favorite teddy have a better vacation than those busy blaming each other for the loss.

When happy couples make vacation plans, they use the same comfortable problem-solving strategies that work for them in other areas of their married lives. The rest of us struggle along as best we can. Parents may decide plans together or appoint one of them the trip "czar" who handles everything. Other parents split roles so that one parent researches the trip and makes the reservations and the other supervises packing. How you coordinate doesn't matter as long as it is comfortable for everyone. Know your kids and your spouse, and be sensitive to your style and theirs. Including even the tiniest family member's needs in making plans can become part of the good memories of the vacation.

Travel Tips with Kids

- Talk about the trip with your spouse and kids in advance. Focus on what you expect to enjoy about the trip as well as behavior expectations.

- Plan how and who will entertain the kids and what the rules will be.

- Discuss how your child's age will affect this trip.

- Figure out together how you can have couple time alone.

- Ask what has been challenging for each of you about previous trips and talk about what to do to make this trip better for each of you.

- Consider how each of you will get relaxation time to yourself on the vacation.

- Ask each other if you are planning to alternate watching the kids or use another form of childcare.

- Allow extra time each step of the way because traveling with kids always takes longer than you think.

- Review the plans on the ride to the airport.

18

Birthday Battles, Christmas, and Other Catastrophes

Everyone knows supermoms who plan and organize perfect parties. The invitations arrive early. Everything has a theme. I believe that these parties and all such events are possibly a threat to your marriage. I learned the hard way.

I used to do these parties—well, as close an approximation to them as a founding member of Nitwits Anonymous can possibly manage. The results were disastrous, although the kids enjoyed them enormously. My husband complained grumpily that I spent too much money and that our children would be spoiled. As each birthday drew near, we would each have our private depressions. I would do all the work for the kids, thinking I was doing Neil a favor to take over the job, all the while feeling lonely and unappreciated. Neil would show up late for the party, hang back, and generally have a terrible time. I would, of course, be furious about his lack of participation. We viewed these parties from completely different perspectives.

The crowning party had a pirate treasure theme. I had read about sprinkling the table with gold wrapped chocolate coins and making treasure boxes. My husband in a token gesture of helpfulness said he'd seen some at the corner convenience store. I was running late with both kids in tow. I ran in the store and located the coins at the checkout counter. Just as I was about to pay, my younger son said, "I have to poop *NOW* Mommy!" I hurriedly paid the man, grabbed the coins and rushed for the exit. The coins looked gorgeous and everything went pretty well, despite the fact that my husband decided to build a child-size table for the kids one hour before the party so the guests arrived to the buzz of a saw and flying sawdust. Shortly after everyone left, while we were still basking in the glow of the festivities a mom called. She cautiously told me the gold coins that I had thought were chocolate were, in fact, condoms. "I was pretty sure you hadn't intended to start sex ed that early!" she said giggling. I reflected on the startled look of the clerk when I cleaned out his condom supply in such a desperate rush. Fortunately, all the mothers I called to warn, found this hysterically funny.

After that party disaster, I decided to send my husband to the store to buy the party favors with the kids. I'd been doing the buying alone for years, to a chorus of criticism. I had splendid visions of the kids running riot in the party store with him alone and me being truly appreciated. At the last minute I weakened and we all went together. Two parents and two boys were a lot better than one parent and two boys in the party store. Dad ended up spending more than I did. The stuff was totally tacky and without any theme, but we had a good time together and all the kids loved the stuff.

The next party I asked Daddy's advice every step of the way. As years of parties passed, the kids reinforced Dad for his "good judgment." He got so into giving birthday parties he eventually insisted on giving a party for a friend's child who had never had a party because his parents were both afraid to do it.

So why are these occasions a threat and how do you avoid this? Lots of couples sink into this arrangement where Mom handles the party and both mom and dad feel resentful.

One couple recalled this nice party they once threw for their daughter. Mom was diligently scrubbing craft paint from the table, thinking to herself, "Look at him sipping lemonade under the tree and acting like a guest!" Meanwhile he was thinking, "If I offer to help I will never do it up to her standards, so I am better off here out of the way." She was furious. Think how differently this day would have gone if he had said, "I could never do the great job you are doing on that but I give good hugs." Or if she had said, "I need a hug of encouragement." Then she could add, "Would you mind bringing out the paper plates so I can set this up?" They hadn't planned the party together and both had negative expectations.

Holiday Crises. A harried woman acquaintance, mother of two under three years old suggested it would be great if Christmas could be like the Olympics—once every four years! Another creative acquaintance sends her cards only every other year. I was ready to sign up. Wow! We'd have more time as a couple. Yet, Christmas is my children's favorite holiday. For many adults, Christmas, Hanukkah, or Kwanzaa is their favorite holiday, filled with meaning. One of these may be yours as well. These occasions can be wonderful times to get close as a family and reconnect with friends, receive holiday photos and read their cards. But there is so much more work with kids that adding the "normal" holiday expectations of cards, massive gift giving, party planning and attending, and visiting families cross-country, can severely stress your marriage and your family.

Because family responsibilities change so dramatically with the advent of children, when holidays hit couples can be plagued with hassles and crises that put them at odds with each other. Time, energy, patience, and resources run out rapidly. I see too many grown-ups in therapy who remember Mom making them run the vacuum Christmas morning instead of enjoying their Christmas stocking. Often clients remember being asked what they wanted as a gift only to have their wishes ignored or made to feel ashamed for answering. When I get cranky with my spouse or kids I try to remember to ask myself if this is what I want them to remember about a holiday, so I will pull it together and get on track.

Given all this, it came as a surprise to me when clients once confided that their favorite time together was their annual Christmas shopping date! They loved the time alone and felt truly blessed to have the money to shop. They saw it as a celebration of the husband's success and their success as a family. Talk about having the right perspective! The point here is that the holidays are what you make of them. You can make some things a priority and skip others. You are creating memories, so enjoy the chance to set a tone for your family. Christmas may be a big romantic deal for you as a couple and may intensify your feeling about your new family or it may be casual and fun. Whatever, make it a time you all enjoy. That, my friends, is harder than it sounds.

Here are a few thoughts on how you can cope and create connection with your partner and children during this challenging time:

Discuss the meaning of a holiday first. Talk with your husband or wife about what a particular holiday means to them. And what it means to you. You will probably have very different wishes depending on what you loved and hated about your own childhood holidays. Don't be surprised if what makes a perfect holiday shifts dramatically once you have children and keeps shifting as they grow. What happened when you were kids and what do you want for your children? What really makes this a

holiday? Is it surprises represented by presents? Is it the link to
their religion or spirituality? Is it the spirit of giving? Is it music?
Is it the chance to express gratitude to all the people in your life
who have brought you joy during the year? Is it the chance to be
with family? Pictures and videos? What are your partner's worst
memories and biggest disappointments? Chances are it is expectations about what holidays *ought* to be. Reality often falls far
short of the image. Discuss what is realistic and what is Hall-
mark nonsense.

Having kids suddenly makes these questions loom larger. A
holiday that was never that important to one partner may be extremely important to the other. When partners see holidays differently, defining these holidays after kids may suddenly become
a struggle. Cross-cultural couples can create cross-cultural holidays. Many mixed faith households include, for example, a
menorah and a Christmas tree. Many students of family relationships suggest that all marriages in America are cross-cultural
because of the many cultures represented here. Hear each other
out. Respect, trust, and listen. Each of you probably won't have
the same important meanings for holidays. Build your own
Christmas rituals by sharing one activity that means the most to
each of you, and build from there. You can create traditions and
rituals for your family that celebrate what is important and
meaningful to each of you in your family life.

This is particularly true in newly formed stepfamilies. They
do not have a history of resolving this year by year. Now they
are suddenly presented with new children and new expectations
and two or more sets of new grandparents and extended families. They have two sets of memories: those from the family of
origin and the family of divorce—some good, some bad.

Whatever your situation, take the time to define the holiday
for yourselves. Ideally, try to make your expression of the holiday with the following thoughts in mind.

Create new traditions. Some people invest a lot of energy trying to make their partner do Christmas like it *should* be done—that is, the way they remember it! Think about what kind of memories you want to have about Christmas when you look back with your children in five or ten years. When they write that fifth-grade essay on my most memorable holiday, what do you each hope they remember? Talk about it with older kids.

One family I know who usually invited a lot of relatives who drank heavily, talked over the holidays with their kids and decided to forgo the presents (and the relatives) and take a ski vacation. They invited the extended family for Thanksgiving, then skipped all the Christmas decorating and eating and took off with just their immediate family for an intimate ski vacation. The trip was bliss for them all, and they started a new family tradition. Nobody got drunk. What a relief to plan the holiday to be what you want it to be. As kids get older, having them take part in the planning teaches them to take ownership of their lives as well.

Plan a couple event. First and most important, schedule a couple event that celebrates your relationship, so you will enjoy many more shared holidays to come. Even if it isn't a shopping date, à la my couple, schedule something just for the two of you. Discuss your expectations and make sure your priorities are clearly in hand, so you know what is important to you. Consider starting a holiday tradition that bonds you as a couple that will be meaningful even when the kids are grown and gone. Buy at least one gift or spend one time together that is just for the two of you. I know couples who have a dinner together separate from everyone on a particular day during the holidays. Others buy a nightgown or negligee each year for her and some goofy sex thing for him. Whatever you do, the idea is to exchange something private that's just between you.

Calendar Events: On a more practical level, get a calendar and write in what you are going to do when. Consider what you both consider important and decide which jobs to do solo, which to delegate and which to share. Schedule the shopping trips with individual children to shop for siblings, or make something together for gifts. Even though it takes time, get kids involved in selecting presents for their parents and siblings so they are excited about giving as well as getting. It is especially memorable for siblings if they have time alone with Mom or Dad to shop, make cookies, or play a game. Decide when you are going to wrap.

Schedule social dates only with people you really want to see. Once you see how full the calendar is, and that you have too much planned to actually do it all, you start making choices more easily. What's more important, a meaningful evening out with friends or running around like mad looking for party clothes (when no one remembers what you wore anyway)? If you make a plan before Thanksgiving, you have plenty of time to let friends and family know anything new.

Don't be the only elf in the family. I remember the first Christmas I wasn't working because I had just had a baby two weeks earlier. I bought all the kids' presents. My husband thought I had overspent and was angry. I was exhausted. The next year I let him do it. He spent as much or more than I did, but I wasn't so tired, and we were both happier. Now we do it together, and although we haven't achieved the state of shopping bliss my clients have, we enjoy it and don't feel resentment either.

Consider money together. Talk about your holiday finances early so you can avoid spending January lamenting your excesses or blaming each other. This can be a big strain on your marriage. If your child won't get that dream present because you can't afford it, see if other family members will chip in. Do tell your child if you think Santa can't afford it. By the time children are old enough to long for really expensive presents they usually are old enough to know that sometimes Santa has a budget and may not be able to bring what you ask for. It is better to be realistic *before* Christmas than to substitute something they do not like and send a message that what they want is bad or that they are bad for asking.

Eliminate some things. Look for ways to ease the load. I am so grateful to my friend Christy who, like me, had zillions of relatives and first suggested that we celebrate each other's birthdays and skip Christmas presents to each other. One family agreed to give up all presents over five dollars and pooled what was left to buy a family computer. Another family just skipped all presents over five dollars. Some decide to draw names among the adults and focus on the kids.

One close friend and I really simplified gift giving when the kids reached awkward ages when only a few gifts are acceptable. We each bought gifts for our own kids, wrapped them and swapped just before we met for our annual Christmas get together. The kids were mystified by how that friend always brought the perfect gift.

One family skipped the glitzy presents when the kids were older in favor of a big relaxing restaurant dinner. Other families would be horrified not to eat at home. Obviously, with small children the restaurant dinner can be a terrible idea because it is too constraining for the kiddies unless you get a private room. And no little kid wants to eat for long in a restaurant and be away from his gifts.

Our best plan was that we would alternate years with Neil's large family and mine. Each of my sisters fell into the plan and we meet even number Christmases and do alternate Christmases with the other in-law families. This eliminated a lot of stress because everyone could count on the deal.

Whatever you eliminate, the aim is to create meaningful time. We make a ritual of buying the tree and having hot chocolate with just our family. The kids would never let us take that special night off the calendar. Dad makes hot cider and plays Christmas music for the tree trimming.

Speak up. This is a time that you and your spouse may need to be a little assertive with relatives who have forgotten the realities of small children. If you can't stand dinner at a restaurant, tell them to come by for dessert. You'll find great peace in marking a polite boundary, and sharing with your kids and friends what was important to each of you. If you want Christmas morning as a family in your home, say so. Once you and your spouse have decided what will be meaningful to you, speak up to friends and family. As one mom said, "I'm grateful now (though I wasn't then) that after Paige was born, Dan made his Christmas commandment: 'We are always going to have Christmas in our home from now on. Anyone who wants to come is welcome. But we are not going anywhere.' It pleased me, even then, that he felt our family was first priority now."

Consider a giving tradition. Consider teaching kids to remember others. Teach by example. While acts of charity are time-consuming, they make memories and are character building. Your church, synagogue, or school may have great ideas for craft parties or giving opportunities so you don't have to do it all. I know a group that does a "Giving Party," where kids make Christmas decorations and collect money for a homeless shelter. In another group, kids make things to sell to each other, and the money is donated to help abused children. A representative of the group speaks to the children and parents about the people who will receive the items and money. In another group, kids deliver the money and visit the shelter. If you as a couple know what you want to communicate to your kids about holidays, you don't have to do it all by yourselves.

One grandmother said that she would try to make sure her kids had a chance to serve dinner in a soup kitchen or disaster line at least once a year to give them some perspective. This is

best started before twelve. Before ten it may be better to participate in a commitment that is shorter like delivering meals on
wheels or making sandwiches for the homeless because children's patience is limited. One word of caution: Such volunteer
work, while laudable, can stress your marriage if you don't do it
as a family or don't make sure it is something you both support
enthusiastically.

Use your village. Trading baby-sitting with another couple can
give each couple shopping or date time alone. Bail out a friend
with a new baby by buying a gift for her to give someone else.
She may return the favor later. Appreciate the magic that others
bring to the holidays. Invite someone you know who has a special talent to be in charge of the music or family plays this year.

Keep presents in perspective. Consider the developmental
age and stage of your child when opening presents. A really
young child, an infant or toddler, is often more interested in the
wrapping than the present. Allow plenty of time for gift opening. Don't rush. Opening more than one or two presents can be
overwhelming to a small child. A large extended family or older
sibs often can't wait to see what the little one's reaction will be,
but it's often disappointing when the little one just wants to tear
into whatever is next and shows little interest in her new toy.
Adults may need help slowing to a child's pace. The Hanukkah
tradition spreads the presents over several days. This works better, considering what young children can handle, and gives kids
a chance to comprehend and enjoy their gifts.

Talk this issue over with your spouse and make an agreement
in advance about how you will manage gifts so that you have
similar expectations. A common conflict would be the person
who likes a giant stocking filled with many inexpensive presents
married to someone who likes one expensive present. Any compromise plan will work, or you can each buy what the other likes.

Share this plan with family and friends in advance so things

go smoothly. Magazine columnist John Rosamond, Ph.D., recommends only allowing children to have ten toys at one time so
that the glut of things doesn't become overwhelming to clean up,
organize, and feed batteries. They inform family members of
this policy so that the family learns to buy things other than toys
for birthdays and holidays. Other people routinely say please
don't buy anything with batteries or loud noises. I know a loving grandma who presented her grandkids with a beautiful five-
piece drum set she saw at a garage sale. I teased her about
whether it was an act of love or hostility.

Appreciate, Appreciate. People often love genuine appreciation more than gifts. Consider thoughtful notes instead of
gifts for some people. Teachers have real experience with well-
intended, but strange, presents. I discovered that teachers love
notes of appreciation even more than gift certificates, especially,
if you quote your children or have them help you write them
(and may appreciate it even more if you send a copy to the prin-
cipal!). Older relatives and friends, who have everything, enjoy
notes of appreciation and school pictures or photos of them
with your kids. I express my deep gratitude to my kids and husband for being cheerful about the grueling cross-country trip to
visit my relatives, to friends for their friendship, and to coworkers just for being great people. Appreciation feels great, and
doesn't bust the budget or take a lot of time.

Stay realistic, flexible, and do not strive for perfection. Following these key principles makes it easier to delegate and ask
for help when your kids are small. If you are less concerned
about making everything perfect, you can feel more comfortable
asking for and appreciating the help you get. Talk to others
about the holidays to get ideas about how they keep perspective
and don't overspend and over stress. In the end, those details do
not matter as much as how you and your family enjoy the holiday together.

Summary: Holidays can be overwhelming before you have kids. After having kids, they can crowd your couple relationship right out of the picture. By agreeing about what really has meaning for you as a couple and saving time for it, you are insuring that together you will share many holidays to come.

Give Yourself a Break: Holiday Tips

- The best breaks are hug breaks. When you are rushed, stop and give your partner a hug. Hold hands. Kiss and hug your kids.

- Appreciate. Tell your partner all the things you are grateful for. Tell your kids what you are proud of. Write them down and post them. Tell people what you appreciate about them every day. It's free. It's quick and it means a lot.

- Stop and read a Christmas story together, even if every little thing doesn't get done.

- Skip a party if you don't really want to go.

- Don't send the cards one year, or skip the handwritten notes.

- Watch Christmas videos like *Prancer* or *The Grinch Who Stole Christmas* with the kids instead of doing the next thing on the list.

- On your master calendar, have one day in the holiday season when nothing is scheduled.

- Schedule special Christmas couple time on that master holiday calendar.

- Schedule "just our family time" for special Christmas rituals.

- If your spouse is gone a lot, take a day off work by yourself to shop.

- Schedule a baby-sitter and go with your spouse early in the morning or late at night, when fewer shoppers are out.

- Have a cup of tea, breathe, and focus.

- *Most important*, enjoy your family and spouse *your way.*

19

When Crisis Strikes

When my sons were four and six, I received a call at work one day from my architect who had been planning a remodel for us. He told me that my house was sliding down the hill and asked if I could authorize some work. Thus began our first crisis. Even as I write these words, I feel as stunned as I did then. We wouldn't learn the cause for weeks. (It turned out a broken, leaking pipe up the hill was washing away the neighbor's house and taking our backyard and foundation with it.)

I arrived home to a swarm of fire trucks flashing lights and yellow "DO NOT CROSS" tape. Three hours later we had evacuated the contents of our home. We went to stay with friends for three weeks. After that, we lived on the floor of our house for two more weeks with only mattresses for furniture. The reconstruction seemed endless and was still not complete six months later. Then the whole city was swallowed in the flames of an out-of-control brush fire. We were evacuated again.

This time our house survived because our architect, an everyday hero, hosed down the roof and wooden decks. I decided remodeling was bad karma, and we have never completed it.

Because I live in a disaster-prone community, I have seen firsthand the effects of different disasters on several marriages with kids. I saw that, as a general rule, if the marriage was troubled before the crisis, it got significantly worse afterward and often ended. Marriages that were unhappy and that had little emotional connection sometimes ended because people decided life was too short to go on like this. Good marriages became stronger, though. Wives would often express the gratitude that the crisis occurred. Nearly losing everything made them realize that people matter more than possessions and helped them to appreciate how well they worked as a team with their partner. Some crises connected couples to their supportive community in a new way. Fortunately for our marriage, we handled external crises well. We even gained the perspective to handle unresolved marital issues that had lingered since our children were born.

Every family faces crises. Death of family members, loss of a home, illnesses, loss of a job. The larger the crises the better people around you respond, if you need to miss work, everyone understands. Your friends understand if you forget to call. People spontaneously relieve you of obligations you have assumed. You feel guilt-free, eliminating those things you just can't do. Crises bring the opportunity to rely on each other in a new way.

As I reflected on the parallel between the crisis of a baby entering a marriage and exterior crises in our life, I could see certain things we did well in a "real" crisis that we hadn't done when adjusting to the birth of our children.

After a disaster, conversations about time, money, and plans take on a survival quality. There is often much more than ordinary emotional sharing. Many couples comment that they just stop fighting and start talking more.

Little crises, and unrecognized crises like the birth of a child, seem more difficult. I had lived through fires, floods, landslides, and evacuations, but the worst disaster of all was when my housekeeper had a complicated birth and took an unexpected eight weeks off in the busiest time of my year. There was no sympathy or outpouring of community support for that. The marital balance and our personal routines were thrown completely out of whack. Couple time dropped to zero. In such situations you and your partner need to take quick action together to focus on getting done what is important and letting go of some things.

Typical Reactions to Crises: Everyone reacts differently to crises. Some people (about a third) are eerily calm and rational, only breaking down in a safe place by themselves or with a trusted other. Another third come completely and thoroughly unglued, expressing their feelings by crying and being generally hysterical. A third group is nearly catatonic and don't say much nor seem to respond at all. Other people generally react to this latter group as being in shock.

None of these reactions are better or more or less pathological. They're just different. As long as you talk about the event fairly quickly and assign it a meaning, you are likely to bounce back regardless of your initial reaction. Those who remain hysterical or in shock, or deny that anything happened, have more difficulty. Knowing your crisis style and your spouse's is helpful in handling the terrain ahead.

In a relationship, different styles become a problem when a person who likes to talk about the event and his or her feelings is married to a stoic. The talker believes the stoic must be suffering mightily. The stoic muses on the mental stability of the talker. Marriages survive best when the partner understands the other's emotional needs.

Each person also works through crises differently. I know two happily married gentlemen who report that their wives responded to separate ongoing crises by going in the closet and sobbing because they didn't want to scare their kids. Trauma triggers can make crises linger. A trauma trigger is an event that vividly brings up the emotions and memories of an earlier crisis. Six months after our landslide crisis, I ran into a trauma trigger. I came home, crawled into bed and pulled the covers over my head. I greatly appreciated that when I told Neil what had upset me, he took the kids out for the afternoon so I could cry, sleep, and recover. Like the husbands of the women who cry in the closet, Neil didn't share my particular upset feelings, but cared that I was hurting and respected my need to deal with my feelings alone.

Partners often have very different needs, post crisis. Some people need to tell the story over and over. Some people need more listening. They thrive in a crisis group with lots of activity and expressiveness. Others tell one person how they felt about it all and then they are done. Others like to have a memorial while many people prefer simply participating in rebuilding when possible. The critical issue in recovery is that each person, including children, be able to talk about their feelings at least once relatively early on, and that they not be judged for their reactions just because they are different from their partner's or someone else's.

Meeting the Special Needs of Your Kids: Children react to crises in many different ways. The most common reaction is fear. Parent's reactions make a great difference in their child's recovery from disasters and crises. When parents are calm, their kids are calm. When parents are agitated and talk about how awful it is, the kids get more worried. Children are most fearful when they don't understand what is happening around them. Talk to your kids about both the facts and feelings surrounding what happened. Get their view of the disaster. Their perspective is often quite unique.

Give children accurate information in terms that make sense. My friend Ginger, who was diagnosed with breast cancer and had a double mastectomy, talked to Eve, her three-year-old, about the booboo's in her breasts. "I don't really feel bad at all. My booboo is deep inside my breast, so deep that you can't see it. It's called cancer."

As the events unfolded and friends arrived to help, she explained things to Eve. She didn't overload Eve with details she couldn't understand. "Will you be different when you come home?" asked Eve. "Not really," Ginger said. "But my breasts will be different, and I won't be able to hold you like this for a while. I might be very tired, but I'll still be able to love you and kiss you and tuck you into bed at night."

After the landslide I explained to the kids that our house was broken and would need to be fixed. When I explained we would have to stay over at his friends, Clark objected. After a long day at his friends, he said, "I am ready to go home now and play with my toys." When I explained that they had been packed on big trucks like when we moved. Xander said, "You remember moving, Clark, boxes, boxes, boxes!" Clark decided we were better off at Matthew's where the toys were already handy.

Reestablish family routines like stories at bedtime as soon as possible. Allow a little extra time with them. These intangible, fun family rituals help cushion the shock of the disruption in the household.

Acknowledge your children's feelings. I told the kids, "Dad and I miss staying at the house, too. But work crews will be there early in the morning to fix the house and I think they would wake us up."

Try not to spill your anxieties on your children. We didn't talk about our concern that the house would continue down the hill, which would leave us homeless. Neil let me get up at 5 A.M. each morning while he stayed with the kids so I could check progress, relieve my anxieties that the house was still standing, without risk of scaring the kids.

Encourage kids to deal with their feelings through play. Given play materials like family figures, blocks, toy houses, and fire engines, children will often do the same play activity over and over. Ginger let Eve participate by playing doctor, taking Mom's temperature, putting Band-Aids on her booboos and playing nurse by rubbing Mom's feet. This is how kids get a sense of control over the crisis. Talking about it repeatedly is another way to gain control. They can do some of this with other trusted adults, so that you have time to talk about your feelings with your partner as you will need to process what happened as well.

Assure them often that they are safe. "I don't think it is safe to be in a broken house right now, but we will be safe there when it is fixed," we told our kids. Be patient. With this, as in all things, children may ask repeatedly for more information about what happened. Avoid giving them too much information. A short but true answer satisfies them.

Help kids develop a sense of control by participating in activities. After we spent three weeks at friends', we talked to the kids about how it would feel to move back and camp in our house even though it meant sleeping on the living room floor for two weeks until the house was restored enough for our furniture to come back.

Plan on spending extra time with your kids. They will need it. If you can't do it all, friends may help. Eve had Aunt Susie and Godmother Ellen to stay over while Mom had surgery and for the first days of recovery, allowing Daddy to spend more time with Mom.

Plan on needing extra time as a couple, too. Our dear friends swooped down from forty miles away and offered to take the kids overnight while we evacuated the contents of the house and discussed our options. They were close friends, and the kids happily went off with them.

Many children begin sleeping with their parents after a disaster. This is comforting and fun, but needs to end eventually to give the couple private space again. Help children gradually return to their own sleeping space. You may need a mini-step method. For example, they move from the parent's bed to a cot or a sleeping bag in the parent's room. Consider celebrating the return to the child's own room with a special treat like a special dinner or activity.

Expect regression. In crisis, kids often retreat to old outgrown habits of six months or more ago. They may be potty trained and start having accidents. Nightmares, lack of interest in usual activities, extreme withdrawal, temper outbursts, inability to concentrate, thumb-sucking, bad dreams, fright fantasies, hair pulling or twisting, crying, clinginess, unusual inattentiveness to parent requests, and other behaviors of concern are common reactions. If these persist more than four or five weeks, contact your doctor or a counselor trained in trauma with kids. Do not blame your spouse for these problems.

The good news is that kids are resilient. Even a small amount of group therapy or EMDR, a trauma therapy mentioned earlier and frequently offered in crises situations, can help resolve the crisis more quickly. You and your spouse will fare better if you work together as a team to understand what the kids need and make sure they are with people they trust, like one of you, as much as possible.

How to Help Yourself and Each Other: Lots of official forms and technical details need tending to in a disaster. Preschool kids will rapidly lose interest in tedious details and yet they may be fearful about separating from you and you from them as you slog through this tedium. Spending extra time and dealing with their fears will make this less unpleasant. You may be irritable and easily lose patience. You may have temper outbursts and trouble concentrating, just like the kids. Go easy on yourself and your partner. Take frequent breaks, and even mini-vacations, such as afternoons or overnights away to readjust your perspective. Stop and hug a lot.

Although people in crisis have a tendency to dwell on their problems, dwell on what you have instead. Express gratitude daily for what you have. Dan told Eve and Ginger repeatedly how proud he was of Mommy for taking care of herself by doing the surgery. Ginger told everyone how grateful she was to have the support of Dan and her friends.

Crises stir up strong emotions. You will need time to deal with your feelings, time to share your feelings with your partner, and time to plan what you want to do. Crises also provide great opportunities to learn to accept help from other people. Choose people who view your feelings as a normal reaction to an abnormal situation, and who encourage you to talk about what is happening.

If they can also play and joke with you, all the better. Ginger can attest that gallows humor helps with cancer. Her family used the cancer crisis to reorganize their marriage roles and priorities in a way that made them all happier. Ginger switched from full-time corporate work to being self-employed part-time so she could spend more time with Eve. Dan moved from consulting to a full-time job. Eve spent more time at home and less time in childcare.

What does all this do to your marriage? Like the crisis of having kids, any crisis can help a marriage grow if you work on it together. Of course, your couple reaction depends on the stage of your marriage. Couples in the "We Are Great Together and Apart" stage generally do rather well, as you might expect. The rest of us ordinary mortals have a harder time. Interestingly, however, a crisis can push each partner in the "Who the Heck Have I Married?" stage to rapidly develop as individuals. As each takes on more responsibility, they quickly move onward to a stage of mutual respect.

This can cause them to pay more attention to each other's feelings because they talk about the crisis so much. This talk creates exactly the habits they need to move toward the "Friends Again" stage. However, working through the crisis may cause couples to ignore or rush through the independence stage too quickly. Although the rigors of the aftermath of crisis sometimes push a couple quickly, they end up being functional partners in crisis without much sense of who they each are as separate people. (See Chapter 7 for a review of the stages.) Like the baby crisis, the many practical tasks that must be accomplished in a crisis sometimes push a couple to work so independently just to get things done that they take no time to be friends and end up feeling that they don't really know themselves or each other.

If, shortly after the central crisis, you skip the independence stage and don't make sure each person's individual needs are well taken care of, the wheels fall off the marriage. To avoid this, check in frequently with your partner about how each of you is feeling.

Summary: In short, a crisis is a great opportunity to let go of the negativity and frustration of trying to change the other person and instead focus on a problem together. Working together creates a communication bridge that makes it possible to rediscover what you loved and respected about each other enough to get married. Be sure to tell your spouse how much you appreciate all they do. Focus on what you have and not what you have lost, and your marriage will emerge stronger.

Crisis Tips

- Avoid driving or be extremely cautious when you do. Statistically, you are extremely accident-prone in this distracted state. If someone offers to drive, let them.

- Avoid drinking or starting to smoke again. These old habits may seem to reduce stress but they are unhealthy and will add stress, even if you and your partner do them together. Drinking and drugs, although relaxing, make making good decisions more difficult.

- Use prescription antidepressants and antianxiety drugs cautiously and only as prescribed because they likewise can affect your judgment, especially when you are just starting them.

- Divide the labor but make many decisions jointly.

- Show respect for each other's decisions.

- Respect the differences in each other's emotional reactions to the crisis. One of you may want to talk a lot and may need a group. The other may need to meditate more.

- Focus repeatedly on what you have, rather than dwell on what you have lost.

- Find whatever positive lessons you can in the experience, and share them with each other.

- Hug each other a lot.

Part Four

Let's Talk: Protecting Your Marriage

20

Healed by Listening

Most of us believe that we are pretty good listeners. If the topic is positive and about us, or about our beautiful child, what we hear is probably pretty accurate. If talk is negative about someone we don't like, we may find it funny. But when negative news about us reaches our ears, few of us retain a sense of humor or even an average ability to listen.

"I love you, but I am not in love with you."

"I don't think you have ever really loved me."

"I can't imagine having sex with you ever again."

"The things I used to like most about you irritate me now."

"Why don't you ever do anything around here?"

"Don't you care about our kids?"

"Don't you care about me?"

"I don't respect your work anymore."

"I don't trust you."

"What kind of father (or mother) would do such a thing?"

These are all things I have heard loving partners say that were hard for their partners to hear. Yet really listening to their partner opened a discussion that made the marriage better.

Most people aren't good listeners in a crisis, because they focus, quite appropriately, on the tasks at hand. Since having kids is a multi-year crisis for most marriages, developing and using your listening skills can work magic in your marriage. Practicing these skills helps you and your partner feel closer. Your multi-year crisis may become a healing crisis, making your marriage stronger than ever.

For good marriages to thrive, each partner needs to be able to express feelings of discomfort, distress, and dissatisfaction— and be heard. This doesn't mean anyone needs to tolerate, nor should they let loose, a torrent of abuse. Indeed, many women marry with the idea that their partner is a sanctuary where they can share negative feelings. Women often see themselves as a sanctuary for their partners as well. Most men didn't read that notion in the fine print of their marital contract. Most men find the idea of sharing negative feelings scary, depressing, useless, perhaps bizarre, and sometimes unmanly. Men initially see a good marriage as one where no one needs to talk about problems. But over time in happy, long-term marriages men and women learn to listen even when what their partner says is negative and about them.

Research suggests that if a husband feels he can't express negative feelings and be heard, the marriage will not survive. Likewise, wives must find a way to influence their husband without harming the relationship. Happy marriage partners get very good at eliciting each other's opinions, reservations, and negative feelings while working together to create something positive. With the crisis of kids, the need to influence each other easily and smoothly goes up dramatically.

In a marriage with kids it is common for parents to complain about needing more help or not having the energy for sex.

Sometimes, sadly the complaints fall on deaf ears. Yet if partners learn to *listen* to each other and try to understand the other partner, sharing with someone who deeply cares about you and working out problems becomes a healing experience—a healing listening for each partner and the marriage. Even better, if you learn to check in regularly with your partner, the negative messages will become less frequent and easier to hear.

Good listening heals wounds from the past and creates a good family life for both you and your kids. Mastering these skills will not only strengthen your marriage now, but will also help your relationships with your children as they grow. And it's great modeling for your children.

In my clinical practice I love teaching the listening skills I'm about to share with you to someone who claims her husband never talks to her. Then the next session, she says, "This stuff is magic!" Or I teach them to a husband, and the wife comes in and says, "What did you do to him?" What I "do" is focus on teaching *one* of these healing listening or active listening rules at a time. After the first four rules are mastered, most people are up and running. Some people have bad habits or difficult partners and need extra work, so I add the other guidelines to help them.

So how do we overcome our natural resistance to hearing something that we don't particularly want to hear? How do we listen in a way that is healing to our partner and healthy for our relationship? How does bad news become a stepping-stone to a better relationship?

Rule 1. Let the person know you are listening intently. This does not mean you agree with them. This means giving them direct eye contact and doing nothing else while they are talking—that includes clicking the remote or listening with the mute on while you watch the screen. Look riveted with attention. Sit still and quiet. Nod your head gently and slowly, yes. If the person is saying, "You act like such a jerk sometimes!" nodding your head slowly may seem inappropriate or insincere, although it may have an element of surprise. Do it anyway. Your rapt attention will be rewarded. Your instinct will be to respond, deflect, or interrupt. Don't. If the phone, a waiter, or a child tries to interrupt, use the moment to pointedly and gently refocus on your partner's comments.

Rule 2. Repeat back what the person is saying as accurately as you can. If they are really angry, repeat it word for word. Otherwise repeat back the central feelings that you are hearing. When someone says you are a jerk, it will have an amazing impact if you say back, "So you think I am a jerk?" What you may realize is that while you heard "You are a jerk!" the person may in fact have said, "When will you ever change diapers!" By repeating the words back, you will discover whether you actually heard what was said. This is hugely important for many women and men. Repeating gives your partner the chance to soften what they said for a better startup. They may even come up with a more positive statement like, "I wish you would change J's diaper right now."

Many partners go through the motions of listening, and assume they already know what their partner is going to say. If this is you, try *really* listening. Your partner will be stunned if you look them in the eye and say anything that lets them know you were actually tuned in. It is the beginning of a real conversation.

Rule 3. Sympathize, reflecting the feelings as accurately as you can. Some people call this approach "Oh, poor baby" or "tea and sympathy." Don't worry. This does *not* mean that you agree with what the person is saying. "Oh, you sound like you have had a really long day and you need a break!" helps the other person know you care that he or she feels bad. That may be all that is required. Even if you think they brought it on themselves or caused the problem (thus being a real jerk, in your opinion), reserve judgment, be sympathetic, and wait for the whole story. You will often be pleasantly surprised.

Rule 4. Ask, "Is there anything more you want to tell me about this?" or "Do you feel I got the heart of what you are saying?" When you feel that you fully understand what your partner has said and you have done a great job of repeating back and sympathizing with his or her point, check to see if you are right by asking. Often they will soften what they are saying or begin to resolve whatever the issue is on their own. What sounded in the first sentence like, "You are a lazy unreliable jerk!" may change. Miracle of miracles, they may say something like, "I love you to death, but I am just so frustrated with my life right now." Your sensitive questions give your partner a second and a third chance to discover subtler feelings that they haven't recognized, and shift to a calmer, more neutral place.

True active listening is often a turning point, helping move couples from Stage 2, Who the Heck Are You?, to the third stage of Separate Identities, or even Stage 4, Friends Again. Midge described the moment in her marriage when active listening began to turn things around:

> We had been sniping at each other and very grouchy all morning. I have always had a very sharp tongue, which my husband, Bo, enjoys as long as it isn't directed at him. Suddenly I stopped and backed up to the edge of the bed and sat down and thought to myself: "I was happy when I woke up this morning and I am not really upset about anything important now. I am just firing back at him."
>
> So I said to Bo, "You know, honey, I wasn't mad when I got up this morning, and now listen to us snarling at each other. You sound really tense and unhappy. Is something upsetting you?"
>
> He growled a bit about this and that and I just actively listened to each thing without problem solving. Then he blurted out that Monday morning he was going to have to

fire his second in command, who had worked for him for over ten years. He felt he couldn't tell anyone because of confidentiality. I was floored and very sympathetic.

I began to try active listening whenever he got sarcastic or grouchy instead of shooting off my mouth. Some amazing stuff would come out.

We started solving little problems that had irritated us both for years. We laughed more at ourselves instead of making fun of each other. Gradually I realized that we both felt closer and more secure than we ever had before. It's great now. Our relationship is very different. I feel so emotionally safe with him. I think he feels safer with me, too.

Refinements: *Control your fear that your partner will never stop talking.* Many people fear that when someone has a complaint about them, or about anyone, that the person will never stop talking. I will teach you how to soothe long-winded partners so they wind down much sooner. When they feel calm, it will be easier to move to problem solving. Although if you do good listening, there may be no problem left.

Do not agree or disagree when your partner is upset. Agreeing or disagreeing, changing the subject, or giving your opinion will cause your partner to escalate intensity, repeat him/herself and prolong your misery. *It's not about you.* Even if they are saying "You never do anything around here!" It is not about you. "Draw a circle," mentally, around your partner's emotional issues and gripes about work, life, or whatever. Picture his stuff in a big bin. Your couple issues are in another box.

When I first try to teach someone active listening, men usually say, "It works great if I just agree with everything she says! But I feel like a wimp and I never get my point across." While full agreement may stop arguments, it breeds resentment. You feel resentful if you go along and your mate feels resentful if you agree and then do something else. These folks miss the point. *Good listening, not agreement, is a better first step.*

Make sure each of you has a full turn to talk before you propose a solution. You *each* need to feel that you have said all you need to say before you try problem solving, especially if you are dealing with a hot issue. Ask how your partner feels about any potential plan before proposing it as a solution. "When you have tried (old stuff) in the past, how did it work?" "Have you considered (new plan or plans)?"

Do not offer solutions unless and until you are asked. Men are famously accused of this, but many women do this as well when they feel attacked or just want to be helpful. *Listening is not about you and your solutions.* Those are distractions that will interrupt the listening process. **Listen first; solutions *much* later.** Maybe not even later. If you are primarily trying to build communication and not solve a problem, let your partner fully express a concern. You may not both need a turn. Listening may be all that's needed for a job issue or boredom with staying home or wishing that you could quit your job. Even when you are asked for solutions, double-check first that you understand the whole problem by restating what you think they are asking.

Stay focused on your partner; don't make it about you. Anything that is about you, including your very interesting opinions, is a distraction and will either shut the person down or prolong the negative part of the discussion. Your solution is probably brilliant, but that isn't listening. When your partner is upset, even if your name is in the story a lot, remember the issue is his/hers not yours.

Ask for what you need so you can listen well. Many upset wives talk in long complicated paragraphs with footnotes and examples. One trick that therapists use is to ask a long-winded talker to put a complaint in one sentence. Sometimes I teach guys to ask their wives to "Please, boil down the main idea of what you just said to three sentences or less so I make sure I have your core point."

Recognize the right times to listen. Notice when you and your spouse communicate best, and try to arrange those times together regularly. Sometimes healing listening isn't required. When your spouse is asking you to please hand them a diaper, hand them a diaper. Nobody asking directions or giving directions wants you to reflect their feelings. Listening is hardest to do when someone is upset with you. Yet that is the best time to listen. Good listening really calms and soothes your partner.

When you just can't listen, make a plan to talk. If you just can't listen (because you are watching a great game on TV or the baby is screaming), say something like "This sounds really important and I would like to talk about it when I can really focus on you. Can we talk about this when the baby is asleep?" As one mom said, "When my husband is too crabby, I say, 'We'd better talk about this later.' He doesn't necessarily apologize later, but when we try to talk again I can tell he has regrouped and we do better."

If your partner is screaming and you just can't think, leave a note that you want to talk when both of you are calm. Write in a journal, call a counselor, or talk to a happily married friend before you talk again, but talk as you promised.

When the rules don't apply. If your partner is drunk, listening is a waste of time. Tell him or her that you will talk tomorrow. If you are afraid for your physical safety, leave and then call or have a friend call and say you will contact them when you feel safe to do so. Even if the marriage can't be repaired, your life will be easier if you treat your partner with respect while you take the time you need to get focused.

Teaching Your Partner to Actively Listen to You

Many people, especially women, long to have their partner listen to them. My basic belief is that you can only change your-

SALLY FORTH By Greg Howard and Craig MacIntosh

self. You can't change someone else. However active listening is so important to the long-term health of the marriage that if someone really, really wants to work on having their partner actively listen to them, I try to teach them how to change the way they talk so their partner naturally listens. The hard part is focusing on changing *yourself* enough that your partner learns to listen. People would rather teach their partner to active listen. In other words, now that you know how to listen, let's review how to talk so you can be heard.

Make sure you have eye contact. If he is watching TV, there will be no active listening. If he is reading, he may listen but you won't feel heard and healed, and he is likely to miss large chunks of what you have said. Wait for or ask for full, undivided attention.

Pick a time free from distractions. My husband, Neil, is naturally gregarious, outgoing and easily distracted. Like most men, he hates talking about anything that might be a problem in our relationship or with the kids, both of whom he considers perfect. He can, however, tolerate such a discussion if he is also doing something else, which is why I discovered I loved skiing. For twenty minutes on a two-person lift, I can talk about an issue and he can't jump out. Walks, car rides, and dinner alone can have a similar effect. However—and this is important—don't *always and only* have serious talks at these times or your partner will begin to avoid these once fun times.

Start with positive feedback and mention shared values. Remember the five-to-one rule. People listen better if they are in a good mood, so prime them with kindness. If you want to talk about increasing his contribution to the housework, make five positive statements first. Talk first about how hard you know he works making money for the family and what a great daddy he is. Joke about how the clutter drives you both crazy and mention how great you both seem to enjoy when things are picked up, if that is true. Or say how much more serene and easygoing you feel when things are picked up like they were before the baby, or last week when you both had cleaned up before company. Then say something like, "I hesitate to bring this up because I think you will take it as a criticism and not be able to really listen to me about this. But I really need to talk about my feelings about the clutter since the baby arrived."

Learn to use "I" messages. "I feel really overwhelmed by all the clutter we have now," clearly works better than: "Why don't you start helping more!" Similarly these messages, while not as good, are still a much softer startup: "I can't relax when the house is messy, but I don't want to be one of those naggy women who complains all the time, or a pushy wife who throws out stuff without asking." "I don't want to make threats either like clean it up or else." "I feel like a maid with a master's degree when I go around picking up all our stuff. I don't want to be resentful, but I am."

Learn the difference between "Change Requests," "Problems" and "Weather Reports." *Weather Reports:* Sometimes you just need to talk through your feelings. You want to know your partner hears you; you want some sympathy and maybe a few questions. You do not want the other person to take it personally or feel criticized. You don't want them to fix anything. That's a weather report. No action required.

Problem: A problem, on the other hand, is something you want advice about. A problem is an issue that needs a discussion, some proposed solutions and a plan of action. Problems may involve the kids, friends or family, but usually are not directed at your partner.

Change request: A change request is an action item. You are unhappy and you need something to change that involves your partner. You may or may not know the solution, and you may or may not need to change yourself to make it better but something in your life needs improvement.

Teach your partner the difference between weather reports, problems, and change requests. This is a complicated lesson and you need to focus on this concept alone without trying to apply it to several issues. When you signal upcoming discussions by labeling them as a weather report, or a problem, your partner will feel safer if they clearly know what is expected.

Label for your partner whether this is a weather report or an issue. Say up front whether an issue is a weather report, a problem for you, or something that needs to change. When you have a change request, say, "I have an issue. I want something to change about this." Try to phrase complaints as issues. Ask for help ahead of time so you don't need to make complaints after the fact. For example, imagine his family is coming for their annual weeklong visit and you know you felt like a house slave the last time they visited. You might sit down or take a walk together before the visit and say, "Last time your parents were here I felt really exhausted. I wonder if we could plan to make it easier for me and everyone this time?"

Let your partner know if you want advice by saying, "This is a problem. I want advice about this." If it is a weather report: "I need some talk time to get my feelings out about something."

Pick just one issue. Only complain about one thing a week, and raise one issue at a time. Figure out what your complaint of the week is and only address that. This will be difficult. Some people ask, "One issue is okay if it is big like. 'I wish you would stop drinking.' But can I have more issues if they are little like,

'You always buy the wrong coffee filters'? The answer is *no*. Your partner still hears coffee filters as a complaint. You need to at least improve the coffee filters issue to the level of a curiosity: "Why do you buy these coffee filters?" or a problem that you need advice about, or give it up for this week. When you are so happy that your only complaint this week is about coffee filters, you will have a very happy marriage.

One complaint a week is enough and a good goal to shoot for. (Even though, as my husband will tell you, I will probably never achieve it!) But one complaint a week is an important guideline if you actually want to encourage listening. People quickly stop listening to someone they feel complains a lot. For the same reason, try to keep bad weather reports or serious venting to only once a week also.

Good weather reports can occur any time. Asking for advice—but not giving it—can happen any time as well.

One Thought at a Time. When you figure out what the single hot issue is, decide how to present it in *three sentences or less*. Be sure the first two are about appreciation and gratitude. You can add a fourth, if it is also positive. "You do so much around the house and you are great with the kids. But I still feel overwhelmed with the mess. I am wondering if we can try to get the house picked up each time before we leave for the park so that it is clean when we get back. I think it would be soothing to come back to a clean place." Be careful to stick to one issue and not start talking about the remodeling that you want to do after the house is cleaned up. Keeping to three short, focused sentences avoids this problem.

After each thought wait for a response or request feedback. You need to know what your listener heard. If you say, "I don't want to just throw your stuff out." And what he hears is, "I am going to throw your stuff out," listening is over. He won't hear anything else you say. You will need to interpret what he is hearing and adjust the message so that he hears a clear nonthreatening message. When you say, "I said I am *not* going to throw your stuff out, but I don't want to have to nag you either," you gently refocus on your message.

When Your Spouse Offers a Solution: Say, "Thanks, honey, but I need more talk time to figure out what feels right for me first." If he says, "Let's hire a housekeeper," don't say, "We can't afford it," because it brings up money issues, which is a distraction and may be his or her hot button. Say, "I am not sure a housekeeper would help what I am feeling," unless, of course, you want a housekeeper. The point is don't argue. Stay focused.

Assume good intentions. Even when your partner is an inattentive listener, give him or her the benefit of the doubt. When we see the best in people, they often rise to the occasion. Even if their words sting, remember they love you and consider the possibility that they are unskilled at communicating or that they are feeling badly and so are expressing themselves poorly.

Accept unsolvable differences. Some therapists and couples believe that if partners are at different ends of a continuum—like willingness to ask versus persistent asking or craving neatness versus being comfortable with clutter—that they unconsciously got together so they could each learn from the other. The trick is to learn to work the issue out between you and strengthen your marriage rather than battle it out. An even better trick is to learn to love and laugh at your differences, to see clearly the advantages of the other's annoying habits, and not simply focus on the disadvantages and on trying to change the other person. For example, clutter bugs are often fun, creative, and spontaneous. Neatniks are often reliable and well organized.

Consider a marriage where one partner is an only child and is used to being regarded as the golden child. The other partner comes from a childhood family that tolerates and uses a great deal of criticism under the guise of "standards." They could argue about his lack of standards and her excessive criticism. They could have conflict over how each washes the counters and performs various chores. This would create a great deal of marital strife and conflict and worry for the kids. In many cases, this fundamental rift could push Dad to retreat to a job across the country, or simply to work long hours at a job where he feels more appreciated. Mom could retreat to charity work and involvement with the kids. Or the two of them could focus on which family traits would make their kids happy and productive. And they could laugh together about the fact that nothing they do will matter because their child may be hard-wired to be just who they are!

Basically, teaching your partner active listening is training yourself to talk so that your partner wants to listen. Both of you will feel better for it. Active listening heals the listener as well as the speaker. By listening, and not jumping in to help, you really hear and feel what your partner feels. When both partners work on being better listeners and better communicators, the combination is powerful. Even the thorniest issues can be worked out in ways that make each partner feel considered, cared for, and most important, heard.

Listening Tips

- Give full eye contact.

- Repeat back the core of what is being said in neutral words.

- Assume your partner has good intentions even when the words hurt.

- Repeat word for word if the speaker seems upset.

- Wait to be invited: Don't ask questions, agree, or offer opinions until your partner has finished saying everything they have to say on that topic and invites a response from you.

21

Fight Like the Windows Are Open

When couples fight, most partners will say things they wouldn't dream of saying to anyone but their partner, even to someone they do not like. In the heat of battle, many people feel they are fighting for their survival, and they feel compelled to respond to defend themselves. Fighting like the windows are open means speaking your piece effectively without hurting your partner or provoking a vicious counterattack. In other words, fight like the neighbors can hear you. When you fight with kids in the house, they are listening and learn your good and bad habits. When they hear tension in adult voices, even infants will burst into tears. As they grow to understand language, toddlers and preschoolers become more sensitive.

Yet, couples need to disagree to be happy. As I said before, one research study actually correlated a husband's ability to effectively express discomfort or "disgust" with long-term marital happiness. Happy couples need to learn to disagree in a way that not only doesn't harm their marriage, but that is also fun and a little playful. Fighting well is a great gift to both yourselves and your kids, and one worth fighting for.

Almost by definition when you are fighting, as opposed to discussing or disagreeing, you have lost your mind somewhere along the way. At home, couples break all sorts of communication rules that they wouldn't consider breaking elsewhere. I hope to teach you some ways to gain perspective, prevent senseless and repetitive fights, and perhaps even help you learn to laugh at yourselves as you fight.

Consider one husband's description of a common fight.

> My wife is always trying to perfect our relationship and especially me. "I wish you would help me more around here and keep up your end of things. I feel like a maid on the weekends while you play with the kids." Sometimes I answer sarcastically so she will just drop the whole subject: "If you were earning a salary as a maid, you'd probably have to do a better job." It's mean, but I just want to relax sometimes, not always run around cleaning. I would rather do something fun together than discuss our relationship.

Most everyone recognizes a bad fight. This typical fight is bad because the wife assumes the problem is her partner's fault. He recognizes the problem but doesn't want to talk about it like this. He responds with something mean to deflect her away from the problem. They manage to break several rules in just a few sentences and end up feeling bad and going nowhere. Good fights and good discussions should strengthen both of you and the marriage.

Often fights at home have a scripted aspect. They are repetitive, and each of you takes the same roles over and over again. To break up these chronic fights it helps to step back and figure out the pattern. Sometimes a friend or counselor can help you back away and see the part each of you plays in the drama.

Learn your partner's role and your own in most of your fights. Over the years I have given names to these fight roles, which I share with my clients to help them laugh at themselves and get a different perspective. I encourage them to recognize the patterns in their fights, and then together we find ways to solve problems and approach the drama differently. See if you can recognize any of your fights here. In all these conflict patterns, nothing is ever settled and the same fight is revisited repeatedly. However, there are many opportunities to start over and have a happier ending if couples could see how they are stuck.

Lawyers in Love. Lawyers in love argue logically—like that matters in a feeling discussion. They are usually quite good at it. Very logically, they argue that their relationship would be better if the other person came home when he or she said, had sex more often, or helped out more with the kids. And they are right. The problem is that their partner feels demeaned and not one bit like cooperating. They both end up feeling miserable and frustrated.

Would you rather be right or be happy? It is far more effective to try to change yourself than your partner. So I must teach them to reflect upon and change their own behavior first.

Generally there are two versions of lawyers in love. *Civil lawyers* in love are quite calm and cold when they argue, although they can manage to sneer, belittle, and blame. *Litigators in love* are passionate and dramatic. They cross-examine each other and set traps. "Ah-ha, see. Gotcha!" Both civil lawyers and litigators are equally miserable, although litigators tend to have more fiery divorces. Sometimes these partners have law degrees, but many articulate, devastating "lawyers in love" function scathingly without any legal training. Civil lawyers married to litigators will often tell them if they just fought more civilly everything would be fine. Litigators say that their civil partner doesn't understand passion. And so their fights continue.

Legal Remedy. There are three simple ways to derail lawyers. (1) Recognize that litigators feel like five-year-olds inside—powerless and vulnerable. Talk to them as gently as and sympathetically as you would a worried child and all the huff goes out of them. (2) Say, "You look like you need a hug, come sit here and let's start over." While some "lawyers" balk at this, most melt. (3) Take a time-out and write down your complaint in the same kind but firm words that you might say to a friend. This eliminates the belittling tones that flood a partner. Making yourself write down a complaint forces you to consider whether it is really important, and not just your way of shooting off a trivial complaint.

Princess (or the Prince) and the Peace Seeker. The Princess always has a clear idea of what she wants and is used to being attended. The Peace Seeker, a.k.a. the conflict avoider, wishes to keep the peace. He knows the Princess will stomp her foot if she isn't happy or yell in an embarrassing way, so he tries to maneuver about so she won't be disappointed. Often she complains that he won't communicate. He doesn't communicate because he doesn't want to disappoint her.

She usually requests therapy to learn how to communicate with a partner who retreats . . . and retreats . . . and retreats or just ignores her requests and needs. The Peace Seeker often feels like a peon and forgets to come to a scheduled date or reports that they have to work at the last minute to avoid unpleasantness (and therapy appointments). He often treats her like a princess because he sees her as especially beautiful or talented or both. Yet he wonders why, if he married the Princess, he hasn't become a king by now. He secretly thinks he should be treated as a king and that she should make as many attempts to soothe and guard his feelings as he does for her. Yet he is constantly subjected to her whims and criticized for not meeting her standards or anticipating her needs.

Connecting with a Peace Seeker. The Peace Seeker has great difficulty saying what he or she wants since they have been trained to make everyone else happy. Then they explode. Prevent fights with a Peace Seeker by asking what they want often. When they say, "What do you want to do?" don't answer first. Instead, learn to say, "I want to do what my honey really wants to do!" Then mean what you say and follow through even if it is a very unappealing idea.

Don't demand their help. Instead, ask them to consider the problem and tell you what they would ideally like to contribute? Praise whatever they offer enthusiastically. Often they will continue stepping up and do more than you ask. The best way to get their assistance is to ask them what they think needs to be done and what part they want to play. "What would you like the first birthday party to be like and who would you really like to have come?" Most frequently the Peace Seeker will say, "It doesn't matter," while thinking, "You are going to do what you want anyway." Or they'll say: "I don't know. What do you want to do?" Then, if you are trying to change the pattern, you will say, "I want to do something that you are excited about doing." Then, be sure to do it or at least incorporate the ideas you have elicited.

Prince and the Former Princess. Frequently the Prince makes a lot of money, and the wife is exceptionally attractive or much younger. Together they decide that it will be best if she stays home with the kids. She is used to getting a certain amount of attention for being attractive, vivacious, and competent. Now she stays home and usually gets considerably less social attention. If she was formerly successful in a career field, she feels even more isolated. He doesn't feel as competitive for her attention as he did when he was wooing her so he often says that things just aren't that exciting after marriage. He believes they aren't supposed to be exciting and is puzzled by her complaint, seeing it as irrational. Both want to settle down and be taken care of by the other. He dreams about coming home to an adoring wife who frequently says how much she appreciates how hard he works, and who wants to do little favors for him as his mother did.

She feels lonely, and as a Former Princess, feels poorly attended by her Prince. He feels poorly cared for and retreats from much contact except that he seeks out sex in which she now has no interest because she is chasing a child all day. She feels like she has been demoted from princess to scullery maid. He has no idea what she is feeling or why she is so upset because he feels they have an agreement and he is carrying his part out to the letter, by earning money. She finds his behavior confusing, insensitive, and appalling—anything but the partnership she expected.

At first she may try being sweet, kind, and engaging. However, as a former Princess, she knows how to give orders and how to throw one heck of a fit when she gets fed up with the treatment she is receiving. She may resort to becoming a screamer and frequently fantasize about escaping this miserable marriage for something more satisfying. Even though she loves her kids, she fantasizes about going back to work. She would to like to wave her hand airily in her husband's face and say, as he does when problems come up, "I need to go to work now." Then leave him to feed the squabbling kids. He may be a very attentive father or a very inattentive one, depending on how he sees the original agreement and his role.

The Magic Wands. The Prince, the Princess, and the Former Princess all have a similar underlying problem. As children their achievements, either good looks or good deeds or successes, were more important than their feelings. Active listening, carefully and sympathetically, is extremely healing to them because no one has ever cared how they felt. The best response is a big hug and "Let's start over," followed by lots of attention and concern.

Never give into a Prince or Princess when they are stomping their foot. Wait until they are calm again. As children, they were forced to give in to their parents' solutions and do the "right" thing. So they expect their partner and children to do the same. Take time to discuss compromises and possible outcomes in moments of calm. Take complaints under advisement and consider them very seriously. Resolving their drama often requires a Prince or Princess to reconsider the original contract and decide how they can each contribute to make it work.

The Prince and Princess both respond well to praise. "My, how clever you are for making so much money (or being so beautiful or handsome)!" Princes love to help damsels in distress and are often quite helpful when their partner is having a bad day as long as it has nothing to do with them.

Meet the In-Laws. One of life's great mysteries is how often our partners can get us to act out the role of the opposite-sex parent they had growing up. That role may be a Prince, Peace Seeker, Lawyer, Rule Maker, or simply Angry One. By doing whatever they did to protect themselves from a difficult parent, they provoke us to react and act like that parent.

Managing the In-Law Problem. The solution is to remind your partner how different you are from his or her parent. When you find yourself acting like your husband's mother, you know you have played out his fantasy of what he expects a woman will be like, whether it is you or not. Often in these fights you will have a distinct feeling that this is *not* me! A woman said to me, "I love sex but when he talks like that, he makes it sound like I have never liked sex and never will and then I don't feel like having sex with him."

Try to be curious when your partner is upset. Try to figure out what is happening rather than reacting. Notice when you are about to do something that you told yourself you would never do. Then learn to act in a surprising way that doesn't confirm whatever negative expectation or preconceived role your partner has for you. If he or she expects you to blow up and yell, don't. If they expect you not to help, help and then ask them how it feels when you follow through. Eventually they will begin to notice the differences between you and the old parent role.

Stage Your Fights. Poor fight scripts are like a Greek tragedy where the marriage dies at the end. In this play, the lines are repeated over and over until the players can anticipate each other's responses perfectly. The actors or partners have stopped listening as soon as the play starts and each has little awareness of how the other actor feels while playing the part.

The best fights are more like improvisational theater. One person is upset and initiates the dialogue. The other listens and helps the skit along, taking their cue from the partner until they reach a thorough understanding of each other's feelings and a workable solution.

Switch Roles: Understanding your Partners Script. The best way to switch roles is to actively listen to your partner so well that you can play your partner's part perfectly. Most people can play the words out but cannot understand the feelings underneath. Partners can reverse roles more easily in therapy or counseling. I ask people to role-play their partner with me so that they can feel what that person is feeling. I play the upset partner's part in a reasonable, nonblaming way. The upset person feels soothed because I articulate their feelings, using the rules below and an understanding of their feelings from the scripts above.

The other person responds differently because I am presenting the partner's story (and feelings) in a way that doesn't attack them. They usually turn and say to their partner, "Is *that* how you feel?" The partner nods an emphatic yes, relieved to hear what they are feeling presented in a way that seems reasonable and clear and doesn't upset the listening partner. Then I take the other partner's role and demonstrate that it is reasonable from their point of view, too. Now it is the listening partner's opportunity to feel understood and the first partner's chance to see the argument in a new light.

I demonstrate that no matter who changes the interaction of their usual script or argument, the other partner responds differently, and the conversation takes a better turn. Each feels better understood if they present what they are feeling differently.

Getting in character. Before you play a part though, you need to understand the underlying feelings of your partner. Naming the roles helps if it helps you understand what lies beneath your partner's feelings.

Lawyers in Love, from the examples above, often see situations as unfair and believe someone is trying to take advantage of them. They believe their partner undervalues, underestimates or disrespects them.

Such a partner often takes the role of blamer or shamer: "Were you where you were supposed to be at the moment in question?" "Why didn't you change the baby?" He or she feels that no one sees how hard his or her job is. They feel that with enough blaming, shaming or complaining you will finally see how hard their job is and be of more help. They were blamed and shamed as children so that they would learn to follow-up on their responsibilities. Now they are trying to help you learn to carry out yours.

Rule Makers, who are often lawyers in love, believe that you have to do it this way because it is the *right* way. They have created safety and order in their own life with rules and want to extend that safety and order to the partner and to their children. They think, "You *have* to do it this way, because if you don't chaos and bad outcomes will follow." They believe that people who won't work harder to have more order are out to hurt and sabotage them.

Princesses, Princes, and Litigators and various drama Kings and Queens often feel that no one is listening. "I am dying over here and you can't hear me." They exaggerate, repeat, raise their voice, hiss with intensity, set traps, and genuinely feel that they will never be heard. One Princess, turned scullery maid, pitched her purse out the car window on the freeway in a fit of anger. I was never sure whether she was out of control angry, tried to hit him or was merely demonstrating he was too uptight about money. She and her husband decided it made perfect sense to get the highway patrol to run a traffic break for a twelve-lane free-way so they could search for it. He could be the Peace Seeker and she could feel that she got the royal treatment. For a short while they felt closer. They didn't find it and didn't solve their problem. In the uproar, they never discussed the real issue, which was about how they managed their child and handled money.

Princesses and Princes often have no idea that what they are saying or doing actually hurts or upsets their partner. They feel the partner doesn't care. If your feelings are hurt, they genuinely feel they have acted with the best of intentions and only done what it took to get your attention. When they feel heard they quickly become calm.

Hearing their stories, I am reminded of this story about a prince in action: A patient bursts into his psychiatrist's office waving a gun at the doctor. The doctor promptly throws up on his desk. The patient runs around the desk, horrified, and com-forts the doc saying, "Doc! I only meant to get your attention. I didn't mean to scare you." The Princess only means to get your attention, she doesn't want you to leave. Princesses are generally soothed with attention and acts of kindness, such as getting them a glass of water and asking how they feel. Very good active listening can lead to real problem solving.

The *Belittler* is often an unappreciated Prince or Princess who, with a sneer and a word, makes you feel like you are shrinking. This person usually thinks that you believe you are better than he or she, and decides you need to be cut down to size.

The *Peace Seeker* who retreats and retreats and retreats

wants life to be fun and to be peaceful. Peace Seekers perceive suggestions as criticisms of their behavior, the opening gambit to a fight, and a chance to disappoint. They just want to love and be loved and avoid unpleasantness. In general their partners were first attracted to them because they were so agreeable, adaptable, and charming. People often seek them out.

They can't understand why their partner gets so mad at them when everyone else likes them so much. Others do see them as quite generous because they love to *volunteer* to help others. When directly asked to help, however, they will often balk and refuse in startling ways. Or they will simply agree to a request to avoid a fight, and then simply not do what they said they would do. Their spouses often see them as passive aggressive. Peace Seekers often feel that their wants and desires were ignored or punished as children. Usually they have great difficulty expressing what they want and feel quite vulnerable. If or when they do risk hinting at what they might like, they often experience their partner and others as ignoring them because the hint is so subtle that the concealed request passes unnoticed.

In-Law Act. People who act out a role from their family of origin are usually completely unconscious of what they are doing. They are defending against something they anticipate, which doesn't exist in the present situation. The more that you follow the rules of fighting like the windows are open and use active listening and make polite requests, the more obvious it will become that their reaction has nothing to do with you. The interesting thing about these roles is that people who act out their own old issues can actually get partners to play the reciprocal role. Once you realize you are playing an unconscious role or opposite one, you have taken the first step to rewriting a new script.

Rewriting the Script. After each player understands their role and their partner's, and is ready to change, we can begin to rewrite their script using the following rules.

Rules for Marital Misunderstandings

All of the rules I am going to write about I have broken, often without disastrous results.

Learn to apologize. When you break the rules apologize quickly and either take a break or move on.

Always make full eye contact. In improvisational comedy and in marriage, making eye contact is the way we say I am here and I am paying attention to you. I care and you matter to me. It is a grounding mechanism that says we are in the same conversation. Many couples resolve issues without further discussion with good, loving eye contact.

Start with five positives. I always reiterate what we as the couple value and have in common before I move on to the hard part of confronting the problem. In good fights I start by establishing why I care about my partner enough to talk about a difficult subject.

Avoid your partner's hot buttons. One couple was struggling with bitter fights early in their marriage when their therapist asked them to each make a list of their partner's vulnerabilities and hot buttons. They double-checked the list to make sure they had every trigger point on the list, and then agreed never to use them again. Now they are very happily married and rarely fight. They attribute their clean fight style to simply avoiding each other's hot buttons.

Attack the problem, not the person. Don't try to change your partner. Remember they married you because they thought you thought they were perfect. Instead invite them to help you solve the problem. When you each start to repeat your positions, say, "Remember, we agree about this, this, and this. I am on your team. What can we do together about this problem?"

Use a soft start-up, not a harsh one. Think before you speak. Then think again. Researchers have demonstrated that they can predict in the first three minutes of a disagreement whether a couple will have a good resolution. They simply watch whether the couple has a harsh or soft start-up. Either the words or the tone of voice can be harsh. I often ask people to listen to themselves and see if they would speak to a close friend, a boss, a housekeeper or a child the same way they are talking to their spouse. A gentle start-up avoids flooding.

Avoid flooding. Most men become upset and flooded with emotion well before most women as I said earlier. Many men are overwhelmed simply by an annoyed tone of voice. Their hearts pound, and they are flooded with adrenaline and fight or flight chemicals. They no longer think clearly. They either want to flee or fight to make a point. Useful problem solving is over. This means that, in an argument, the woman is going on with her discussion well past the point where a man is emotionally present and able to comprehend or remember what she is saying. If you were to ask the partners to repeat back what each has said, you would quickly see how little is heard in this agitated state. A soft start-up, slowing the conversation down to a few sentences at a time and using soft voices or putting a problem in writing dramatically improves understanding and reduces fighting.

Plan time-out breaks together. When you are not fighting and are both calm, go over some ground rules that are comfortable for you both. Some people say simply, "Let's discuss this later." Some take a walk or go to the gym. Some hug. Some use truce triggers discussed in Chapter 8. The key in all cases is that both partners know they will come back and try again.

Throw down your guns. Don't threaten divorce or separation and don't use any labels like lazy, messy, critical, fast-talking, hypersensitive, liar or even in the kindest possible terms compare their behavior to detested behavior of someone in the family they grew up in. Threats create a wedge between you even if they temporarily force a solution.

Skip the Greek chorus. Don't say that you know several other people who agree with your assessment of their behavior.

Recognize good intentions. In marital requests, consider how different it sounds if you say, "Our relationship makes me feel so protected and connected, I wish we could find more time together." Compare this to "Why can't you schedule more time at home? Don't you care?" In role-plays, I often highlight the good intentions of the person I am role-playing and the good intentions of the partner.

There are no mistakes, only opportunities. Find a silver lining. In a marriage issue, if you attribute good intentions to your partner's blooper, the relationship gets on track more easily. So if your partner indicates that she is afraid you will turn out just like your father and leave the family when your son turns sixteen, even though he is now only six months old, you might say, "I am glad you can share your fears with me. I am really curious: What made you worry about that today?"

Use your truce triggers. Find a key word that signals, we don't have to have this fight. Some people use a hug, a wink, a word, a phrase, or a funny face. Anything works as long as it is your personal signal.

Trust your partner and take chances. If you spin a safety net of understanding for your partner and thank them when they listen to and support you, your exchanges become emotionally safe. You'll have more fun together. "I know you are trying to be efficient, helpful, and thoughtful when you run errands on the way home. And you are helpful. But I miss you and want to see you sooner. Can we reorganize how we do that?" Compare this to landing on your partner's head with, "Why do you always stop on the way home? Are you trying to avoid being with us? Don't you want to see your child? What kind of mother (or father) are you anyway?"

Get a little goofy. Take a tip from comedy experts and go with whatever material comes up. Work it. If your partner says you are a slob, say "oink, oink" and grin engagingly.

Be truthful and extremely sincere. Have fun, but the sincerity makes it work. After the "Oink, oink." say with a sincerely concerned and contrite face, "What are we going to do with me?" Don't say, "I am not!" Even if you aren't a pig, this scene is about his or her upset and not yours.

Do not let even a hint of a smile or the slightest sound of sarcasm come from you. Act like someone who doesn't understand punishment and only relates to instruction. But, if you respond with, "I am not a pig!" or "I cleaned out my car last week and what about your tool bench," the argument starts circling down a sinkhole and nothing gets resolved.

Don't deny. If he says, "You are always late!" say, "That must be so disappointing for you!" And you might add, "What do you do while you wait for me?" Don't change the subject. Instead, focus on what it feels like to wait for you. Give eye contact and show that you care about your partner's distress. Become an active listener. The conversation will be more interesting.

Ask for what you want instead of describing what you don't want. Saying what you don't want is whining, negative, and saps the other person's energy and motivation to talk to you. If you want to understand this idea better, simply stand, close your eyes and repeat, "No, no, no!" to yourself in your childhood language. Repeat the exercise, saying "Yes, yes, yes!" Many people are surprised how they react inside their body.

Compromise on unsolvable problems. As most people live together they learn that they react very differently to some issues. Learn to work together in ways that protect each person's vulnerabilities. For example, Bill hates talking about money and it often worries Sue, so they agreed to talk about it only on Sundays. That way Bill doesn't fear being shanghaied when he wants to relax, and Sue can count on having a chance to obsess about it once a week, even though she sometimes forgets her turn. She confesses she sometimes cheats and brings money up in an e-mail when she has forgotten her turn, but she titles the e-mail "financial check" so he doesn't read it until he is ready.

THE POSITIVE GAME

I first started playing the positive game with my kids. We first called it the "No Nots" game, but that didn't match the spirit of the game. We have various versions, but the person who can make all comments and requests without using a negative word wins. My son liked to set traps for me. So, for example, if Xander says, "Do you want to buy me an ice cream?" I must say, "I prefer that you have ice cream after dinner." Likewise, if I want something done, instead of saying, "Why don't you pick up in here?" I must say, "Please start picking up now." In the drop-dead version of the game, the person who uses the first negative loses. Sometimes we play for the most positive points or the lowest negative points during a trip to the store.

I use this with clients who are so discouraged about their marriage that they only have negative talk about what is wrong. I teach them to ask for what they want instead of what they don't want. Instead of saying, "I don't think you find me attractive because we never have sex anymore!", which produces a defensive barrage and no action, I ask them to rephrase it to say exactly what they want, as in, "How can we get some quiet time together to have sex?"

Pick a solution that is positive and countable. When you get around to picking a solution for a problem in your marriage, try to make the solution something that you do rather than that you do not do. And make it an action that you can count. For example, a goal like "helping more" is hard to count. A countable goal would be if the wife agrees to take the trash out every day. In exchange, the husband could agree to do two diaper changes. If either one falls down on the deal, they owe that job plus another duty, so the problem is not ignored and both partners are involved and accountable.

Check the solution for comfort. When you have gotten this far, now ask: Can you each picture yourselves doing what you agreed to do? Does the solution address the problem? "Would you feel better in a week if we did it that way?" If the solution involves, for example, making requests in a different way, check how the new way of asking feels and ask how your partner will respond. After you have a comfortable solution, decide on a trial period for a week or two.

Pick a time to check in with each other about how it worked. When couples in therapy are working on problems and solutions, the next session is the obvious time to check in. In real life, I encourage people to make a regular time to check in with their partners and make points by inquiring how they feel the issues they've discussed are working out. Start each check-in by congratulating yourselves on successes first.

Resolving marital misunderstandings seems awfully slow when I describe it on paper. However, generally people resolve emotional issues slowly. This slowness provides a safety net and prevents flooding and endless repetitive arguments. And when you go slowly and carefully, you are more likely to reach a true resolution so that you never need to have that fight again.

Often, but not always, couples who come to see a therapist have fairly comfortable disagreements with people at work and elsewhere. In other words, they already know how to fight. They just blow up at home. I have even asked couples who come to therapy to fight politely in front of me, to audiotape their fights at home, and bring them in. I don't plan to listen to the tapes, but want them to see that they can be more civil at home, too, and *they will be* if they think someone's listening.

Summary: My best advice about how to fight like the windows are open boils down to these three tips: (1) Learn how to fight well. (2) Learn when not to fight. (3) Marry someone who knows how to fight civilly. Then concentrate on fixing your own mistakes, because that is all you can fix, and there will be plenty of those. Nobody does this perfectly, but the good news is you can learn a few rules to make your discussions good and your fights clean. Gradually, as you spend more time together, your fights may even become fun.

Tips for fun fights

If You have a Complaint, Suggestion, or Request:

- Make fun of the problem, not the person.

- Make fun of yourself, but not your partner or your kids.

- Commiserate about the problem if you can.

- When your partner makes a blooper and looks remorseful, be gracious or say nothing. This can pay big dividends next time.

- 'Fess up to your own part in the problem first.

- Try to talk about a problem situation just before it may come up again.

- Choose your problem wisely, no more than one a week, if you can. Write the others down for another week.

- Sincerely compliment your partner on several wonderful and amazing attributes before you try to bring up a problem.

- Highlight (exaggerate) all your shared values before addressing the problem.

- Keep it light. Come up with as many silly solutions as serious solutions.

- Ask what your partner thinks is a good solution and what he wants to be responsible for.

If Your Partner Has a Complaint:

- Give full attention and be concerned. Big eyes and sincere, full attention often help resolve the problem quickly.

- Strive for a curious rather than a frustrated or angry tone.

- Try to reflect the depth and extent of the problem. Restate your partner's feelings and the problem as best you can and as often as necessary. Then ask, "Do I understand completely?"

- Ask, "Is there any more I missed?" Or "What is it I am not getting?"

- If you think your partner does the same thing they are accusing you of, ask them in a sincere, if confused, way how what they do is different than what you do.

- Ask all the possible things they have considered or tried to resolve the problem and any other ideas they might have to solve the problem.

- Suggest goofy solutions as well as serious solutions only after your partner feels you understand well enough and says he or she is ready to try and look at the solutions.

- Check back to see how you are doing in resolving the complaint. You get many, many emotional points for that.

22

Taking Care of Yourself

After the birth of your baby, time for yourself is the first thing to go. Sometimes the reaction to losing time for yourself comes right away. Other times the explosion comes years later. Nevertheless, frustration and irritability inevitably follow when you don't care for yourself.

As a new parent, allow yourself to be a little sad about the carefree life you left behind. Think about what you miss most from your old life and give yourself a little of whatever you miss if you can. Remember, your new life will have new joys, but will not be like the life you had before. So celebrate what you like in your new life. Granted, much of what is new in your life you will not be able to control, because the baby's needs will dictate what happens. See if you can learn to enjoy not having control. Enjoy using the baby as an excuse not to do something you didn't want to do anyway! (I secretly loved telling people I had to leave a party early because of the kids' baby-sitter so I could indulge my need to be a zombie in the evening.)

Giving to a child is easy at first, just as giving to your spouse is easy in the honeymoon phase. But if you don't take care of yourself, you will run out of energy for you, your partner and your child.

Many women suffer from a Cinderella complex and expect more help as they become more drained. Even if you are married to Prince Charming, he is unlikely to truly understand what you need unless you take the time to discover what you need yourself and tell him. And he is likely to be feeling overwhelmed and deprived of his special time. Likewise, many guys work intensely at moneymaking yet never ask if their own work or life gives them joy. This chapter is to encourage you to develop habits that protect you both from waking up one day a "stranger in a strange land"—your marriage.

The hardest step is choosing and creating personal time. I can almost guarantee that you will read the tips list and think, "Right. When am I going to do that!?" The true creativity comes in carving out the time. At first many moms start by trying to include the baby in their personal time. This isn't really personal time, though it is a testament to female creativity. My friend Pam uses the treadmill while feeding her placid and happy daughter. My friend Nicole delivers meals on wheels with her preschooler with the idea that her child is learning to volunteer.

Another new mom found a videotape called *Baby and Mom Yoga—Post Natal* at the library. The video focused on doing yoga with a newborn. Another mom has "Mom Time" when she comes home from work. She curls up for half an hour with each kid so she can recharge and enjoy her kids before plunging into dinner. She feels rested and recharged, and her kids get some welcome special time with Mom. These are wonderful activities that recharge both Mom and child. They reduce the chaos and

BABY BLUES By Rick Kirkman and Jerry Scott

create a nice routine. The problem is they don't create personal time for the parent.

To feel centered, each parent needs definite alone time set aside, with no little person in tow. Neil counted listening to blaring rock music alone in the car as his alone time. That wouldn't work for me. Many mothers tell me they find focus time by getting up early or staying up late, to be alone in the house on their computer or reading or exercising. This is a workable solution for many but has another significant snag. Sometimes the partner staying up has such a good time, he/she gets sleep deprived, irritable, and is anything but recharged. The other partner often feels avoided and left out if alone time means skipping couple time to cuddle before falling asleep or early in the morning.

Janice's husband would stay up late on the computer rather than come to bed. She felt that he was avoiding sex with her. Jeff's desire was to become a Web designer so he would no longer have to work in an uncreative job. He felt that the late hours were his only chance to create the work life he wanted without threatening their finances. He saw it as extra work he was doing for himself, the family, and his own sanity. When Janice understood his goal, she was able to be more comfortable. They decided to make certain nights his, hers and ours so they could each have private time as well as couple time. Jeff then set an alarm so he wouldn't work too long and be cranky. Another couple solved a similar problem with Dad cuddling with Mom until she fell asleep and then getting up to play on his computer.

Some of your recharge time needs to be energetic like exercise, and some needs to be quiet or spiritual, like meditating, listening to music, going to church, writing in a journal, or reading inspirational literature or a good novel.

A necessary part of self-nurturing for both partners is connecting with people other than your spouse, so that your spouse doesn't feel either required to, or drained by, trying to meet all your social needs. Socializing with others also makes you a more interesting partner. Sometimes connecting with people can be combined with exercise like walking with someone, or it could be attending church. I have a wonderful "bad girls" group. Every two months or so, we meet without kids, dress nicely and eat, drink, and talk all afternoon. I also love walking with my friend Suzy. We can laugh about the latest nightmare thing we have done as parents or puzzle about the idiosyncrasies of our spouses or kids.

Make sure that if golf or marathon shopping is your thing that your partner has as much time as you do for his or her activities, and that whatever you choose doesn't rob from your couple time together.

Leaving the Kids with Your Spouse: Depending how this is handled, this can actually enhance your relationship with each other and your relationship with your kids. As a general guideline, however, it only enhances up to a point. Too many traveling days away from your kids begins to feel like single parenting to the parent at home, and, to the traveler, like visitation in a divorce.

Many couples with one spouse who travels a lot send the other on a getaway at least once a year so that the one normally at home can experience time away from kids and the other can experience time alone with kids. The switch in roles gives them greater empathy for each other, and the kids sometimes love the change in routine. As one mom said, "My kids love when Daddy's on duty because he gives them soda. We all know it is okay on his watch, but not on mine. They can handle that we don't always have a united front." Not only can kids handle it; it models flexibility in their parents' relationship. She thought about it and added, "When I go away, the girls learn moms don't always stay home. I want them to have a life when they grow up, too!"

If you don't feel safe leaving your child alone with your spouse, this is a big warning sign of trouble in your relationship. This warning sign can mean a lot of things, none of them is good.

Bottom Line: If you don't feel safe leaving your kids with your spouse, you may want to consider why this is a problem. Can your kids be left with anyone else? Is there a major problem, like drug or alcohol abuse? Or is it just that you need to have things done your way? If you decide the problem is yours and not your spouse's, you will benefit from occasional time away from your kids. Meanwhile, the kids and your spouse will benefit from their special time together. However, if you really can't imagine doing this, you may want to closely consider what your partner and you each are doing to contribute to this lack of trust and find a way to remedy it.

As you can see from my examples, recharging self-care activities don't have to be wildly original. Anything that you really love to do and that makes you feel recharged works. I hope that through the work you have done in the other chapters, you will have created space for yourself.

Use self-nurturing time as an opportunity to carry out some of the exercises I have talked about in the preceding chapters. Reflect on the incredible changes that you and your marriage are experiencing.

Taking care of yourself and feeling content with your priorities and choices are terrific contributions to your couple relationship. Help your partner get the time he or she needs, and take the time you need. The key questions are: "Do we get the time we need as a couple? Do each of us get about the same time alone?" If the answer to both is yes, then you are taking good care of yourselves and each other.

Tips for Self-Nurturing

- Focus on healthy escapes. Go for a walk alone. Stay in the shower longer. Call a friend regularly to go for walks.

- Pamper yourself while your spouse takes the kids to the park or a movie. Have your hair or nails done. Get together with a friend and do each other's hair and nails. Get a massage. Read a book. Lock yourself in the bathroom, turn up the music, and take a bubble bath.

- Center yourself. Meditate. Practice yoga. Keep a journal.

- Exercise. Dance. Schedule a regular tennis game with a friend.

- Nap.

- Stimulate your creativity. Start a hobby, like quilting, painting, or making scrapbooks for the family.

- Rediscover an old hobby that has nothing to do with the baby.

- Rent a movie.

- Read spiritual books.

- Go to the mountains.

- Take a class and let your husband watch the baby.

- Watch the History Channel. (I never do this; but my husband loves it!)

- Go to an art museum alone or with a friend.

- Listen to your favorite music rather than kiddie music.

- Make a romantic meal to eat together when the kids are asleep.

- Get out and do volunteer work.

- Do nothing and don't feel guilty.

Protecting Your Marriage
with Warmth and Persuasion

JUMP START By Robb Armstrong

The formula for taking care of your marriage is fairly simple. The execution when you have young children is difficult. Happy marriages have certain critical markers. The trick is to establish routines that encourage these habits. John Gottman says that happy marriages need about five hours a week spent in the following ways:

Warm Good-Bye: Say good-bye with eye contact and affection. Make sure you know at least one significant activity that your spouse has to do that day—a meeting, sales presentation, finishing a chunk of work, a scheduled phone call with a friend or avoiding an annoying colleague.

Twenty-minute Reconnect. Make twenty to thirty minutes in your day to do a stress-reducing check-in about what is going on in each other's lives. Take turns being the star and either brag or complain about what is tough. Don't give unsolicited advice. Show genuine interest. Communicate understanding of bad feelings and good. "That's fabulous!" "You must feel so proud of yourself!" "I am so sorry she said that. What in the world makes her think that is okay." Let your partner know her feelings make sense to you. Use the same intensity you use for fights. Take your partner's side. See it entirely from your partner's point of view for this time. You can come back and talk about a different angle on it later. Let each other know that you are in this together and will support each other, all things you would do for a best friend and more.

Warm Greetings: Show your happiness when you see each other at the end of the day. Even if the baby is screaming or you are chasing the kids around, stop and share a hug. Give that special, "Hey, you!" glad-to-see-you hello that no one else gets.

Affection and Appreciation: Hug your partner or pat them when you walk by. Touch or cuddle when you are reconnecting. If you don't feel up to sex on a given day, do some special stroking or touching so that you feel connected when you do have energy for sex. Make sure you kiss each other before going to bed.

Weekly Date: Am I repeating myself? Yes, because it is important. Remember M.A.D. Plan some questions and discussions ahead of time. Think back to your dates when you first got together. Did you rehearse questions? Even if you didn't, you may need to now that you are tired and distracted. "How are you feeling about our decision that you stay home with the kids?" "Where do you think that we should take our next vacation? Have you thought about how different vacations will be with Tonya than by ourselves?" "How are you feeling about your job these days?" "You haven't mentioned Sam lately? Is that getting better?"

Protect the Civility of Your Marriage: Don't Foul the Nest. Under the stress of kids it is easier to start yelling, swearing, and engaging in other unpleasant and crabby behaviors that you didn't do before kids. Watch out for those. Couples who have high expectations for civility and who talk about and eliminate sarcasm, irritability, and meanness of any kind when it creeps into the marriage, do better. Although I have encouraged you to lower your expectations about what you can get done in a day, now that kids are here, *don't* lower your expectations for how you treat each other. Use signs of anger as a way to detect problems and improve your marriage. Don't let your expectations for treating each other respectfully slide just because you are tired and grouchy.

If you detect a problem, remember the goals for good communication. Don't flare up and start a discussion with someone who is cranky. Use the soft start-up. "Hey you sound unhappy, honey. What is going on?"

I know many a husband or wife in a happy marriage who also knows when not to be around or try to talk. Pilots who fly overnight trips and are sleep-deprived have a grump day when they get home. A smart spouse plans to run errands or take the kids on a play date then. Some people aren't fun on a deadline, and a smart partner takes the kids to visit a friend. Whatever your strategy, work together to make sure that you don't foul the nest with unpleasant words. Join together against an issue or problem. Fight it together.

Study the Fine Art of Persuading Your Spouse.

Many people think that persuasion is manipulative. I don't. I think it is a loving act to study your spouse and their reactions and learn to present your ideas in a way that works for them. Trust me, many moms spend hours deciphering the needs and personalities of their babies, and many more hours as they mature to teenagers. If they spent just a bit of time figuring out how to work with their spouse, both partners and children would be much happier. What is amazing to me is that clients can often recite chapter and verse about what doesn't work, but are in a fog about what does work.

In all my years of doing marriage counseling, and talking with my friends, I cannot think of any couple in which both partners read self-help books and few who both wanted counseling. I assume that one of you will make it to this chapter and one will not. Even if you both read self-help books, or readily exchange books, most likely one of you will be more excited and motivated about working on your marriage. The other will see a new idea as criticism of the marriage, if you are lucky. More likely, and worse they'll see suggestions for change as personal criticism. This will lead to conversations like "Our marriage is just fine. We talk more than most couples I know." Or "Why do you read that stuff?" The process will quickly derail.

In order for a marriage to succeed, each person needs to be able to influence the partner to participate in plans and ideas that are exciting and enlivening to them and to halt things that just don't work. I have given you tons of specific suggestions of what to do. Now I would like to talk about how to suggest them to your partner in ways that will be comfortable for both of you and will get good results. You will need to experiment and find the method that actually works for you and your partner, one that feels comfortable for the two of you.

Some people love indirect methods because they feel as if it gives them the most choices. Others like the direct method because the indirect approaches make them feel manipulated. Try out the various approaches and avoid those that don't work in your marriage. I've tried all these. For me, some work better than others when I'm trying to pass on the "wisdom" of favorite self-help books to my Neil. See what works for you.

Think about a time that you have easily talked your spouse into something they were reluctant to do. *If you compare your successes with these methods and combine them, you are likely to achieve a home run the quickest.* I have given them pet names.

Indirect Persuasion Methods

Nose in the Tent: In this method you start with one comment, and over the course of days, add a bit to the idea. For example, if you want to establish a habit of going somewhere alone together, you go on and on about how great it was when you went to the lake, just the two of you. After a few days, when this sinks in, then you add how you're afraid that she is such a wonderful mother and community member that the two of you will get too busy to schedule anything together. A few days after that you say, again, how happy you feel every time you think of your time at the lake. Then add that you were wondering if you could possibly plan another weekend away in a few months, so that you could have something to look forward to and daydream about. Then you might add that planning ahead is great because you would have plenty of time to find a baby-sitter, and so forth. The key is to get a commitment to do it one more time rather than moving directly to asking for it to be a ritual. Eventually, you suggest that since it makes you both so happy, maybe you could make it a ritual to plan your next weekend away on your first date night when you return. The point is that if you have a good time and begin planning for the next good time it will become a habit or ritual.

Creating a Chief: I once used this approach with astonishing success with Neil. He refused to go over our finances in any way. He always felt he should be making more money, although I thought he made plenty. I was feeling overburdened and said I wondered if he would look into how the children's and our family's mutual funds should be invested. I told him he was quite good with numbers. (He is fabulous.) I said he was really smart at learning things quickly and applying what he learned and that he could probably do a better job than I could. He agreed to take on the job and become chief mutual fund man in our family. Fortunately it was just in time. I had everything in aggressive growth funds and he invested some of our money in value stocks just before the tech wreck of late 2000. This was a big ego boost for him, and he has maintained his specialty. Soon we started having brief family meetings every six months or so, complete with handouts provided by Dad, to discuss where we were investing and why! I was shocked and thrilled.

I have also helped clients create a chief in their marriage when a problem stalled. I had a client that really wanted more fun in their marriage and I asked him to become the family "funmeister" and kidnap everyone on Saturday mornings. Mom agreed. This stopped an ongoing family feud that went "You aren't any fun anymore" and "I am a fun person and I always have been" and got them moving in a direction of having fun.

Pleasant Surprise Approach: Let's say that you want to get a regular date night started because you haven't dated in a long time. You check both your calendars, pick a spot, hire a baby-sitter, and announce the plan as a pleasant surprise.

Some spouses get stalled in the surprise approach because they have never hired a baby-sitter. If you have never hired a baby-sitter, you can ask, "Suppose I wanted to surprise you with a baby-sitter for a date, who would I call to find out who you think would be a good baby-sitter?" Or, if you know who her best friend is, you can call and ask who is an acceptable baby-sitter. Or you can call the last baby-sitter you used.

A simpler solution is to ask your partner to pick a day, get a baby-sitter, and promise to surprise her with the rest of the fun.

Trial Balloon Approach: Bring up an idea *very* tentatively and include some of the reasons it isn't such a great idea. This works best if your partner always says no to new ideas and if you have the reputation of coming on too strong or too suddenly. "You know sometimes I feel like with all the rushing around we do with kids that we need to sit down and talk together about our goals for our family, our kids and our marriage. But I don't know where we would ever get the time to do it. And you probably wouldn't want to spend a lot of time doing that. It might make you feel antsy." Then you wait for them to say, "Well, what would you talk about?" Also if you give a small sample of goal setting and have it work out and then fan the flames before going on to bigger plans like a whole goal-setting weekend, it works better.

Another example from a friend reverses the approach and leads with the positives. Here is her story:

A friend of mine called and invited my family and me for a weekend at a beach house in Mexico. I knew Donny wouldn't go for this because he doesn't like traveling with other families and he doesn't like Mexico. But I wanted to go so I said it like this, "How would you like to spend a free weekend at a great beach house right on the sand. There are only two catches."

("Free" works because the main reason we don't go away right now is money.) I didn't mislead because I said there were two hitches up front. But by then I had his interest. Because I presented the good before the bad, he bought it, and we went and had a great time.

The point of the method is to pique your partner's curiosity with an idea and mention that you know there might be drawbacks, so he or she doesn't feel forced.

Fanning the Flames: It helps to be a southern belle, which I am not, to pull this one off. The strategy involves finding an example of something that you would like more of and carrying on about how fabulous it makes you feel. Let's say that you like positive feedback. So you say, "The other day when you said I looked good before work, it made me happy all day. I told Jane how happy it made me feel. She said how lucky I was to be married to a charmer like you." Then you tell someone in front of him how wonderful he is about compliments. Most people think that this will not work and that the other person will realize you are angling for something. But you would be surprised how many people just love this approach and will do more of whatever it is that made you feel so good that you keep commenting on it. The key is to let your partner experience your enthusiasm and how happy this makes you.

Raise the Issue Approach: The key to this approach is to raise the issue without proposing a specific solution, so your partner has plenty of room to give suggestions. Saying "I sure miss going out on dates with you" is an example. Now this will produce a rain of practical objections from some people like, "Where will we get the money? Who can baby-sit? *When* can we do it?" Just listen and say, "I know you are absolutely right, but I still wish we could figure out a way."

In some spouses, especially those who might otherwise argue the point into the ground if pressed, this will produce action or a suggested solution in a week or so. If a week seems like a long time, I point out to clients that they have a spouse, who was perhaps rushed and forced into activities as a child, who must always say no before saying yes. So I encourage them to ask early and be patient.

Sometimes though the suggestions or response will blow

your socks off. Let's say that you are looking for more sex or more cuddling and affection in sex. If you say, "I'd like to try some new things sexually to see if we can have more excitement," and your partner might say, "Let's get a porno flick to watch together!" You might be thrilled or you might feel like you got more than you bargained for.

Consider the Big Picture: In this approach you bring up the big picture of your relationship and how you would like it to improve. "How are you feeling about our relationship lately?" This is a hard question for men to ask and an easy one for women to ask. Men are always afraid to hear the wrong answer. Women assume any answer is interesting. But a woman gives a man big points just for asking, whether the woman feels positive or negative at the moment. Obviously, asking the big question about the relationship scores men more points than women. I think men deduct points if you ask this question.

If you ask the question and your husband complains about money, pretend he has a spendthrift wife, and you are just the sympathetic colleague instead of his wife. If your wife complains you don't help enough, pretend you are meeting her for the first time and she has a rotten roommate. Later you two can solve what to do about it. First, just listen.

Carefully rehearse the question about the relationship in your mind so the tone is warm, or write it out in a note. Share some positive feelings that you have to set a warm tone. Without the right friendly tone, the question may sound as though you are threatening to ask for a divorce or asking for such a big change that your partner will feel intimidated and inadequate. If you are angry, this is very hard to pull off well without sounding grinchy, depressed, insecure and/or critical. Don't tie a general relationship question to any specific change request, and especially don't tie it to a change in your partner. Even more importantly, don't tie it to a change that you have asked for already and been refused. Done well, though, it is a magical question that invites the partner to talk about what is good and not so good and leads to productive conversation.

Direct Persuasion Method

Just ask. Many men will tell you that this is their favorite approach. Keep it short, positive, clear, and to the point. Indicate the positive benefits or rationale for the request. In many ways the creating a chief approach above had these characteristics. A simple suggestion with genuine positive enthusiasm works wonders. "Let's go on a date this Saturday night. I miss you." You can expect there will be minor negotiation like "Will you get the sitter if I pick the place and make a reservation?" Sometimes, if you have a good idea, your partner just says yes.

The critical thing is do *not* say: "We haven't been out in forever" or "Why don't you ever take me out?" Keep it simple, straightforward and positive. I tell clients to look for the word "not" in the sentence. If it is there, rephrase the sentence. (Remember the Positive Game.)

If the person says, "We can't afford it" or "I can't find a baby-sitter," don't take it personally. Recognize that if the date or whatever you are requesting hasn't happened before, it will probably take more than one request and perhaps an offer to help. Say, "Can I help by calling so and so to find a sitter?" Or offer to do something really cheap like take a romantic walk and have a picnic. The point is to indicate how much you want their company and treat discouragement as just a step to success.

Try this technique first on simple requests. Before using the technique on something more loaded, see how it works when you want help with a task. I've found that saying, "Would you please take out the trash?" in a pleasant tone without sarcasm works a lot better than: "I can't believe you could continue to walk by this trash can and not take it out!"

When and Why Persuasion Fails

Avoid negative predictions and discouragement. In my practice I most often see attempts at persuasion sabotaged by a man or woman who, once the partner says yes, says something discouraging like, "He says that here but it will never happen." "Why are you saying yes now when you said no before?" "Why didn't you say that sooner and we probably wouldn't be spending all this money on counseling." Or my personal favorite: "Yeah, but he doesn't really want to. He is just doing it because I asked him to." They have little insight into the fact that their discouraging response stops the action. Then they can't understand why the partner is suddenly unwilling again.

So if you have a partner who always says no, think what you do when they say yes. And think about what you say when they say no. Ask yourself: "How would I respond to a friend who asked the same thing? How do I respond when I need a friend's help and they say yes?"

Ask for counseling or therapy. If neither of you can really talk about the changes you need in a constructive way, you may need to ask your partner to go to therapy. Obviously you don't say, "You seem so miserable, you need therapy!" Likewise it is better not to say, "I am miserable, you need therapy! (you sorry . . .) " although you would be surprised by the number of cases that start this way. Instead try, "I am really unhappy and I would like to find out why. The Joneses, who are really comfortable and happy now in their marriage, say they saw a counselor named Mr. Blah and I would like us to talk to him, too." Or say, "I can picture us in a happier marriage, but I don't know how to talk about it to you in a way that doesn't upset you and hurt your feelings. So, I would like us to talk to a counselor about it. Jane and Jacob are really happy. They saw a Dr. So and So, who really turned things around for them."

If your partner refuses or isn't ready, then go alone and work with your counselor to change yourself in gentle ways that will strengthen you and the marriage.

Serenity to accept what I cannot change. Every marriage is filled with unresolvable differences. Sometimes it is the thermostat wars or differences about who sleeps with the window open and who sleeps with the window closed. "I love loud rock music!" versus "That hurts my ears!" Most of these issues can be settled with creative compromise, like earplugs or headphones or an extra blanket. The compromises are easier if you show concern for your partner. "Well I don't want your tender ears to hurt, but I need some time to unwind to music. How can we work this out?"

Summary: The greatest thing you can do to take care of your marriage is learn to talk about difficult things in a way that doesn't hurt you or your partner. Then build on that by learning to persuade each other in ways that allow you to experiment and try new activities together. Learning this one thing opens the door to a long and happy marriage.

Marriage Care Tips

- Put as much—or more—effort into keeping your conversation clean and supportive as you put into looking good or caring for your kids.

- Remember when you stand your ground about something, being right in an argument is not as important as being warm. Being right and not being warm doesn't get you very far.

- When you are balancing your budget and assessing what you own, count how many times you laughed together this week, too.

- When your partner is upset, let her or him know she or he is first priority with you.

- Search for simple things to praise.

- Make happy comments regularly.

- Keep symbols around the house, in the car, and at work that remind you of each other. Pictures are great. People also use jewelry, crosses, stones from their hikes, framed children's art at work, and delightfully creative items.

Use those symbols to remind you to express happiness and gratitude to each other regularly.

Closing: Happy Endings

Friends of ours sent out the notice for their twenty-fifth anniversary celebration listing five years of bliss, five years of fun, five years of doing it all wrong, five years of getting it right, and five years of renewal—not necessarily in that order. Obviously, they know from experience that long marriages are a mix of ups and downs, stages, and ages. Understanding how marriages evolve (or devolve) can help you to weather the inevitable rough spots in your marriage, just like understanding your kids' developmental stages can help you sail through the rough seas with them.

When your marriage is in the bliss stage, and you can both share the bliss of having children, you are lucky. But don't expect it to last. Happy couples celebrate this stage and recall visions of it often to cheer themselves up. As the workload increases after the baby arrives and you divide the labor to survive, you also move into a sense of profound differences. You enter the "Who the Heck Have I Married?" stage discussed earlier. Sadness wells up about what will never be because of your differences. Some women and men retreat at this point and dutifully begin plodding through their roles and responsibilities, unhappily and alone. They don't emerge to see who their partner really is until the last child leaves home.

When you discover that your soul mate isn't quite the person you thought, you begin to mourn the loss of your fantasy. There is a temptation to find another partner, a new soul mate, and start over to recapture the bliss. Instead this realization can be the beginning of an exciting process of consciously creating the life you want for yourselves and your kids. Together you can build in the fun and values that you want for your family.

As you watch your young children develop, you will see a process unfold that is parallel to the one unfolding in your marriage. If you carefully nurture your marriage in its infancy and formative years it will sustain you for the rest of your life. The bliss stage is parallel to infancy. The baby can feel no difference between herself and the caregiver.

Eventually, the baby discovers the differences and frustrations of being separate. By two, she is saying no just to experience the fun of being a different and separate little person. "This is me and I am not you!" In the same way, partners discover that they are different. Some people are frustrated and angry about these differences. But happily married people learn to laugh and enjoy the differences. At first you respect and tolerate the differences, though they seem impossible to enjoy.

Hang in there and you may actually enjoy them, just as a good parent enjoys a child's "no" because it is a sign of independence, though frustrating. Meanwhile, the good parent learns to work with the child so tasks that need to get done get done, without spanking, hitting, or spoiling. In a good marriage, the partners each recognize that their differences are a normal part of the development of the marriage and important to their personal growth. They learn to disagree in a way that is not dismissive, critical and hurtful. Sometimes it is playful, idiosyncratic, and fun.

A good parent sees that the child's crude attempts at independence are not aimed at hurting them. A good partner recognizes that separate interests, tastes, wishes and desires aren't intended to hurt them personally. Often people struggling in the discovery-of-differences stage (the "Who the Heck Are You?" stage) focus so much on how they are different that they lose sight of how great their connection is. Acceptance seems the biggest stretch that newly independent people must extend to each other. The pain and disruption of an affair or flirtation can derail this stage or serve as an unusually difficult place from which to develop acceptance and reestablish connection.

Just as some parents try to raise their children as little replicas of themselves or to fulfill their unfulfilled ambitions, expecting them to pursue the careers and goals they see as valuable, so some spouses demand their partners behave in certain expected ways. Children suffer if they are expected to be just like their parents without regard to their own wishes, needs and temperament. They don't develop their own identities. They succumb easily to the influence of their peers in their teens because they haven't made their own decisions or found their own voice. As married adults they may tend to have secret lives, like an affair, or they have an abrupt departure from the family, like a divorce.

> You need to learn to let your marriage grow, just as you let your child find out who he or she is.

Like college students who hide their true career dreams from their parents, some people drop out of a marriage because they are afraid to tell their partners who they are until it is too late. Other people won't let their partners say who they are. Good parents are curious along the way about who their kids are and what they feel. Likewise in a good marriage both partners are genuinely curious about how the other feels.

Just as good parents often grieve privately about what they dreamed for their kids but may never be, so couples must give up any fixed notion of what they imagined would be in the marriage. My family sat around the dinner table and talked every night. I remember the exact restaurant I was in crying (while Neil was hoping the floor would swallow us) because I realized that with our careers and lifestyles that the classic family dinner experience would never be in our family. Yet once I gave it up as a demand, Neil began making sure we had more meals with the kids. Now he is more fun at the table because he doesn't feel forced to be there. Some people feel that when the grieving sets in the marriage is over. But sometimes the grieving and letting go of having to have something exactly your way is a first step to a better marriage. That better relationship isn't just your fantasy marriage or just your partner's dream marriage but a true partnership between both your fantasies.

By age three, the young child often begins a pattern of play where she runs to Mama or Daddy and hugs a knee and then runs off to play with peers only to return frequently and touch base. A good mom enjoys that running-and-returning pattern because she can see that the child is developing an independent sense of self that feels good because of the trust in home base. Likewise in a solid marriage there are times to create your own identity and have wonderful experiences, and then return to the safety and connection of a good marriage. Loving your children and setting good limits while providing safety and fun is parallel to creating good solid structure in your own marriage and keeping the safety and fun, while allowing you each to have room to grow in your careers and friendships with other people.

As the marriage grows, you become best friends in a way that you couldn't have dreamed of or understood in the bliss stage. This is a critical transformation. In a strong marriage,

partners are curious about each other's feelings, wishes and desires. They make time in the marriage to ask these deeper questions and really listen and hear the answers. The marriage
becomes strong and vital as you each begin to see each other as
you really are, with a sense of deep acceptance, and encourage
each other to develop into the strong, interesting person you
each can be.

Happily married couples intrigue me. I remember a brief
conversation I had with a woman after overhearing her cheerfully saying into her cell phone, "Honey, I love you and can't
wait to get home so we can talk more." Someone waiting with
us commented, "Honeymooners are so great to watch." She
laughed and said she had been married ten years and had an
eight-year-old daughter. When I told her about the book I was
writing, she told me that after the birth of their child, she and
her husband had started fighting. She said that at the time she
complained that he didn't take care of the baby just the way she
wanted and that he didn't change diapers enough. She had griped
to her friends about not getting enough help and even thought
about divorce. She said, essentially, "He wouldn't go to counseling, so I went alone at first. I realized that in my desire to be a
good mom I had become a bad wife. I had changed as much or
more than my poor husband. I forgot my husband and I needed
time alone, just the two of us. Eventually he came to counseling
with me. We learned that when you give a little, you get a little
and when you give a lot, you get a lot." She inspired me and it
struck me at the time that many happily married couples had reported a rough spot a few years after the baby was born and a
brief period of counseling before their marriages got back on
track. I came away from our discussion with a renewed faith in
the resilience of people and marriages. In our brief conversation
she described moving through the five stages to a very happy,
grateful place.

Strong families and strong marriages change often in response to the changes in the lives within them. In a good marriage with kids, people change often. Learning how to change together and support these changes is the biggest task you face when you have children and as you respond to their rapid normal growth and change. Succeeding at learning to change gracefully sets the stage for a long and happy life.

Good marriage habits make a protective shield around the family so that they can weather change and differences with as little stress as possible and spend more time enjoying one another. The formula for taking care of your marriage is fairly simple. The execution when you have young children, however, is difficult.

Although I have encouraged you to lower your expectations about what you can get done in a day now that kids are here, *don't* lower your expectations for how you treat each other. Use signs of anger as a way to detect problems and improve your marriage. If you detect a problem, remember the goals for good communication. Don't flare up and start a discussion with someone who is cranky. Use the soft start-up. "Hey, you sound unhappy, honey. What is going on?"

Above all, remember, during the kid crisis in your marriage, you will experience moments, days, even weeks, months, or years when you wonder why you ever thought that marrying this partner and having kids was a good idea. The trouble is normal and the effort to fix it well worth the time, energy, and commitment spent. People who achieve a long, satisfying marriage with children gain what is possibly the most personally enriching, fulfilling experience we can have in this life. What could be more important than creating an enduring, healthy relationship that your children will carry on to future generations? When the going gets tough, I hope you will think back to this little book and find some words to inspire you to be kinder and gentler and, ultimately, to have more fun.

Enjoying Your Marriage with Kids

- When you are moving from a life of movies and dinner out to a life of takeout and videos, take time to make eye contact and kiss.

- When she leaves her purse on top of the car and drives away because she was strapping the baby in the car, laugh; don't lecture.

- Count those battle scars on the furniture as tributes to a relaxed Mom or Dad. This says, "You are more important to me than stains on the furniture."

- Focus on what a thorough job she does packing for a picnic, rather than how she slows things down.

- Accept apologies.

- Learn to take "do overs" when either of you need them.

- Ask for breaks when you need them.

- Calm yourself down before you load and fire with your mouth.

- Recognize that most of the time your partner has good intentions or is clueless. He or she is rarely out to get you.

- After an argument, comment on how well you work things out and how good other aspects of the marriage are.

- Schedule fun and downtime into every day.

- Find fun and different ways to tell your partner you love them each day.

- Tell your partner often that you are proud of them.

- Celebrate your marriage as much as you celebrate your kids.

Resources and References

Books and Articles:

Anderson, Judith Z., and Geoffry White. An empirical investigation of interaction and relationship patterns in functional and dysfunctional nuclear families and stepfamilies. *Family Process,* 25, 407–422, 1989.

Bader, Ellyn and Peter T. Pearson. *In Quest of the Mythical Mate: A Developmental Approach to Diagnosis and Treatment in Couples Therapy.* Brunner-Routledge, 1988.

Bach, George Robert. *The Intimate Enemy: How to Fight Fair In Love and Marriage.* William Morrow & Co., 1969.

*Bakos, Susan Crain. "Beyond the G Spot." In *Redbook* magazine, 2001.

Barrett, Nina. *I Wish Someone Had Told Me: A Realistic Guide To Early Motherhood.* Academy Chicago Pub., 1997.

* Highly Recommended.

*Brown, Emily M. *Patterns Of Infidelity and Their Treatment,* 2nd ed. Brunner-Routledge, 2001.

*Chapman, Gary. *The Five Love Languages: How to Express Heartfelt Commitment to Your Mate.* Northfield Publications, 1992.

*Chopra, Deepak. *The Seven Spiritual Laws of Success: A Practical Guide to the Fulfillment of Your Dreams.* Amber-Allen Pub., 1995.

*Covey, Stephen. *How to Develop a Family Mission Statement.* Audiocassette. Covey Leadership Center, 1996.

*Covey, Stephen and Sandra Merrill Covey. *The Seven Habits of Highly Effective Families: Building a Beautiful Family Culture in a Turbulent World.* Golden Books Pub. Co., 1997.

Crittenden, Ann. *The Price of Motherhood: Why the Most Important Job in the World is Still the Least Valued.* Owl Books, 2002.

Crittenden, Danielle. *What Our Mothers Didn't Tell Us: Why Happiness Eludes the Modern Woman.* Touchstone Books, 2000.

Cusk, Rachel. *A Life's Work: On Becoming a Mother.* Picador, 2002.

*Davis, Michele Weiner. *The Divorce Remedy: The Proven 7-Step Program for Saving Your Marriage.* Simon & Schuster Adult Publishing Group, 2001.

*Davis, Michele Weiner. *The Sex-Starved Marriage: A Couple's Guide to Boosting Their Marriage Libido.* Simon & Schuster Adult Publishing Group, 2003.

Doherty, William J. *Take Back Your Marriage: Sticking Together in a World That Pulls Us Apart.* Guilford Publications, 2001.

Ferber, Richard M.D. *Solve Your Child's Sleep Problem.* Fireside, 1986.

---

* Highly Recommended.

*Glass, Shirley P. with Jean Coppock Staeheli. *Not "Just Friends": Protect Your Relationship from Infidelity and Heal the Trauma of Betrayal.* The Free Press, 2003.

*Glenn, H. Stephen and Jane Nelsen. *Raising Self-Reliant Children in a Self-Indulgent World: Seven Building Blocks for Developing Capable Young People.* Prima Publishing, 2000.

Godeck, Gregory J. P. *1001 Ways To Be Romantic.* Sourcebooks Trade, 1999.

*Gottman, John Mordechai and Nan Silver. *Seven Principles to Making Marriage Work: A Practical Guide from the Country's Foremost Relationship Expert.* Crown Publishing Group, 2000.

*Hendrix, Harville. *Getting the Love You Want: A Guide for Couples.* Owl Books, 2001.

*Herman, Frances. *The ABC's of Hiring a Nanny: How to Find a Nanny Without Losing Your Mind; Expanded Version.* McGavick Field Publishing, 2000.

Hochschild, Arlie R. *Commercialization of Intimate Life: Notes from Home and Work.* University of California Press, 2003.

Hochschild, Arie R. with Anne Machung. *The Second Shift,* Penguin, USA, 2003.

Hochschild, Arlie R. *The Time Bind: When Work Becomes Home and Home Becomes Work,* Henry Holt & Company, Inc., 1997.

*Katie, Byron and Stephen Mitchell. *Loving What Is: Four Questions That Can Change Your Life.* Harmony Books, 2002.

Lerner, Harriet. *The Mother Dance: How Children Change Your Life.* Perennial, 1999.

Lew, Amy and Betty Lou Bettner. *Raising Kids Who Can: Use Good Judgment, Assume Responsibility, Communicate Effectively, Respect Self & Others, Cooperate, Develop Self-Esteem & Enjoy Life.* Connexions Press, 1998.

* Highly Recommended.

Linton, Bruce. *Finding Time for Fatherhood: Men's Concerns as Parents.* Berkley Hills Books, 2000.

Maushart, Susan. *The Mask of Motherhood.* Penguin Books, 1999.

Myers, Gary and Patty Barthell Myers. *Smart Mom's Baby-Sitting Co-Op Handbook: How We Solved the Baby-Sitter Puzzle.* Tukwila Publishing, 2000.

*Nelson, Jane and Cheryl Erwin and Roslyn Duffy. *Positive Discipline for Preschoolers, Age Three to Six: For Their Early Years—Raising Children Who Are Responsible, Respectful and Resourceful.* Crown Publishing Group, 1998.

*Nelson, Jane. *Positive Discipline.* Crown Publishing Group, 2003.

*Oxhorn-Ringwood, Lynne and Marjorie Vego-Krausz and Louise Oxhorn. *Stepwives: 10 Steps to Help Ex-wives and Stepmothers End the Struggle and Put the Kids First.* Fireside, 2002.

*Pantley, Elizabeth. *The No-Cry Sleep Solution: Gentle Ways to Help Your Baby Sleep Through the Night.* McGraw-Hill Companies, 2002.

Pittman, Frank. *Private Lies: Infidelity and the Betrayal of Intimacy.* W. W. Norton & Co., 1990.

Rapoport, Elizabeth. "How Many Working Fathers Does It Take to Screw in a Lightbulb?" In *Mothers Who Think: Tales of Real Life Parenthood,* Camille Peri and Kate Moses, ed. Washington Square Press, 2000.

Schnarch, David. *Passionate Marriage.* W. W. Norton & Company, New York: 1997.

Shapiro, Francine. *Eye Movement Desensitization and Reprocessing: Basic Principles, Protocols, and Procedures,* 2nd ed. The Guildord Press, New York: 2001.

*Spring, Janice. *After the Affair: Healing the Pain and Rebuilding Trust When a Partner Has Been Unfaithful.* HarperCollins, 1997.

* Highly Recommended.

Webb, Michael. *The RoMANtic's Guide: Hundreds of Creative Tips for a Lifetime of Love.* Hyperion Press, 2000.

Weiner-Davis, Michele. *Divorce Busting: A Step-By-Step Approach to Making Your Marriage Loving Again.* Simon & Schuster Adult Publishing Group, 1993.

————. *How to Change Your Life and Everyone In It.* Simon & Schuster Adult Publishing Group, 1996.

Wolf, Naomi. *Misconceptions: Truth, Lies, and the Unexpected on the Journey to Motherhood.* Bantam Doubleday Dell Publishing Group, 2003.

Video

The Method: Baby & Mom Postnatal Yoga. Cal Pozo and Gurmukh Kaur Khalsa, 2001.

Websites

www.cavemania.com
www.comamas.com
www.fathersforum.com
www.happilymarriedwithkids.com
www.parentsplace.com
www.smartmarriages.com

* Highly Recommended.

Credits and Permissions